Writing Research Papers

A Complete Guide

Third Edition

Writing Research Papers

A Complete Guide

Third Edition

James D. Lester
Austin Peay State University

Scott, Foresman and Company

Glenview, Illinois

Dallas, Tex.   Oakland, N.J.   Palo Alto, Cal.   Tucker, Ga.   London

Library of Congress Cataloging in Publication Data

Lester, James D.
  Writing research papers.

  Bibliography.
  Includes index.
  1. Report writing. I. Title.
LB2369.L4   1980   808'.02   79-27837
ISBN 0-673-15327-4

1 2 3 4 5 6—CON—84 83 82 81 80 79

Preface

I first started the project of writing a style guide for research papers fifteen years ago. What began as a small pamphlet for the Kansas State Teachers College English department grew into a small booklet and then finally became *Writing Research Papers* in 1967 when published by Scott, Foresman. Later, in 1971, a special Diamond Printing followed, supplanted in 1976 by the Second Edition. Now we present the Third Edition in an effort to serve today's college and university students.

The primary goal of the first two editions was to make the guidelines of the *MLA Style Sheet* as comprehensible as possible for the student inexperienced in research paper writing. We also intended the book to serve as a reference source for graduate students and professors who wanted a ready answer to questions on correct documentation. In addition, we tried to aid the student in handling reference material and in writing and styling the research paper.

The Third Edition continues to try to meet these goals. As before, it adheres to the stipulations of the Modern Language Association and continues to offer students guidance in locating sources, organizing their thoughts, incorporating references into their writing, and expressing their results in a polished paper.

For the sake of greater clarity, usefulness, and consistency with MLA standards, several improvements have been made. Chapter 1 places greater emphasis on choosing and restricting the topic, two initial stumbling blocks. Chapter 2 ("Gathering Data"), which received favorable reviews as a thorough and workable guideline for library investigation and the development of the working bibliography, has been updated. Chapter 3 ("Taking Notes") features new sample note cards that distinguish more clearly between different types of notes—personal, précis, paraphrase, summary, and quotation—and their techniques. The section "Avoiding Plagiarism" was updated with new examples.

Chapter 4 ("Writing Your Paper") was extensively revised to improve the sections on outlining, handling reference material, format, and technicalities of the manuscript. This chapter also features a new sample research paper on a nonliterary topic, "Creative Marriage." Many instructors requested a nonliterary subject because they use the text in a course other than English composition; others said they simply preferred to suggest topics from fields other than literature. However, for those instructors who prefer a literary paper, we incorporated the sample paper from the Second Edition ("The Theme of Black Matriarchy in *A Raisin in the Sun*") into the Instructor's Manual.

The "Raisin in the Sun" paper offers another alternative: It continues to feature footnoting and single-spacing of such items as long quotations, footnotes, and bibliographies. The new sample paper in Chapter 4 demonstrates double-spacing throughout for all materials—long quotations, notes, and bibliographies;

as a result this edition of *Writing Research Papers* is longer than the first two. The sample paper also places notes at the end of the paper as endnotes rather than at the bottoms of the pages as footnotes. All this is in keeping with the MLA stipulation that only a thesis or dissertation—which must look like a published paper—should have footnotes. All other papers, whether a freshman research paper or scholarly treatise for publication, should be in manuscript form and thus employ endnotes.

Chapter 5 ("Endnotes and Footnotes") was revised to accomplish several purposes. First, it now distinguishes between endnotes and footnotes, explaining the rationale for notes at the end of the paper. Second, it carefully delineates the various note forms for a great many entries so that the student can find samples of even the most difficult documentation problems. Third, we added entries for such items as "Art Work," "Microfilm," "Musical Compositions," "Tapes," and "Transparencies" to achieve more comprehensive coverage of documentation form.

Chapter 6 ("The Bibliography") was, like Chapter 5, updated with many new samples of proper bibliographic form. Chapter 7 ("Documentation of Science Papers") remains a guide to the "Name and Year System" or the "Number System" as used by scientific disciplines.

An Instructor's Manual will again be available to accompany the Third Edition. It features research questions and exercises, all geared to the book's organization, plus, of course, the alternative sample research paper. The manual enables instructors to test the progress of their students at nearly every stage of their research project.

Finally, it would be impossible to thank all those who have contributed to the success of *Writing Research Papers*. I am indeed grateful to the many instructors who have written with suggestions. In addition, I wish to remember Ted Owens, and William Elkins for their help and encouragement along the way; Dick Welna, who helped to inspire the original manuscript years ago; my editor on this edition, Vicki Stewart; student Pamela Howell for her research paper; and of course my wife Martha and sons Jim and Mark.

James D. Lester

Table of Contents

CHAPTER 5

Endnotes and Footnotes   97

CHAPTER 6

The Bibliography   128

CHAPTER 7

Documentation of Science Papers   149

APPENDIX I

A Glossary of Additional Research Terms   157

APPENDIX II

A List of General Reference Books and Journals   168

INDEX   197

Writing Research Papers

A Complete Guide

Third Edition

THE PRELIMINARIES

Introduction

● Why write a research paper? That is like asking, why do research at all? Obviously, research in many fields has brought our society from a horse-and-buggy era to one that is so exuberant in its use of automobiles and electrical gadgetry that today we need research on methods to conserve fuel. In the medical sciences research has helped doctors attain such levels of efficiency that persons can now be kept alive by machinery, thus creating new research problems in philosophical areas. In the area of books the output is enormous; more books and articles are being written today than ever before. Somebody must be doing something right! New fiction, new poetry, new essays—all are awaiting our examination and, importantly for the scholar, awaiting our critical judgment.

So why write a research paper? The answer is twofold. First, you add new information to your personal storehouse of knowledge by collecting and investigating facts and opinions about a limited topic from various sources. Second, you will add to the knowledge of others by clearly and thoughtfully communicating the results of your research in the form of a well-reasoned answer to a scholarly problem or question.

Perhaps more importantly, learning to master research techniques will be of great help in your other courses and in your life after college. Since you will probably face several instances in your career that will require careful research, you should, as soon as possible, acquire the techniques for retrieving information, knowing where and how to find it, and using it to your best advantage. Sound research means going beyond encyclopedia articles and getting into special indexes and reference books, scholarly journals, and specialized studies of all sorts. With today's sophisticated communications systems, there is an abundance (some would say an overabundance) of information available to the researcher.

No longer is the card catalog the ultimate answer for retrieval of information in a library. Sophisticated equipment now enables libraries to store enormous amounts of information on microfilm (for example, a full year's issue of the *New York Times* in one small container). Cassette tapes store additional pieces of information. Indexes and bibliographies in every field are more detailed and sophisticated than ever before. Thus, learning proper research techniques will help you identify and process the information you retrieve with a minimum of time and effort.

Another long-term advantage in doing a research paper will be learning to shape your material into coherent, logical patterns. Any adequate research assignment, whether in or out of the classroom, will ask you to inform, interest, and, in some cases, persuade the reader. You must be able to critically judge the merit of the evidence which you have collected through careful research techniques and then be able to express precise conclusions about it. Such a task requires imaginative molding of your material.

In this respect, it is all too easy to submit a poor manuscript. For example, you might put together a paper by paraphrasing a few authorities and by inserting quotations abundantly. But such a paper would prove seriously inadequate since it would merely present facts and opinions in a research paper format. In such a paper, the thesis—if there was one—would not be developed or explored. In other words, you would have offered a recital of investigations without the personal expression and explanation that is the ultimate purpose of most research writing.

Research techniques and the ability to shape the material derived from research—these are two of the more important things you will learn in writing your paper. Along with these, you should also acquire a working familiarity with research writing style and the handling of quoted materials. This book will help you: it explores the complete scope of research writing, includes a sample paper, and contains full information on style, format, and note and bibliography forms.

If you are concerned that your research is insignificant and your writing is inadequate, do not despair. The undergraduate research paper is primarily a learning and training experience. That is, you study a selected topic thoroughly and train yourself in writing that generally conforms to an established style and format. At first the task may appear insurmountable: locating sources, reading books and articles, and taking notes; then outlining, footnoting sources, and writing; and still yet rewriting, typing, and proofreading. Perhaps at some point you will begin to question your ability to express yourself in English at all!

Obviously, you need to apply some kind of order to this procedure. You can learn to do that by studying basic research techniques, strategies for selecting and arranging evidence, and methods for presenting your ideas in a clear and logical fashion. College students are not expected to know everything, but they should possess the ability to find accurate information about any subject and to communicate their facts and conclusions to the reader. Self-reliant library research and competent writing will be valuable assets in meeting several kinds of demands: assignments in other courses, research articles for publication, seminar papers in graduate study, and reports and studies for business and industry.

Choosing a Topic

Perhaps the most important advice is to select a topic of interest to yourself. Your choice requires more than passing attention because you may discover, too late, that an impulsive choice has led you into a dull subject, difficult research problems, or disappointing results. Before deciding upon a final topic, ask yourself if you can live with that topic for several weeks of intensive study.

In addition, there are several other principles you should consider in the selection of a topic. The first thing to keep in mind is that the topic should offer opportunities for investigation, for discovery of something new, different, or original, and for the formulation of judgments. It should demand, therefore, much more than a brief study of one or two encyclopedias which, though they may get you started, will provide only a report at most and are not sufficient for investigative research. For example, subjects such as "Poetic Imagery" or "Auto Production" are seldom suitable because all reference sources would provide almost identical information, and you would have little opportunity for the discovery and formulation of judgments. Restricting yourself to a specific topic might help, such as "Poetic Imagery in the Poetry of Langston Hughes" or "Auto Production: A Key to America's Economy." You would then have a narrow topic demanding a careful examination of the issues and the comments of experts in those respective fields.

The second principle requires that you be wary of topics that are too recent, too specialized, and too geographically removed for you to obtain adequate materials. First, a news item in this week's newspaper might appear interesting, but research materials would most likely be limited to recent articles and editorials in newspapers and popular magazines that would permit little depth for development. Most instructors prefer your topic to be one that critics, experts, and authorities have examined in books, scholarly reports, and learned journals found on library shelves, not at a corner newsstand. Second, some topics are so specialized and classified that research itself becomes the sole end. You may get as technical as you wish as long as you don't get so bogged down in technical jargon and procedures that the paper becomes a report rather than a research tool in which you draw some conclusions about the general significance of your topic. For example, a paper on the differences between Euclidian and non-Euclidian geometry would get rather technical; but as long as your instructor approves, you are capable, and the conclusions are valid, this topic seems to be a pretty good one. Third, a regional topic is permissible, even encouraged, if it centers around your own geographic region. For example, a student in Michigan might consider the ecological crisis in the Great Lakes area while a student in Louisiana might examine the same issue by focusing on Lake Pontchartrain. In short, select a topic for which you can readily obtain the material.

Research studies usually avoid certain topics. Avoid topics that can be handled only by restating the research material; avoid straight biography that summarizes a person's life, though acceptable topics may be developed on either the influence of a historical period on a person or the importance of one aspect of a person's work; avoid sensational topics that merely titillate, such as "Political Sex Scandals"; avoid topics that are too broad, such as "The U.S. Presidency"; and avoid topics that are not scholarly—there is seldom any place in research writing for such topics as "Fishing for Trout" or "The American Hot Dog." However, as you will see, all these topics can be the basis for valid papers if they are properly restricted by your thesis and then adequately developed.

Carefully determine the nature of the assignment. First, you may need to prepare a *process paper* that documents the step-by-step procedures used to reach your findings. The sciences—biology, physics, psychology—popularized this type of research format. In this case your instructor is mainly interested in your research techniques, that is, how and where you found the information. Second, the instructor may require a *product paper* that gives the factual results of your research with listings, graphs, charts, maps, and so on. This sort of writing is popular in the social sciences—economics, sociology, political science.

Both of the above areas have been aided in recent years by computer technology, which enables the researcher to store and catalog great quantities of data and then retrieve it in various forms of printed readouts—lists, charts, graphs, and so on.

Yet most instructors will require the *critical paper,* one in which you arrive at judgments about the topic based upon your research procedures (first above) and findings (second above) as supported by secondary sources (other critics who have studied and written about this topic). In other words, you must go through step-by-step procedures, arrive at certain findings, and present your critical commentary about the subject.

Finally, you should select a topic that will permit you to express your reasoned judgments and your guarded opinions with support from your source materials. A thorough examination of all the available evidence should result in responsible, impartial findings. All topics are controversial to some degree, but guard against unfounded personal opinion and prejudice. Bias has no place in the research paper, which requires careful assimilation and presentation of the evidence to prevent any appearance of prejudice and rash generalization. Therefore, you will need to be especially cautious in your assessment of findings about controversial topics such as abortion, gun control, and the death penalty.

In brief, research demands the search for and discovery of information, an evaluation of that information, a formulation of unbiased judgments, and a demonstrable conclusion. The topic you choose must offer an opportunity for full development of each of these four points.

Preliminary Reading

You will need a thorough familiarity with your material before attempting to restrict the subject. To that end, your introductory reading will serve several purposes: it will provide an overview of the subject, it will furnish the beginning of a working bibliography (see pp. 11–15), it will enable you to determine the availability of relevant reference material, and it will make possible a careful restriction of the subject.

This preliminary reading does not normally require taking notes, since you cannot yet be certain of your needs. As a starting point, you might begin with a book or journal article recommended by your instructor or librarian (see pp. 15–35 for a full discussion of the use and resources of the library). You might also start with a general survey, such as *Literary History of the United States* (see Appendix II, pp. 168–96, for a list of general reference works and journals in your field). Or you may begin with an encyclopedia, a biographical dictionary, or some other general reference work, as listed below:

ENCYCLOPEDIAS

Chambers's Encyclopaedia. New rev. ed. 15 vols. Fairview Park, N.Y.: Maxwell Scientific International, 1973.

Encyclopedia Americana. 30 vols. New York: Encyclopedia Americana, 1978.

The New Columbia Encyclopedia. 4th ed. New York: Lippincott, 1975.

The New Encyclopaedia Britannica. 15th ed. 30 vols. Chicago: Encyclopaedia Britannica, 1979.

BIOGRAPHICAL DICTIONARIES

Universal

Deceased

Chambers's Biographical Dictionary. Rev. ed. London: W & R Chambers, 1969.

Webster's Biographical Dictionary. Rev. ed. Springfield, Mass.: Merriam, 1976.

Living

Current Biography Yearbooks. New York: H. W. Wilson, 1940–date.

Dictionary of International Biography. Cambridge, England: Melrose, 1978.

A Dictionary of Universal Biography of All Ages and of All People. Ed. Albert M. Hyamson. 3rd ed. Boston: Routledge and Kegan, 1976.

Index to Women of the World from Ancient to Modern Times: Biographies and Portraits. Ed. Norma O. Ireland. Westwood, Mass.: Faxon, 1970.

International Who's Who. New York: International Publications Service, 1935–date.

Twentieth Century Authors: A Biographical Dictionary of Modern Literature. Ed. Stanley J. Kunitz and Howard Haycraft. New York: H. W. Wilson, 1942. Supplement 1955.

Webster's Biographical Dictionary. Rev. ed. Springfield, Mass.: Merriam, 1976

Who's Who in the World: 1978–79. 4th ed. Chicago: A. N. Marquis, 1978.

American

Deceased

Dictionary of American Biography. 10 vols. New York: Scribner's, 1974.

National Cyclopedia of American Biography. 71 vols. Clifton, N.J.: J. T. White, 1978.

Who Was Who in America. 7 vols. Chicago: A. N. Marquis, 1963–date.

Living

Contemporary Authors: A Bio-Bibliographical Guide to Current Authors and Their Works. Detroit: Gale, 1962–date.

Encyclopedia of American Biography. Ed. John A. Garraty and Jerome L. Sternstein. New York: Harper & Row, 1974.

National Cyclopedia of American Biography. 71 vols. Clifton, N.J.: J. T. White, 1978.

Webster's American Biographies. Springfield, Mass.: Merriam, 1975.

Who's Who Among Black Americans. 2nd ed. Northbrook, Ill.: Who's Who Among Black Americans, Inc., 1978.

Who's Who in America. Chicago: A. N. Marquis, 1899–date.

Who's Who of American Women. Chicago: A. N. Marquis, 1958–date.

British

Deceased

Burke's Landed Gentry. 18th ed. 3 vols. Elmsford, N.Y.: British Book Center, 1965–69.

Dictionary of National Biography. Ed. Leslie Stephen and Sidney Lee. 22 vols. 1882–1953; rpt. New York: Oxford Univ. Press, 1971. 6 Supplements.

Who Was Who: Companion to Who's Who. 6 vols. New York: St. Martin's, 1952–62.

Living

Who's Who. London: A & C Black, 1849–date.

ALMANACS AND YEARBOOKS

Americana Annual 1978. Danbury, Conn.: Grolier Educational Corp., 1978.

Annual Register of World Events. Ed. I. Macadam and H. V. Hodson. New York: St. Martin's, Annually.

Britannica Book of the Year. Ed. James Ertel. Chicago: Encyclopaedia Britannica, 1938–date.

Facts on File Yearbook. New York: Facts on File, 1941–date.

Information Please Almanac 1978: Atlas & Yearbook, Maps, Charts, Index. New York: Viking, 1977.

Kane, Joseph N. *Famous First Facts: A Record of First Happenings, Discoveries and Inventions in the United States.* 3rd ed. New York: H. W. Wilson, 1964.

Kane, Joseph Nathan. *Facts About the Presidents.* 3rd ed. New York: H. W. Wilson, 1974.

The Negro Almanac: A Reference Work on the Black American. Ed. Harry A. Ploski and Warren Marr. New York: Bellwether, n.d.

The World Almanac and Book of Facts. New York: Newspaper Enterprises Association, 1868–date.

The Statesman's Year-Book: Statistical and Historical Annual of the States of the World. Ed. S. H. Steinberg. 6 vols. New York: St. Martin's, 1961–67. Supplements 1973–76.

Yearbook of the United Nations. Lake Success, N.Y.: United Nations, 1947–date.

ATLASES AND GAZETTEERS

Atlas of American History. Ed. Edward W. Fox. London: Oxford Univ. Press, 1964.

The Atlas of the Universe. Chicago: Rand McNally, 1970.

Atlas of United States History. Maplewood, N.J.: Hammond, n.d.

Atlas of World History. Maplewood, N.J.: Hammond, n.d.

Britannica Atlas: Geography Edition. Ed. William A. Cleveland. Chicago: Encyclopaedia Britannica, 1974.

Commercial Atlas. Rev. ed. New York: American Map, 1974.

Goode's World Atlas. Ed. Edward B. Espenshade, Jr. 15th ed. Chicago: Rand McNally, 1977.

Grosset World Atlas (originally: Hammond World Atlas). New York: Grosset and Dunlap, 1973.

National Geographic Atlas of the World. 4th ed. Washington, D.C.: National Geographic Society, 1975.

The New York Times Atlas of the World. In collaboration with *The Times of London.* New York: Times Books, 1975.

Oxford Economic Atlas of the World. 4th ed. London: Oxford Univ. Press, 1972.

Oxford World Atlas. Ed. Saul B. Cohen. London: Oxford Univ. Press, 1973.

Shepherd, W. R. *Shepherd's Historical Atlas.* 9th ed. 1964; rpt. New York: Barnes & Noble, 1973.

The Times Atlas of the World. Comprehensive ed., produced by *The Times of London.* New York: Times Books, 1975.

DICTIONARIES

Concise Oxford Dictionary of Current English. Ed. J. B. Sykes. 6th ed. London: Oxford Univ. Press, 1976.

Funk and Wagnalls Standard College Dictionary. New updated ed. New York: Funk & Wagnalls, 1977.

Oxford English Dictionary. Ed. James A. H. Murray et al. 13 vols. New York: Oxford Univ. Press, 1933.

Random House College Dictionary. New York: Random House, 1975.

The Shorter Oxford English Dictionary. Ed. William Little et al. 3rd ed. 2 vols. New York: Oxford Univ. Press, 1973.

Webster's New Collegiate Dictionary. Ed. Henry Bosley Woolf. Rev. ed. Springfield, Mass.: Merriam, 1977.

Webster's New World Dictionary of the American Language. 2nd concise ed. Cleveland: Collins-World, 1975.

Webster's Third New International Dictionary, Unabridged: The Great Library of the English Language. Springfield, Mass.: Merriam, 1976.

BOOKS OF USAGE, SYNONYMS, AND DIALECT

Americanisms: A Dictionary of Selected Americanisms on Historical Principles. Ed. Mitford M. Mathews. Chicago: Univ. of Chicago Press, 1966.

A Dictionary of American English on Historical Principles. Ed. Sir William Craigie and J. R. Hulbert. 4 vols. Chicago: Univ. of Chicago Press, 1938–44.

Dictionary of American Slang. Ed. Harold Wentworth and Stuart B. Flexner. New York: Crowell, 1975.

Ebbitt, Wilma R., and David R. Ebbitt. *Writer's Guide and Index to English.* 6th ed. Glenview, Ill.: Scott, Foresman, 1978.

Fowler, H. W. *A Dictionary of Modern English Usage.* Rev. Sir Ernest Gowers. 2nd ed. Oxford: Clarendon Press, 1965.

Partridge, Eric. *A Dictionary of Slang and Unconventional English.* 7th ed. New York: Macmillan, 1970.

Roget's Thesaurus of English Words and Phrases. Rev. Robert A. Dutch. New York: St. Martin's, 1965.

Webster's Synonyms, Antonyms, and Homonyms. New York: Barnes & Noble, 1974.

This initial reading need not be extensive since it is intended to provide only a general survey. You will have accomplished your purpose in preliminary reading when you have enough understanding of your material to decide on the restricted phase of it that you wish to pursue.

Restricting the Subject

You should not be too ambitious in what you attempt to cover. For one reason, research writing requires you to probe deeply and to present accurately facts and ideas that demonstrate the validity of your contentions. Your support for various judgments and opinions will be effective only if detailed. Furthermore, you will realize no sense of accomplishment if you present only vague, indefinite statements about a too extensive, too generalized subject.

Another reason why you should limit your subject to a specific problem or question is that the research paper is a relatively short work, often no more than about ten typewritten pages in length, excluding title page, outline, endnotes, and bibliography. The subject, accordingly, should be one that can be handled within these limitations of space, not one that would require twenty or thirty pages for adequate presentation.

For example, you could not deal adequately with "Edgar Allan Poe: His Poetic Genius," but you should get along well with "The Role of the Narrator in 'The Raven.'" Rather than attempting "The Ecology Problem," you might write effectively about "The Ecological Effects of Fish Kills on the Cottonwood River." And though "American Inflation" is probably unmanageable, "The Effects of Inflation upon College Tuition" might well be within your range.

This restriction of subject requires careful study of all available sources. For example, let us say you are assigned the general subject area of the U.S. presidency. A first step in restriction could be to limit the topic to one president— Jimmy Carter. You would discover, however, that there is an overwhelming amount of written data about Carter. Therefore, you would want to limit yourself to one aspect of Carter's administration—for example, his fight for energy control legislation. At this point you should read the related documents, articles, and government reports, noting particularly all material about energy waste and methods of controlling the problem. You might then decide that Carter's proposals were effective or ineffective. Either way, you have a manageable topic in "President Carter and His Energy Policy." You may, of course, select any policy or proposal of the president and, by handling it in this restricted fashion, write an acceptable political science paper.

If you need specific devices for narrowing a subject, consider the following techniques:

1.   Examine the table of contents and index of your textbook, which are divided into major headings.

2.   Read an encyclopedia entry which provides a summary of major issues about a subject as well as a brief bibliography listing of new sources.

3.   Check the library's card catalog (see pp. 29–34) which, under subject headings, will indicate study areas. This search will also reveal the number and kinds of books available on a topic.

4.   Relate your subject to your own special interests. If your general subject is poetry and your special interest is ecology, you might join the two by studying poems about ecology and nature in general. In like manner, you might join the subject "Crime" with your interest in detective fiction, or you might join the subject "The State Legislature" with legislation affecting your special interest— for example, marijuana, abortion, or tuition and fees.

Remember that it is usually the uninformed, uncertain writer who feels he or she must take refuge in the "safety" of a large, generalized, unrestricted subject.

Developing a Preliminary Thesis
Sentence

The next great influence upon the success of your work is your development of a *preliminary* thesis sentence to limit even further the scope of your study and to distinguish your approach from that of others. As you progress more and more deeply into your subject, you will need more than ever the unity of a central purpose. Early in your work it will be all right to have a sentence which begins with "The purpose of this paper is . . ."; but you are warned against phrasing it so in the formal paper. Also, remember that your preliminary thesis will both control and, to a certain extent, be controlled by your research. It will always be subject to change as you progress in your research.

After note-taking and just before you start writing your first draft, you will arrive at a *final* thesis sentence that will be your controlling force. The final thesis sentence should unite your various findings, serve as the nerve center for all your paragraphs, and lead toward your demonstrable conclusions at the end of the paper.

Let us look at three possibilities. If your general topic is "Demand for Energy Production in the U.S." and you have restricted it to the effects of the energy crisis upon the environment, then your purpose is to examine the critical issues in this push-pull debate. Does the energy crisis require that we sacrifice the environment? Should we allow pollution in order to heat our homes? Can we have a safe, clean environment and also drive our automobiles at will? Asking such questions during research and note-taking will ultimately lead to your final thesis—for example, "The demands for energy production in the United States will increase environmental pollution and delay, perhaps forever, our chances for clean air and water."

If your general topic is Robert Frost's poetry and you have narrowed it to a study of his imagery, then you can ask such questions as: Is there an image or image cluster that appears often? Is it a significant image in several important poems? Asking many questions like these will eventually lead to your final thesis—for example, "As an image, 'snow' is suggestive of mystery in Robert Frost's poetry."

If your general topic is the role of the pediatric nurse, you might ask, "Who does she serve—the child, the family, the medical community? How does she serve? What functions are important?" Such questions and your discovered findings may produce the final thesis, such as, "The pediatric nurse satisfies several needs of the community—the health needs of the child, the personnel demands of the medical community, and the medical education of the family."

The earlier the preliminary thesis is formulated, the earlier a satisfactory working limitation will be set on note-taking. Remember that you may change your working thesis sentence as you progress. You should not bind yourself, early in your work, to a thesis you cannot support or do not believe. In fact, you cannot properly state your final thesis until after you complete note-taking and are ready to begin writing the paper. Nevertheless, a preliminary central idea, expressed in one or two sentences, will aid you in the organization of facts, limit your note-taking, and eliminate needless research.

Keep your thesis flexible at this early stage. Some researchers change it several times during the course of the research.

GATHERING DATA

2

The Working Bibliography

● Early in your research you ought to begin developing a working bibliography, which is a list of reference sources that you will eventually investigate for information about your subject. Therefore, during your preliminary reading you should begin writing bibliography cards for all references that show promise of giving clues about your topic. Specifically, you need to watch for bibliographies and notes that list new source materials. Most books of critical evaluation will contain extensive bibliographies at the ends of chapters or at the end of the book. Journal articles usually have footnotes at the bottom of the page and a bibliography at the end. General reference works, such as encyclopedias and biographical dictionaries, normally offer brief bibliographies at the end of each entry.

Suppose your topic concerns some aspect of Benjamin Franklin's political activities. Your preliminary reading of *Encyclopaedia Britannica* will uncover not only a brief biography but also the following bibliography:

MAJOR WORKS
POLITICAL AND ECONOMIC: *A Modest Enquiry into the Nature and Necessity of a Paper Currency* (1729); *Plain Truth; or Serious Considerations on the Present State of the City of Philadelphia* (1747); *Proposals Relating to the Education of Youth in Pensilvania* (1749); *Observations Concerning the Increase of Mankind* (1755); *The Way to Wealth* (1757); *The Interest of Great Britain Considered with Regard to Her Colonies and the Acquisition of Canada and Guadaloupe* (1760); *Positions to be Examined Concerning National Wealth* (1769); *Journal of the Negotiations for Peace* (1782).
RELIGIOUS, PHILOSOPHICAL, AND SCIENTIFIC: *A Dissertation on Liberty and Necessity, Pleasure and Pain* (1725); *Articles of Belief and Acts of Religion* (1728); *Experiments and Observations on Electricity* (1751).
OTHER WORKS: *Poor Richard's* (1732–57), an almanac containing a number of famous maxims; Franklin's *Autobiography* (1771–88); "Information to those who would remove to America" (1784).

BIBLIOGRAPHY. *The Papers of Benjamin Franklin*, 15 vol., ed. by L.W. LABAREE *et al.* (1959–71), with 25 additional volumes expected, will be the definitive collection. *The Writings of Benjamin Franklin*, 10 vol., ed. by A.H. SMYTH (1905–07), has heretofore been the chief collection. The fullest biography is CARL VAN DOREN, *Benjamin Franklin* (1938); the best brief one is VERNER W. CRANE, *Benjamin Franklin and a Rising People* (1954). The most recent life is THOMAS FLEMING, *The Man Who Dared the Lightning: A New Look at Benjamin Franklin* (1971). An interesting specialized study is BRUCE INGHAM GRANGER, *Benjamin Franklin, An American Man of Letters* (1964).

(T.Hor.)

Fig. 1: From *The New Encyclopaedia Britannica*

Since several of these sources will appear promising, you will want to begin making bibliography cards, such as:

Fig. 2: Sample Bibliography Card

> Crane, Verner W.
> Benjamin Franklin and
> a Rising People, 1954.

Later, at the card catalog, you can insert the proper library call number (see pp. 29–32) and the missing publication information (see Figure 3, p. 13). Then, when you are ready to study this particular book, your card provides the information for finding it. In addition, your card will have the necessary data for the final bibliography.

As you discover each new reference, you should record the bibliographical data onto *individual,* three-by-five-inch index cards. (But if you have a system that works well for you, by all means use it, provided, of course, that your system is accurate and efficient.) Individual cards have one great advantage over other systems: you can shuffle and arrange them to keep them in alphabetical order.

As you record information, check carefully to make certain that each card includes the following:

1. *Author's name,* followed by a period. Arrange the name in inverted order, surname first, for alphabetizing purposes. Provide the name in the fullest form available, for example, "Hart, Thomas P.," not "Hart, T. P."

2. *Title of the work,* followed by a period. Enclose within quotation marks titles of articles, essays, chapters, sections, programs on radio or television, short poems, stories, and songs. Underline titles of books, journals, pamphlets, magazines, newspapers, plays, movies (including television movies), long poems, and operas.

3. *Publication information.* For a book: the place, followed by a colon; the publisher, followed by a comma; the date, followed by a period. For a journal

article: the name of the journal, followed by a comma; the volume number in Arabic numerals; the date in parentheses, followed by a comma; the page(s), followed by a period. Spell in full titles of periodicals, for example, *Journal of Higher Education,* not *J. of Higher Ed.*

4. *Other items of documentation* as necessary (see Chapter 6, pp. 128–48, for exact information about positioning these items on the card):

- name of the editor or translator
- edition used, whenever it is not the first
- series number
- number of volumes with this particular title
- volume number if one of two or more

5. *Library call number* of a book or magazine, placed in the upper right-hand corner of the card. This item is valuable when you are ready to search out and read your sources.

6. *A personal note,* at the bottom of the card, as to the type of material to be found in this source or any special aspect it presents. Perhaps include the name of the index in which you first found mention of this source, just in case you need to go back and double-check the facts (see Figure 5).

Specimen Bibliography Cards

In addition to the examples provided below, you may also study the bibliographical entries in Chapter 6.

973.320
J156b
Jacobs, Wilbur R. Benjamin Franklin: Statesman, Philosopher, or Materialist. New York: Holt, Rinehart & Winston, 1972.
Check items on Franklin as a statesman.

Fig. 3: Card for an Entire Book

Fig. 4: Card for a Journal Article

Korty, M.B. "Franklin's World
of Books." Journal of
Library History, 2 (Oct. 1967),
326-28.
Check this article for those
writers who may have
influenced Franklin.

Fig. 5: Card for Entry Found in *Essay and General Literature Index*

810
Es73g

Aldridge, A.O. "Form and
Substance in Franklin's
Autobiography." In Essays
on American Literature.
Ed. Clarence Golides. Durham:
Duke Univ. Press, 1967.
See esp. pp. 47-62
ESSAY + GEN. LIT. INDEX 1965-69

Fig. 6: Card for an Editor

973.320
F854f

Fleming, Thomas, ed. Benjamin
Franklin: A Biography in
His Own Words. New York:
Harper and Row, 1972.

Good quotations from
Franklin.

**Fig. 7: Card That
Refers to a Portion
of a Book**

```
                              810.9
                              P55 A

Paul, Sherman, ed. Six Classic
American Writers: An
Introduction. Minneapolis:
University of Minnesota Press,
1970.
Study pp. 235-38.
```

Later in your study you will need information from these cards for several purposes. First, you will need to find a book for research purposes. Second, you will refer to its card for note documentation, as in:

> 3 M. B. Korty, "Franklin's World of Books," Journal
>
> of Library History, 2 (Oct. 1967), 327.

Third, you will again need the card for writing the bibliography entry, as shown:

> Korty, M. B. "Franklin's World of Books." Journal of Library
>
> History, 2 (Oct. 1967), 326–28.

Obviously, it benefits you to write carefully detailed bibliography cards. Also, you should keep them in order and in a safe place.

The Library Reference Room

You will need a system of library study that will save time and produce results. Adding a few sources to your bibliography during preliminary reading is only incidental to your main bibliographical development. After preliminary reading and your selection of a restricted topic, you will need to thoroughly investigate all avenues of approach to the subject. To that end, you should follow established procedures which direct you to the important bibliographies and indexes in your library's reference room. In these books you will discover a vast array of source material. Your stack of bibliography cards will grow rapidly, providing a valuable index to the range and scope of past and present scholarship related to your subject.

The step-by-step method of investigation that follows in this chapter should provide a basis for thorough coverage of your topic: it takes you first to bibliographies and indexes, then to the card catalog, and finally to the books and articles themselves. Following this system will ensure efficiency and skill in the preparation of your paper.

Before beginning formal research, you may wish to tour the library to learn its organization. Your tour should include the information desk, the reference room, the card catalog, the periodicals room, the stacks (if they are open to undergraduates), and other specialty areas such as the microfilm room, the photocopying area, the listening area for records and tapes, and the viewing room for films and film loops.

Experienced researchers usually begin their investigation in the reference room. There they gather a list of sources from bibliographies, indexes, and other works of reference. Later, at the card catalog, they supplement their list and record call numbers. Only then do they begin serious reading for note-taking.

You may employ this same procedure. Already you should have a few bibliography cards that you recorded during your preliminary reading in encyclopedias and other general works. Now you need to expand this small list into a full working bibliography. Keep in mind, however, that bibliographies and indexes in the reference room do not provide information for note-taking; rather, they direct you to books, pamphlets, and articles in collections, magazines, and newspapers where you will find detailed treatment of your topic.

Bibliographies and indexes classify their listings according to individual systems that vary from work to work. Before using any index, you should study its preliminary pages to determine its system of abbreviations, symbols, and classification. And, since indexes appear weekly, bimonthly, monthly, and yearly, you should look closely at the date of publication of each one you select. For example, if your topic concerns a contemporary problem, you would want to concentrate on recent listings, but if your subject is a historical figure like Woodrow Wilson, you would want to examine earlier indexes, especially those for the years 1913–1921 when he was president.

Because reference works serve many students, you must not take them from the library. Rather, make notes from them and leave them on a table so that the librarians may return them to their proper position on the shelves.

BIBLIOGRAPHIES

In the reference room you will find separate bibliographies on a wide range of subjects. Some, like *A Shakespeare Bibliography,* are standard bibliographies that list sources in existence for some time. Others, like *Bibliographic Index,* are current bibliographies that list recent publications and that are kept up-to-date by supplements.

Bibliographies also appear within other works. As noted previously, encyclopedias usually contain brief bibliographies at the ends of most articles. Critical and biographical studies often have bibliographies at the end of the book; for example, Thomas J. Fleming's *Man Who Dared the Lightning* has a four-page bibliography. Most scholarly journals maintain up-to-date bibliographies: for example, history students depend upon *English Historical Review*, literature students look to the *MLA Bibliography*, and biology students consult *Biological Abstracts*.

As a beginning researcher, you need a comprehensive listing of major reference materials in your subject field. To that end, Appendix II of this manual contains lists of standard reference works and journals in the following subject areas: applied sciences (pp. 168–73), art (pp. 173–75), biological sciences (pp. 175–76), business (pp. 176–77), education (pp. 177–78), English language and literature (pp. 178–81), foreign languages (pp. 181–85), health and physical education (pp. 185–86), home economics (pp. 186–87), music (pp. 187–88), philosophy (p. 188), psychology (pp. 188–89), religion (pp. 189–90), social sciences (pp. 191–95), and speech and drama (pp. 195–96). A brief glance at these lists will show you that they contain titles of major bibliographies in all these disciplines.

Then, for thorough coverage of your field, examine the following reference sources; each of these books functions as a bibliography that offers a list of other bibliographies:

Bell, Marion V., and Eleanor A. Swidan, eds. *Reference Books: A Brief Guide.* 8th ed. Baltimore: Enoch Pratt, 1978.
Besterman, Theodore. *A World Bibliography of Bibliographies.* 4th ed. 5 vols. Lausanne: Societas Bibliographica, 1965.
Murphey, Robert W. *How and Where to Look It Up: A Guide to Standard Sources of Information.* New York: McGraw-Hill, 1958.
Sheehy, Eugene Paul. *Guide to Reference Books.* 9th ed. Chicago: American Library Association, 1976. Revised, Expanded, & Updated Version of the 8th ed. by C. M. Winchell.
Shores, Louis. *Basic Reference Sources.* Ed. Lee Ash. Library Reference Series. 1954; rpt. Boston: Gregg, 1972.
Walford, Arthur J., ed. *Guide to Reference Material.* 3rd ed. 3 vols. London: Library Association, 1973, 1975, 1977.

Let us assume you wish to proceed with the investigation of Ben Franklin begun earlier in this chapter. You would first examine the listings under "History" (pp. 192–93), "Political Science" (pp. 193–94), and "American Literature" (p. 178) in Appendix II and perhaps one or two of the books listed immediately above. As a result, you would find such works as:

American Historical Association. *Guide to Historical Literature.* Ed. George F. Howe and others. New York: MacMillan, 1961.
Beers, Henry P. *Bibliographies in American History.* 1942; rpt. New York: Octagon, 1973.
Northup, Clark S. *A Register of Bibliographies of the English Language and Literature.* New York: Hafner, 1962.

Examining these and other books like them, you would then search for special bibliographies of Franklin. In this case, fortunately, there are two bibliographies exclusively concerned with our subject:

> Ford, Paul Leicester. *Franklin Bibliography: A List of Books Written by, or Relating to, Benjamin Franklin.* Brooklin: n.p., 1889. Rev. by R. R. Bowker in *Library Journal,* XIV, 425.
> "List of Works Relating to Benjamin Franklin Published Since the Franklin Bicentenary." Washington, D.C.: Library of Congress, 1924.

However, if your thorough investigation uncovers the fact that no bibliography devoted solely to your subject exists, you will still have plenty of other reference material to work with. Even with the Franklin bibliographies above, you would need up-to-date reference sources because new discoveries are made regularly, even about such historical figures as Benjamin Franklin. Scholars are constantly reinterpreting such things as his writings, the circumstances surrounding him during his age, and the effect he had upon others.

Therefore, in addition to such special bibliographies you should also examine the following:

> *Bibliographic Index: A Cumulative Bibliography of Bibliographies.* New York: H. W. Wilson, 1938–date.

Although *Bibliographic Index* originally covered only the years 1937–42, it is kept current by supplements. It is therefore valuable for bringing your investigation of a topic up-to-date. A sample entry from *Bibliographic Index* of 1971 uncovers these sources:

Fig. 8: From *Bibliographic Index, 1971.* 1. Subject heading **2.** Entry of book that contains a bibliography on Franklin **3.** Specific pages on which bibliography is located

Each entry in *Bibliographic Index* directs you to the specific bibliographic section within a critical study. In other words, by consulting this text, you would have discovered not only five books about Franklin but also five additional bibliographic lists. For example, a bibliography on Franklin will be found on pp. 515–20 of Thomas J. Fleming's *Man Who Dared the Lightning* and on pp. 175–76 of Esmond Wright's *Benjamin Franklin and American Independence*. This information should be noted on a bibliography card, as follows:

Paul, Sherman, ed. *Six Classic American Writers: An Introduction*. Minneapolis: Univ. of Minnesota Press, 1970.
Bibliography on pp. 235-38

Fig. 9: Card Listing a Bibliographic Source

Another reference aid of this general nature is *Bulletin of Bibliography and Magazine Notes* (Boston: F. W. Faxon, 1897--date). The first page of each volume contains an index.

TRADE BIBLIOGRAPHIES

You may also want to use the trade bibliographies, which are works intended primarily for use by booksellers and librarians. As a researcher, you will find them helpful in three ways: to discover sources which may not be listed in other bibliographies or in the card catalog of your library; to locate facts of publication, such as place and date; and, especially, to learn if a book is in print.

Subject Guide to Books in Print (New York: Bowker, 1957–date) supplies a subject index that enables you to discover new sources. For example, the 1974 edition contains an extensive listing about Benjamin Franklin. A small portion follows:

Fig. 10: From
Subject Guide to
Books in Print
1. Subject **2.** Dates
of subject's life span
3. Author **4.** Title
5. Date of
publication
6. Price **7.** Publisher
8. Library of
Congress Number
9. International
Standard Book
Number (used when
ordering)
10. Paperback book

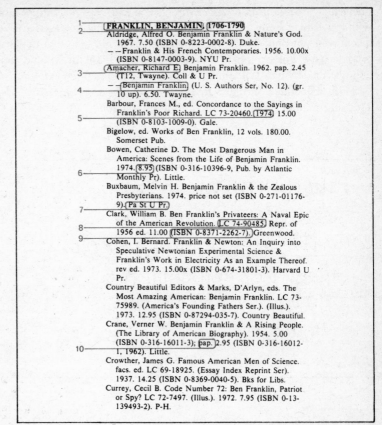

Many items from this *Subject Guide to Books in Print* will lend themselves to your study. Therefore, bibliography cards should be made for the most promising, as in this sample card:

Fig. 11: Sample
Bibliography Card
for Source Found
in *Subject Guide to*
Books in Print
The publisher's full
name and city are
listed in a separate
section of *Books in*
Print

Aldridge, Alfred O.
Benjamin Franklin and
Nature's God. Durham,
N.C.: Duke Univ. Press,
1967

In like manner, you should become familiar with *Books in Print* (New York: Bowker, 1948–date). This work provides an author-title index to the *Publishers' Trade List Annual* (New York: Bowker, 1874–date), a list of books currently in print. Also, *Publishers' Weekly* (New York: Bowker, 1872–date) offers current publication data. In short, you cannot overlook the trade bibliographies as a possible source of information. Others are:

Paperbound Books in Print. New York: Bowker, 1955–date.

Since the publication of paperback books is increasing annually and since important books are occasionally found only in paperback form, you may find this text a necessary tool.

Cumulative Book Index. Minneapolis [later New York]: H. W. Wilson, 1900–date.

This work lists books by author, subject, editor, and translator. Use it to find complete publication data or to locate *all* material in English on a particular subject.

The National Union Catalog: A Cumulative Author List. Ann Arbor: Edwards, 1953–date.

Basically, this work is the card catalog in book form; that is, it provides a list representing the Library of Congress printed cards and also titles reported by other libraries. It supplements the *Library of Congress Catalog.*

Library of Congress Catalog: Books: Subjects. Washington, D.C.: Library of Congress, 1950–date.

This catalog complements *The National Union Catalog* by supplying a subject classification. Separate volumes are available for the years 1950–54, 1955–59, 1960–64, and annually thereafter.

General Catalogue of Printed Books. London: Trustees of the British Museum, 1881–date.

This British publication serves a corresponding function to *The National Union Catalog.* Such listings are available for most nations.

Union List of Serials in Libraries of the United States and Canada. 3rd ed. New York: H. W. Wilson, 1965. Supplements, *New Serial Titles,* Washington, D.C.: Library of Congress, 1953–date.

You may consult this work to determine if a nearby library has a magazine that is unavailable in your library.

Ulrich's International Periodicals Directory. Ed. Merle Rohinsky. 15th ed. New York: Bowker, 1973.

This work is a guide to current periodicals, both domestic and foreign.

INDEXES

A general index furnishes the page number(s) of another book or magazine where you will find specific information. Fundamentally, there are three types: indexes to materials in books and collections, indexes to literature in periodicals, and indexes to materials in newspapers.

Indexes to Books and Collections

First, you should recall *Bibliographic Index* (see pp. 18–19), which refers you to books or collections as well as bibliographies. In addition, you should familiarize yourself with:

> *Essay and General Literature Index, 1900–1933.* New York: H. W. Wilson, 1934. Supplements, 1934–date.
> *Biography Index: A Quarterly Index to Biographical Material in Books and Magazines.* New York: H. W. Wilson, 1946/47–date.

The first index directs you to material within books and collections of both a biographical and a critical nature. Note the following entry from a supplement of *Essay and General Literature Index:*

Fig. 12: From *Essay and General Literature Index*
1. Subject 2. Article by Franklin 3. Book in which Franklin's essay appears
4. Designates that following essays are *about* Franklin, rather than essays written *by* him
5. Author of essay about Franklin
6. Title of the essay
7. Book in which the essay appears

1 —— Franklin, Benjamin
Benjamin Franklin calls for a volunteer militia
In Millis, W. ed. American military thought p 1-9
Experiments and ideas; excerpt from "The ingenious Dr Franklin"
In Shapley, H.; Rapport, S. B. and Wright, H. eds. The new Treasury of science p273-79
2 —— 'On modern innovations in the English language and in printing'
In Bolton, W. F. ed. The English language p174-79
3 ——
4 —— About
Cawelti, J. G. Natural aristocracy and the new republic: the idea of mobility in the thought of Franklin and Jefferson
In Cawelti, J. G. Apostles of the self-made man p9-36
5 —— Conkin, P. K. Benjamin Franklin: science and morals
In Conkin, P. K. Puritans and pragmatists p73-108
6 —— Rossiter, C. L. Benjamin Franklin
In Rossiter, C. L. Six characters in search of a Republic p206-59
Sainte-Beuve, C. A. Franklin
In Sainte-Beuve, C. A. Portraits of the eighteenth century v 1 p309-75
7 ——
Stourzh, G. Sober philosophe: Benjamin Franklin
In Intellectual history in America v 1 p64-93

About individual works
Autobiography
Aldridge, A. O. Form and substance in Franklin's Autobiography
In Essays on American literature, in honor of Jay B. Hubbell p47-62

Anecdotes
Harris, L. A. Benjamin Franklin
In Harris, L. A. The fine art of political wit p41-51

Note that this index sends you to essays *within* books that you might otherwise overlook; for example, J. G. Cawelti's essay appears in *Apostles of the Self-Made Man* and P. K. Conkin's essay appears in a book with the deceptive title *Puritans and Pragmatists*. The publishers and dates for these entries are found in a "List of Books Indexed" at the end of each volume of *Essay and General Literature Index*.

Biography Index is a good starting point if your study involves a famous person. It gives clues to biographical information for people of all lands. (However, for the years 1900–47 you should see *Essay and General Literature Index*.) Note the following short excerpt from *Biography Index:*

FRANKLIN, Benjamin, 1706-1790, (statesman) and scientist
Currey, Cecil B. Code number 72/Ben Franklin: patriot or spy? Prentice-Hall '72 331p bibliog pors
Duane, William, ed. Letters to Benjamin Franklin from his family and friends, 1751-1790. Bks. for libs. press '70 195p por
Fleming, Thomas J. Man who dared the lightning; a new look at Benjamin Franklin. Morrow '71 532p bibliog il pors
Ford, Paul Leicester. Many-sided Franklin. Bks. for lib. press '72 516p il
Ford, Paul Leicester. Who was the mother of Franklin's son? An historical conundrum hitherto given up, now partly answered. Franklin '71 15p
Franklin, Benjamin. Autobiography, and other pieces; ed. with an introd. by Dennis Welland. (Classical Am. texts) Oxford '70 183p bibliog
Franklin, Benjamin. Benjamin Franklin; a biog. in his own words; ed. by Thomas Fleming; with an introd. by Whitfield J. Bell, jr; Joan Patterson Kerr, picture editor. (Founding fathers) Newsweek; distributed by Harper '72 416p bibliog
Franklin, Benjamin. Founding fathers; Benjamin Franklin; a biog. in his own words; ed. by Thomas Fleming; with an introd. by Whitfield J. Bell; Joan Paterson Kerr, picture editor. Newsweek '72 416p bibliog il pors map
Franklin, Benjamin. Papers; vol 13: Jan 1 through Dec. 31, 1766; vol. 14: Jan 1, through Dec. 31. 1767; Leonard W. Labaree [and others] editors. Yale univ. press '69-'70 2v il por facsims
Franklin, Benjamin. Papers; vol. 15: Jan. 1-Dec. 31, 1768: William B. Willcox [and others] editors. Yale univ. press '72 327p il por facsims
Franklin, Benjamin. Papers: vol.16: Jan. 1 through Dec. 31, 1769. Yale univ. press '72 359p il pors facsims
Freedman, R. S. Musical Benjamin Franklin. il por Mus J 28:40+ O '70

Fig. 13: From Biography Index
1. Subject 2. Dates of subject's birth and death 3. Subject's profession 4. Author of the biography 5. Title of the biography 6. Publisher 7. Date of publication 8. Number of pages 9. Contains a bibliography 10. Contains portraits and a map 11. Illustrated 12. Publication data for a periodical

Most indexes published by the H. W. Wilson Company use this same code system. Specifically, note the code for journal volumes and page numbers— "23:81–91 D'71." To conform to the suggestions in this manual, you will want to record this data differently on your bibliography card, as follows:

Fig. 14: Sample
Bibliography Card

Morris, R. B. "Meet Dr.
Franklin." *American
Heritage,* 23 (Dec. 1971),
81-91.

When looking for biographical information, you should also consult a good biographical dictionary (see pp. 5–6).

Other important sources are the cumulated subject and author indexes to *Dissertation Abstracts International* (Ann Arbor: Univ. Microfilms, 1970–date; formerly *Microfilm Abstracts,* 1938–51, and *Dissertation Abstracts,* 1952–69). Issue No. 12, Part II, of each volume contains the cumulated subject and author indexes for Issues 1–12 of the volume's two sections—A, Humanities and Social Sciences and B, Sciences and Engineering. (Note that since 1972 the indexes have included authors only.) In addition to these indexes, the *Comprehensive Dissertation Index* lists dissertations from 1861 to date according to subject and author. For example, Volume 29 includes the following entries for Benjamin Franklin:

Fig. 15: From the
*Comprehensive
Dissertation Index
1861-1972*

FRANKLIN
AN ANNOTATED CHECKLIST OF THE LETTERS OF
FRANKLIN BENJAMIN SANBORN (1831-1917)—
CLARKSON, JOHN W., JR (PH D 1971 COLUMBIA
UNIVERSITY) X1971, p 222
FRANKLIN AND CREVECOEUR INDIVIDUALISM AND
THE AMERICAN DREAM IN THE EIGHTEENTH
CENTURY— AGEE, WILLIAM HERBERT (PH.D 1969
UNIVERSITY OF MINNESOTA) 600p 31/01-A, p 380
70-01830
BENJAMIN FRANKLIN AND HIS BIOGRAPHERS A
CRITICAL STUDY— KUSHEN, BETTY SANDRA (PH.D
1969 NEW YORK UNIVERSITY) 317p 30/09-A,
p 3946 70-03081
BENJAMIN FRANKLIN AND THE ZEALOUS
PRESBYTERIANS— BUXBAUM, MELVIN (PH D 1968
UNIVERSITY OF CHICAGO) X1968, p 172
SPIRITUAL AUTOBIOGRAPHY IN SELECTED WRITINGS
OF SEWALL, EDWARDS, BYRD, WOOLMAN, AND
FRANKLIN A COMPARISON OF TECHNIQUE AND
CONTENT— MILLAR, ALBERT EDWARD, JR (PH D
1968 UNIVERSITY OF DELAWARE) 362p 29/06-A,
p 1873 68-15542
BENJAMIN FRANKLIN A STUDY IN SELF-
MYTHOLOGY— WHITE, CHARLES WILLIAM (PH D
1967 HARVARD UNIVERSITY) X1967, p 175
THE GROWTH OF THE BENJAMIN FRANKLIN IMAGE
THE PHILADELPHIA YEARS — SAPPENFIELD, JAMES
ALLEN (PH D 1966 STANFORD UNIVERSITY) 233p
27/10-A, p 3469 67-04426
FRANKLIN'S STYLE IRONY AND THE COMIC— CLASBY,
NANCY TENFELDE (PH D 1966 THE UNIVERSITY OF
WISCONSIN) 273p 28/02-A, p 622 66-09892

An abstract of the eighth entry, "Franklin's Style: Irony and the Comic" by Nancy Tenfelde Clasby, is to be found in Vol. 28, No. 2A, p. 622, of *Dissertation Abstracts International*. A portion of that abstract follows:*

FRANKLIN'S STYLE: IRONY AND THE COMIC. ————1

(Order No. 66-9892) ————2

Nancy Tenfelde Clasby, Ph.D.
The University of Wisconsin, 1966 ————3

Supervisor: Professor Harry Hayden Clark ————4

Since Benjamin Franklin's style is the product and essence of a lifetime of expressive action, an analysis of it should bring us closer to an understanding of his extremely complex man. My dissertation is aimed at collating and interpreting those elements of his style which will help to fill in the outlines of the figure which modern Franklin scholars have only begun to discover. There are three parts to this dissertation: the first deals with the expressive character of certain elements of style, the second with Franklin's mind, the source of expression, and the third, and longest, section presents and interprets statistics on such features of his style as parallelism, metaphor and tone. The comic and ironic tones which inform so much of Franklin's best work are treated at length in the third section.

•• ••• ••• ••• ••• ••• ••• ••• ••• ••• ••• ••• •••

Reservations about the eighteenth-century world and its values did not, however, dull Franklin's passion for communication. In life, Franklin was an eiron, a maskmaker whose activities were shaped to present various appearances when seen from various angles. He made sure that people saw only those aspects of himself that they were capable of recognizing as parts of some coherent personality. In its myriad delicate adjustments to varied audiences his prose bears the marks of the same consuming effort to clarify, to make sense. The style is concrete and direct, never abstract, seldom merely decorative. It aims at the attractive statement of certain limited truths, and its aspect changes as Franklin adopts various masks. Beneath the multiple surface characteristics of the style, however, is a radical unity, a gestalt which reflects in miniature the quality and direction of a lifetime of communicative gestures. The whole effort of this paper, in its various parts, is directed toward a clarification of the full outlines of a carefully structured life and style.

273 pages. 5

Fig. 16: From *Dissertation Abstracts International* **1.** Title of dissertation **2.** Order number if you desire to buy a copy of the work **3.** Author, school, and date **4.** Faculty chairman of the dissertation committee **5.** Total number of pages of the dissertation

An abstract, of course, is only a brief summary of the entire work. If the dissertation is pertinent to your topic or if you plan an exhaustive investigation, you may wish to order a copy of the complete work from University Microfilms, Inc.

Indexes to Literature in Periodicals

Because they provide four types of information better than any other source, you must use articles in periodicals. Understandably, they contain: the most recent articles on any subject; obscure, temporary, or extremely new materials; the climate of opinion of a particular period; and supplements to professional literature. Remember, too, that materials often appear as journal articles before their publication in book form.

There are two main types of periodicals: general periodicals (for example, *Time, Ladies' Home Journal, Reader's Digest*) and professional journals (for example, *American Historical Review, Journal of Psychology,* or *National Tax Journal*). You will use both types, of course, but you should depend mainly upon the learned journals whose treatment of topics is more critically detailed.

As an index to articles in periodicals, you should first investigate:

Readers' Guide to Periodical Literature. New York: H. W. Wilson, 1900–date.

A sample entry follows:

Fig. 17: From Readers' Guide to Periodical Literature
1. Subject 2. A piece by Franklin himself 3. Designates that the following articles are *about* Franklin 4. Title of article 5. Author 6. Illustrated with portraits 7. Indicates a review: Van Doren's book *Benjamin Franklin* was reviewed in *Commonweal* by J. Cournos 8. Name of periodical and publication data

```
FRANKLIN, Benjamin                                    —1
  Benjamin Franklin meets the press; excerpts
    from his writings. por facsim Scholastic
    67:14-15 Ja 12 '56
  Benjamin Franklin on his religious faith;
    letter to Ezra Stiles. Am Heritage 7:105
    D '55                                             —2
  Excerpts from his voluminous writings. por
    N Y Times Mag p76 Ja 15 '56
  Farther experiments and observations in elec-
    tricity; excerpt from Experiments and ob-
    servations on electricity. bibliog Science
    123:47-50 Ja 13 '56
  From Ben's letters. Time 67:90 Ja 30 '56
  Mr Franklin, self-revealed. facsim Life 40:
    74-7+ Ja 9 '56
                    about                             —3
  Americana page. Hobbies 61:100 Jl '56
  Ben Franklin: an affectionate portrait, by
    N. B. Keyes. Review
      Sat R 39:16 Ja 21 '56. W. M. Wallace
  Ben Franklin, trail blazer for inventors. P.       —4
    Lee. il pors map Pop Mech 105:99-102+ Ja
    '56
  Benjamin and the bell. M. Alkus. Ladies            —5
    Home J 72:180 Ap '55
  Benjamin Franklin and the French alliance;
    adapted from Secret war of independence.
    H. Augur. il por Am Heritage 7:65-88 Ap '56      —6
  Benjamin Franklin, by C. Van Doren. Re-
    view
      Commonweal 63:497 F 10 '56. J. Cournos         —7
  Benjamin Franklin in modern life and educa-
    tion. T. Woody. Sch & Soc 84:102-7 S 29 '56
  Benjamin Franklin the diplomat. por U S
    Dept State Bul 34:50-1 Ja 9 '56
  Benjamin Franklin's grand design; Albany
    plan of union. R. B. Morris. il por map
    Am Heritage 7:4-7+ F '56                          —8
```

Again, you would want to write out bibliography cards for those entries that look
promising, as in the following example:

Franklin, Benjamin. "Benjamin
Franklin on His Religious
Faith: Letter to Ezra Stiles."
<u>American Heritage</u>, 7 (Dec.
1955), 105.

Fig. 18:
Bibliography Card
for Entry Taken
from *Readers'*
Guide to Periodical
Literature

In most instances, this index directs you to general periodicals, though since 1953
certain scientific periodicals have been included. If you wish a more in-depth
examination of the scholarly journals, such as *New England Quarterly* and *Polit-*
ical Science Quarterly, you should investigate the following (listed in chronological order):

International Index. Vols. 1–18. New York: H. W. Wilson, 1907–65.
Social Sciences and Humanities Index. Vols. 19–61. New York: H. W. Wilson,
  1965–74.
Humanities Index. Vols. 1– . New York: H. W. Wilson, 1974–date.
Social Sciences Index. Vols. 1– . New York: H. W. Wilson, 1974–date.

Both the new *Humanities Index* and the *Social Sciences Index* supersede the
Social Sciences and Humanities Index. The *Humanities Index* now serves as an
index to articles in 260 magazines in the following fields: archaeology, classical
studies, area studies, folklore, history, language and literature, literary and political criticism, performing arts, philosophy, religion, and theology. *Social Sci-*
ences Index catalogs articles in 263 magazines in these fields: anthropology,
economics, environmental science, geography, law and criminology, medical
sciences, political science, psychology, public administration, and sociology.

A sample entry from the 1960–62 issue of the *International Index* lists the
following sources on Benjamin Franklin:

Fig. 19: From
International Index
1. Subject 2. Title of
article 3. Author
4. Name of journal
and publication data

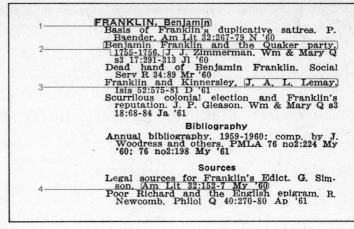

You may also need to investigate:

Nineteenth Century Readers' Guide to Periodical Literature, 1890–1899 [with
supplementary indexing, 1900–22]. 2 vols. New York: H. W. Wilson, 1944.
Poole's Index to Periodical Literature, 1802–1881. Rev. ed. Boston: Houghton
Mifflin, 1891. Supplements cover the years 1882–1906.

> With this work you may locate information on materials from 1802–1906.
> Note that *Poole's Index* has only a subject classification list. See, however,
> Marion V. Bell and Jean C. Bacon, *Poole's Index Date and Volume Key*
> (Chicago: Association of College and Reference Libraries, 1957) for an
> alphabetical title listing.

Newspaper Indexes

Newspapers are an excellent source of information. Therefore, you should
familiarize yourself with the *New York Times Index* (New York: New York
Times, 1913–date). It not only indexes the *New York Times* but also indirectly
indexes most other newspapers by revealing the date on which the same news was
probably reported in other newspapers. Many libraries have the *New York Times*
on microfilm. A sample entry from the *New York Times Index* follows:

Fig. 20: From *New*
York Times Index
1. Subject 2. Cross
reference 3. Date,
section number, and
page number
(November 25,
Section 8, p. 22)

For British newspapers a similar index is the *Official Index* [to *The London Times*] (London: Times, 1907–date). It is available in most American public and university libraries.

Pamphlet Indexes

The principal index to most pamphlet material is:

> Vertical File Index: A Subject and Title Index to Selected Pamphlet Material. New York: H. W. Wilson, 1932/35–date.

Your library may not own many of the items listed, but the catalog gives a description of each entry, the price, and the means by which you may order the pamphlet.

Finding the Call Number

Sometime before completing your work in the reference room, you probably will want to begin preliminary investigations of some of the more promising sources you have listed on your bibliography cards. For that purpose you should turn to the card catalog, which specifies the location of all books in the library. (For periodicals most libraries have a separate, smaller catalog, sometimes called a *cardex.*) With your bibliography cards arranged alphabetically, you can easily find and record the call number for each book. If, after exerting sufficient effort, you cannot locate a catalog card, you may seek help from a librarian.

For each book you will usually find at least three separate entries in the catalog, filed under: (1) the author's name, printed on the first line (see p. 30); (2) the title of the work, typed in black ink at the top of the card (see p. 30); and (3) the subject, typed in red ink at the top of the card (see p. 33). Additional catalog cards are filed for coauthors, translators, editors, illustrators, and for other subject headings.

MAIN ENTRY CARD

As you go through the card catalog you will quickly discover that there is a main entry card for each book you are seeking, usually filed under the author's name. For example:

Fig. 21: Main Entry Card (Author Card)
1. Classification number 2. Author number 3. Author 4. Life span of author 5. Title 6. Editor 7. Place of publication 8. Publisher 9. Date of publication 10. Technical description: size, number of pages, illustrations, etc. 11. Note on contents of book 12. Separate card also filed under editor's name 13. Publisher of this card 14. Order number-Library of Congress 15. Library of Congress Call Number and date

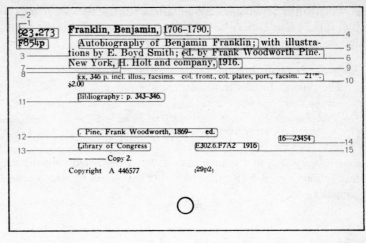

You may gather several kinds of information from this main entry card. Specifically, you should record the *complete* call number—in this case, $\frac{923.273}{F854p}$. Do not copy the first line only! You must have the full number, usually consisting of two (and sometimes three) lines of symbols. In addition, you should record any bibliographical notations, such as "Bibliography: p. 343-46." Data of this sort can direct you to additional sources.

TITLE CARD

Another card is always filed alphabetically by the book title:

Fig. 22: Title Card
1. Title, usually typed in black ink 2. Main entry card filed under "Newcomb, Benjamin H." 3. Subject headings under which you will find this same card

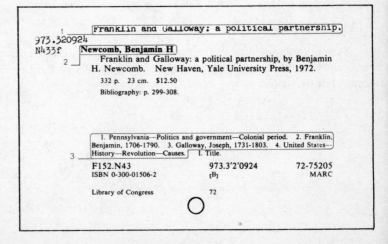

A third type of card found in the catalog is the subject card—but we will come to that in a moment.

THE CALL NUMBER

The library classifies and arranges its books by the call number, which is usually a combination of the Dewey Decimal System and the Cutter Author Number. In a call number such as $\frac{973.320924}{N433f}$, the first line is the Dewey Decimal Number and the second line is the Cutter Author Number. The Dewey system divides all books into ten general classifications:

000–099 General Works
100–199 Philosophy
200–299 Religion
300–399 Social Sciences
400–499 Language
500–599 Pure Science
600–699 Technology (Applied Sciences)
700–799 The Arts
800–899 Literature
900–999 History

The Dewey system then divides each of these ten general classes into ten smaller divisions. For example, the general literature classification (800–899) is broken down into:

800–809 General Works [on Literature]
810–819 American Literature
820–829 English Literature
830–839 German Literature
840–849 French Literature
850–859 Italian Literature
860–869 Spanish Literature
870–879 Latin Literature
880–889 Greek and Classical Literature
890–899 Literature of Other Languages

Next, American Literature (810–819) is divided into the following classifications:

810 American Literature (General)
811 Poetry
812 Drama
813 Fiction
814 Essays
815 Speeches
816 Letters
817 Satire and Humor
818 Miscellany
819 Minor Related Literature

Immediately below the Dewey classification number, most libraries also insert an author number, a set of letters and numerals based on the Cutter Three-Figure Author Table. For example, "N433f" is the author number for Newcomb's *Franklin and Galloway*. The letter "N" is the initial of the author's last name; next the Cutter table stipulates the Arabic numeral "433"; and the lowercase "f" designates the first important letter(s) in the title to distinguish this entry from similar books by Newcomb. Thus, the complete call number for Newcomb's book is $\frac{973.320924}{N433f}$. You must use both items to locate the book.

Some libraries employ the Library of Congress classification system, which features capital letters followed by Arabic numerals to designate the subdivisions. The major divisions of the Library of Congress system follow:

A	General Works and Polygraphy
B	Philosophy and Religion
C	History and Auxiliary Sciences
D	History and Topography (excluding America)
E-F	History: America
G	Geography and Anthropology
H	Social Sciences
J	Political Science
K	Law
L	Education
M	Music
N	Fine Arts
P	Language and Literature
Q	Science
R	Medicine
S	Agriculture and Plant and Animal Husbandry
T	Technology
U	Military Science
V	Naval Science
Z	Bibliography and Library Science

An example of this system might be as follows:

    TD   Environmental Technology
    833 Air Pollution
    .H48 Author Number

This call number for the Library of Congress system directs the researcher to the following book: Howard E. Hesketh, *Understanding and Controlling Air Pollution,* 2nd ed. (Ann Arbor, Michigan: Ann Arbor Science Publishers, 1974). In contrast, the Dewey classification number would be $\frac{628.53.}{H46lu}$

Using the Catalog as an Index

The card catalog indexes all important subject areas by means of subject cards and tabular headings. This is the third kind of card to be found in the catalog. For example, if your subject is Benjamin Franklin, you would discover under ''United States History'' an index to all books in the library on this subject. Note the following subject card:

<table>
<tr><td>

973.320924
N433f

    United States - History - Revolution - Causes   1

    Newcomb, Benjamin H   2
        Franklin and Galloway: a political partnership, by Benjamin
    H. Newcomb.   New Haven, Yale University Press, 1972.

        332 p. 23 cm. $12.50
        Bibliography: p. 299-308.

        1. Pennsylvania—Politics and government—Colonial period. 2. Franklin,
    Benjamin, 1706-1790. 3. Galloway, Joseph, 1731-1803. 4. United States—
    History—Revolution—Causes. I. Title.   3

    F152.N43   973.3'2'0924   72-75205
    ISBN 0-300-01506-2   [B]   MARC

    Library of Congress   72

</td></tr>
</table>

Fig. 23: Subject Card
1. Subject heading, usually typed in red ink **2.** Main entry card filed under ''Newcomb, Benjamin H.'' **3.** Other subject headings under which you will find this same card

The library makes a subject card of this nature for every topic developed within each book. As shown above, the library will index this same book by Newcomb under these additional subject headings:

Pennsylvania—Politics and government—Colonial period
Franklin, Benjamin, 1706–1790
Galloway, Joseph, 1731–1803

In other words, the card catalog of your library is, among other things, a subject index to the books it lists.

Other Catalog Cards

Always be alert for special kinds of catalog cards. Temporary cards are of a different color and usually indicate that a book is not in circulation. However, ask the librarian about the book, for it may be available:

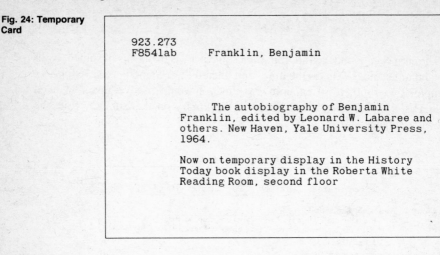

```
923.273
F854lab      Franklin, Benjamin



                 The autobiography of Benjamin
             Franklin, edited by Leonard W. Labaree and
             others. New Haven, Yale University Press,
             1964.

             Now on temporary display in the History
             Today book display in the Roberta White
             Reading Room, second floor
```

Cross-reference cards refer you to alternate or related headings. There are two types. The "see" card indicates the correct heading under which material is listed, while the "see also" card directs you to related subjects that contain additional material:

Fig. 25: "See Also" Card

```
         United States--History--Revolution

             see also

         Pennsylvania--Politics and government--
             Colonial period
```

Your best procedure with the card catalog is a combination of practices: you can easily record call numbers while you search for new sources. For example, with your bibliography cards in hand, you should look first under the proper subject heading—"Franklin, Benjamin," in this instance. There you will find index cards for all books *by* Franklin that precede the books *about* him. At the same time, you will learn the call numbers for most of your sources. Also, you may uncover new sources that supplement your working bibliography.

Getting Your Books and Periodical Articles

THE STACKS

Armed with the correct call numbers, you are now ready to locate your books in the stacks or, in the case of closed stacks, to request the books from a clerk. If a book is unavailable, you may request a "hold" on the book. When it returns, the librarian will reserve it for you.

THE RESERVE DESK

Recognizing the importance of certain books to their discipline, many instructors place them "on reserve" in the library so that a limited number of books will be available to many students. You will want to determine if any books necessary for your research are on reserve. To that end, you should ask the clerk at the desk to explain the filing system employed.

If you use a reserve book, you usually must read it in the library. Some libraries, however, permit overnight withdrawal of reserve books. But under no circumstances should you keep such a book for several days or hide it somewhere in the library for future use. These books must serve many students.

THE PERIODICALS ROOM

You will locate periodical articles in both bound and unbound volumes. The bound volumes, usually in open stacks, contain several issues within a hard cover. The unbound volumes are usually of recent publication. If periodicals are kept in closed stacks, you must provide the clerk with sufficient publication data.

Supplementing Library Materials

Without doubt the library is your best source of information when writing a research paper. But you may also find material in other places. For instance, you could write your U.S. senator or representative for one of the many booklets printed by the Government Printing Office. You will find a list of these materials, many of which are free, in a monthly catalog issued by the Superintendent of Documents, *United States Government Publications Monthly Catalog* (Washington, D.C.: GPO, 1895–date).

Also important are audiovisual materials: films, filmstrips, music, phonograph recordings, slides, and tape recordings. You may find these in the library or in some other location on or off campus.

Other good sources of information are: radio and television programs, lectures, letters, public addresses, personal interviews, and questionnaires.

TAKING NOTES

● All your work prior to actually writing the paper is organic and flexible. Therefore, after preliminary investigations, you need to take stock of your progress to that point. For example, as you gathered material for your working bibliography, you also should have uncovered and dipped into some of the more promising books and articles. Having gained from these an initial familiarity with your general subject, you should have framed a preliminary thesis sentence, thereby determining a little more accurately the direction of your future research. In addition, of course, you now should have in hand a good portion of your working bibliography, to which you will add new references as you come upon them while taking notes. Thus, your general subject will guide many aspects of your note-taking; but, at the same time, your note-taking will lead you to pin down the subject more specifically.

The Preliminary Outline

Before you progress very far in your note-taking, you should prepare a preliminary outline (write a final outline only *after* note-taking). It should be stressed that the preliminary outline is just that, a rough sketch of your major concerns, based upon ideas that you have absorbed while choosing and restricting your subject. It will serve the valuable purpose of giving order to your note-taking, thereby enabling you to evaluate and choose quotations and material for paraphrase more wisely.

To develop the preliminary outline, you should follow two fairly simple steps: (1) jot down your ideas in a rough list and (2) arrange the list into major and minor ideas. Suppose, for example, that your general topic is "Marriage," especially as marriage reflects some of the new life-styles of young couples. Your rough list might look like this:

```
contract marriage
open marriage
marriage by steps
commuter marriage
monogamy
polygamy
marriage vows
```

```
divorce laws
creative marriage
Margaret Mead's steps
alternatives to marriage
        group living
        couples living together
```

Obviously, this list is not even a rough outline, but you now have your ideas on paper where you may examine them and find relationships among them. If you organize the items, grouping main topics and relating subordinate elements to them, you will, in turn, come up with a rough outline for your paper. Two possible arrangements are shown below:

```
Introduction
Society's rejection of monogamy
Alternative choices within marriage
        polygamy
        open marriage
Alternative choices outside of marriage
        group living
        couples living together
How these affect the future of traditional marriage
```

and

```
Introduction
Monogamy in society
The concept of creative marriage
Styles of creative marriage
        Step marriage
        Long-distance marriage
        Contract marriage
        Role-sharing
Future of marriage
```

Obviously, the outlines above are sketchy, but they would serve the purpose of note-taking because you would know the sort of material to search out. Later, before actually writing the paper, you can develop a more formal outline. For now, however, you have a fairly good idea of things to search for in books and articles—that is, a definition of monogamy, the types and styles of marriage and its alternatives, and the sociological consequences of marriage styles upon the participants and society as a whole.

Always be prepared to alter the outline as your focus on the subject sharpens. For example, if you decide that it would not prove fruitful to pursue the topic of the rejection of monogamy, then adjust your outline and your thinking to a new direction, switching perhaps to the topic of creative marriage.

When preparing a preliminary outline, remember that you may arrange it in one of two ways, either general to particular (deductive order) or particular to general (inductive order). If you arrange your materials deductively, you will first present a general statement (thesis) that you will afterwards support with specific details and instances. For example, the paper about marriage might make certain generalizations about alternative marriage styles and then pinpoint particulars about these alternatives that support the generalizations made. Similarly, you could use the deductive procedure in other kinds of research papers: stating the theme of a novel and then proving it with details from the work, presenting the conclusions of a laboratory experiment and then stating the particulars, or declaring the ruthlessness of a political dictator and then presenting the evidence.

In other papers, however, you may wish to use the particular to general procedure. Using the inductive technique, you would reverse the process described in the paragraph above and present first the specifics of your argument and then work carefully toward a general conclusion. For example, the person writing about styles of marriage might examine several contractual arrangements before arriving at any generalizations about the future of marriage in our society. Such an arrangement, of course, would delay the expression of the thesis until late in the paper.

If the project demands it, you may want to use a more structured method of organization, such as cause and effect, comparison and contrast, chronological order, or process analysis. Because these methods call for fuller explanations than can be given here, you should consult a standard rhetoric book for a quick review.

Brief as they are, rough outlines nevertheless help you locate and record the important, necessary data and omit information that looks valuable but that, in fact, contributes little to your overall plan. Preliminary outlines are usually ragged and incomplete, but only you will see them. Such outlines represent the best you can do before your note-taking is very far along.

You should not feel bound by this first outline. Instead, let it develop and grow: add new topics and discard others, rearrange your order, evaluate topics, and subordinate minor elements. In short, as your ideas materialize, you should allow your outline to expand accordingly. (Before writing your final outline, however, see pp. 52–56.)

Evaluating Your Source Material

You should skim all potentially relevant material to determine its relationship to your thesis and rough outline. When you discover something pertinent, you can then write accurate, detailed notes, recording only that material which will aid the development and clarification of your thesis.

Also, you should closely examine each book to see if it contains, in addition to its text, any of the following:

1. A *table of contents* that helps you discover the chapters that deal directly or indirectly with your topic. You may find, for example, that only one chapter is potentially useful.

2. A *preface* that may explain the presence or absence of certain material in the book.

3. An *introduction* that usually serves as a critical overview of the entire book, pinpointing the primary subject of the book and approaches taken toward it.

4. An *appendix* that offers additional materials of a supplementary nature not pertinent to the primary text but perhaps important to your study.

5. A *glossary* that lists and defines complex terminology within the subject area.

6. An *index* that, by listing specific concepts, events, and names mentioned in the text, helps you discover whether the book discusses your subject at all.

7. A *bibliography* and *footnotes* that suggest new sources for later investigation.

You should utilize the most recent, reliable sources of information. Since you are expected to form sound judgments based on the merit of your collected evidence, you should depend upon the most respected authorities in your subject area and should closely evaluate outdated or biased material. The most highly regarded or influential authorities on your topic are most likely not hard to find because they are usually mentioned again and again in the sources you uncover. For example, writers about women's liberation refer often to Kate Millet, a pivotal figure in the movement. If women's liberation is your subject, you certainly must look at Millet's *Sexual Politics*.

Whatever the field, the names of certain authors are going to come up again and again, and it would pay to look at their work. For example, in black studies there is Martin Luther King, Jr.; in early space rocketry there is Wernher von Braun; in James Joyce studies there is Richard Ellmann; in recent American history there is Arthur Schlesinger; and the list goes on. There are several methods of discovering the key people in your area: (1) ask your instructor; (2) watch for certain names that keep reappearing in scholarly materials; (3) if available, check the credentials of an author—Has the individual written several books? Is the individual a chairperson of a national committee on this subject? Has he or she had wide experience in this field? (4) consult reference sources that evaluate books or that index evaluations.

The *Book Review Digest* (New York: H. W. Wilson, 1905–date) is considered a reliable source for checking the critical reception of a book. Here is a portion of the 1970 edition which demonstrates several entries that summarize the reviews for Kate Millett's *Sexual Politics:*

Fig. 26: From *Book Review Digest*
1. Author, title, and facts of publication
2. Call number, subject entry for card catalog, and Library of Congress number
3. Description of the book **4.** Reviewer's evaluation of the book **5.** A review that the *Book Review Digest* has not summarized.
6. Facts of publication of the review—*Christian Science Monitor* (September 10, 1970), p. 15, 850 words

MILLETT, KATE. Sexual politics. 393p $7.95
Doubleday

301.41 Woman—History and condition of women. Woman—Rights of women. Women in literature and art
LC 70-103769

"The relationship between the sexes is and always has been a political one—a continuing power struggle in which women are sometimes idolized, other times patronized, always exploited. So argues [the author. She discusses] how the patriarchal bias operates in culture and is reflected in literature [and] traces the effects of the so-called sexual revolution in the period 1830-1920 as well as the . . . influences of the counter-revolution from which we may be emerging." (Publisher's note) Bibliography. Index.

Reviewed by W. B. Hill
Best Sell 30:189 Ag 15 '70 160w

"As [the author] traces the vocabulary of sexual power in texts ranging from the Oresteia to Henry Miller and Mailer, it is hard not to be convinced that no deck has ever been more thoroughly stacked, and that the same impulse that recognizes 'black is beautiful' must respond to 'feminine is intelligent, responsible, and strong.' This is a richly informative book. Though [Millett] indulges herself in a heavy irony which women may find more amusing than men, she has no space for polemic. She has too much to tell us. . . . [She] works through textual analysis; the book is worth buying for the quotations alone." C. C. Park
Book World p5 Ag 9 '70 700w

Reviewed by M. J. Irion
Christian Century 87:1487 D 9 '70 800w

"'[This controversial book] is currently regarded as the doctrine of the feminist movement. The book, which grew out of the author's Ph.D. thesis at Columbia University, has received an unexpected amount of publicity mainly because it coincides with the mounting feminist insurgence and because it represents the first scholarly justification for women's liberation. . . . [It] tends to be too academic and repetitious. But its heaviness is effectively countered by Miss Millett's remarkable wit and originality. Even though her bias seems occasionally to distort her interpretations, the forensic forces of her analysis of the male-female power struggle inevitably shifts the balance of power in the reader's own attitudes. . . . [The book] is disturbing precisely because it does force this kind of private reevaluation." Diana Loercher
Christian Science Monitor p15 S 10 '70 850w

"On the question of the 'basic' psychology of women . . . the value of Millett's work is diminished by the effects of her missionarism. Results of animal behavior studies and research on the role of hormones, for instance, are either ignored, deemed irrelevant, or explained away on other terms when they indicate fundamental sex differences; yet where such research indicates equivalence of the sexes, it is heralded. Millett mentions John Money's conclusion that gender identity is a matter of social learning but neglects his finding that women given male hormones become more aggressive and sexually desirous. Such eclecticism is unfortunate. It is as if to consider the possibility of natural sex differences is equivalent to acknowledging female inferiority, a curious bias." N. R. McWilliams
Commonweal 93:25 O 2 '70 1500w

Arranged alphabetically by author, the *Book Review Digest* provides an evaluation of several thousand books each year.

You might also examine *Index to Book Reviews in the Humanities* or *Index to Book Reviews in the Social Sciences* (Williamston, Mich.: Phillip Thomson, 1960–date). Although these two works do not contain summaries of reviews or capsule evaluations, they provide additional reference information on current book reviews.

And you will find additional evaluation of source material in any of the following:

The Booklist. Chicago: American Library Association, 1905–date.

> This work offers a selective list of new books that will meet the needs of the average public library. Annotations make it valuable for student usage.

The Reader's Adviser. Rev. and enl. by Hester R. Hoffman. 11th ed. New York: Bowker, 1968.

> This work provides a systematic treatment of many books, as indicated by its subtitle: "a guide to the best in print in literature, biographies, dictionaries, encyclopedias, bibles, classics, drama, poetry, fiction, science, philosophy, travel, history."

United States Quarterly Book List. New Brunswick, N.J.: Rutgers Univ. Press, 1945–56.

> Critical annotations and biographies of the authors make this a valuable reference. However, you will not find recent material because it has ceased publication.

Finally, it will pay you to be curious and somewhat skeptical during research. Curiosity will keep you searching and tracking down facts from the library and other sources. Skepticism will prevent you from accepting the printed word as absolute. Analyze the printed page as you analyze the spoken word of instructors and friends. Verify and document your facts and findings. Your critical perception will enable you to interpret and report your findings in an interesting as well as a reliable manner.

Using Primary and Secondary Sources

Whenever possible, you should make use of primary sources—that is, the original works of an author. Primary sources include novels, short stories, poems, letters, diaries, notes, manuscripts, documents, and autobiographies. Remember, an author's own words are often the most valid source of information for both direct quotation and paraphrase.

On the other hand, you should also make extensive use of secondary sources—books and articles. Articles may be found in magazines, learned journals, and book-length critical studies. However, in reading these sources, you must judge carefully the difference between fact and opinion. Just because a statement is in print does not mean it is valid. You must learn to rely primarily on facts, and then base your own interpretations and opinions upon these. Still, if certain opinions or interpretations seem valuable to the discussion, you might wish to include them in your notes, though clearly labeled as opinion. In your later readings, perhaps, you will discover other authorities lending credence to an opinion. The weight of such evidence would then authenticate what, at first, seemed opinion.

Technique of Note Cards

As with the bibliography cards, you should be exact in recording note card information. The following system may prove helpful:

1. Write the notes legibly in ink—penciled notes become blurred because of repeated shuffling of the cards.

2. In general, use either four-by-six-inch or three-by-five-inch index cards for taking notes. (Some people prefer the four-by-six-inch cards to avoid getting them mixed up with the smaller bibliography cards.) Cards provide adequate space for most notes and, unlike large sheets of paper, are easily shuffled and rearranged.

3. Place only *one* item of information on each card. You may then shuffle and rearrange the cards during all stages of organization.

4. Since material on the back of a card may be overlooked, write on only one side of the card. However, if material should run a few lines beyond the one side on occasion, finish it on the back, but write "OVER" conspicuously on the face of the card. If you use two cards for one note, staple the two together to avoid their separation.

5. Before writing the note, indicate in an abbreviated form the source of the information. Use a brief form, inasmuch as full information on the reference is available on the bibliography card. The identification may be the title of the book, the name of the author, or both. (Some students prefer a key number system, which involves numbering each bibliography entry. When a particular reference is used, this key number is then placed on the card. The danger of this technique, however, is the possibility of losing the key.)

6. Always place the proper page number at the top of each note card, since the bibliography card will not contain this specific page reference needed for documentation (that is, endnotes or footnotes, see pp. 100–103).

7. Also, label the note card to indicate the kind of information it contains. This label at the top of the card will speed arrangement of notes with the outline.

8. Finally, write the note, using one of four basic methods: summary, précis, paraphrase, or quotation. (See below for a discussion of each method.)

Methods of Note-Taking

SUMMARY

Many times you will want to write a brief sketch of your material without great concern for style or expression. You primarily need to put information on your card, quickly and concisely—there is no concern here for careful wording or exact paraphrase. The summary note serves this purpose. Later, if you need the material for your paper, you will write it in a clearer and more appropriate prose style.

Your chief purpose with the summary card, as well as with the other kinds of note cards, is to extract all significant facts. You must devote, at this time, sufficient energy to this task; otherwise, it will still remain to be done if you take the easy way and unthinkingly copy entire paragraphs verbatim. Also, you should remember that the summary requires documentation when placed in the text. A sample note card follows:

Fig. 27: Summary Note Card

```
Long-distance marriage problems    Nichols, p. 54


        Partners must cope with loneliness, change
  child-raising practices, and learn to handle
  difficult situations on their own.
```

This sort of summary note card is valuable for giving you a rough sketch of material you may need but can express more fluently when you write your first draft. For an example of how one student employed this note, see the sample research paper, p. 89.

Another type of summary card is one that briefly summarizes the plot of a drama or story that serves as your primary source. You will have occasion to use this note whenever you write about a novel, short story, drama, or similar work. The following note demonstrates the plot summary card:

**Fig. 28: Plot
Summary Note
Card***

Hansberry   <u>A Raisin in the Sun</u>

      The drama is a problem play that portrays a
black family's determination to move out of a
ghetto to a better life. Mama Younger dominates
the family, shaping and molding the family
members, although each rebels in his own way,
especially Walter who squanders the family
inheritance and brings them to a crisis that
threatens their survival.

Such a summary should be brief, offering only enough information to clarify the plot for your reader. Avoid writing a plot summary that extends beyond one paragraph.

A third type of summary note is one that records your own ideas and thoughts. Unless you jot down your own concepts, your collection of note cards will contain only source material. Yet the majority of your paper should represent your thinking and expression. Therefore, you must make careful notes of your own ideas or they may be forgotten and beyond retrieval when you begin writing your rough draft.

The following note demonstrates the notation of personal thoughts or ideas:

**Fig. 29: Summary
Note Card of
Personal Thoughts**

      All marriage styles discussed by critics
stress the importance of "commitment" and
"relationship." Our society still retains
values inherent in traditional marriage.

---

*Instructors will find an example of how one student employed this note in the sample paper of the Instructor's Manual.

PRÉCIS

The précis is a very brief summary in your own words, differing from the rough summary in being more polished in style and differing from the paraphrase in being more concise. Try to write your précis in a polished form with complete sentences in formal English. (Only the rough summary allows abbreviations and sentence fragments.) Moreover, you must make certain that the précis is accurate not only in its content but also in its connotations. That is, you should preserve the essential truth of the reference material. Do not distort the material in any way or quote out of context, a suggestion which applies to all of your note-taking. You will have success with the précis if you:

1.   Condense the original with precision and directness. Reduce a long paragraph into a few sentences, tighten an article into a paragraph, and summarize a longer work, such as a biography, into a few pages.

2.   Preserve the tone of the original. If the original is humorous, for example, maintain that tone in the précis. In the same way, retain moods of satire, exaggeration, doubt, irony, and so on.

3.   Limit the use of key words or phrases from the original, and write the précis in your own language. However, retain exceptional words and phrases from the original, enclosing them in quotation marks.

4.   Provide documentation locating the source of your material.

A sample précis note card follows:

Fig. 30: Précis Note Card

Three—step marriage   Rice, p. 467

      Michael Scriven suggests three possible marriage levels--preliminary, a legitimized cohabitation; personal, like Mead's individual marriage; and parental, entered into only after success with the previous levels.

This note summarizes in a few words the substance of Scriven's position. The student has examined the textual matter, determined its relevance, and quickly summarized it. The following paragraph is the original material that the student reduced into précis form:

Philosophy professor Michael Scriven has elaborated on Margaret Mead's two-step plan. He proposes three types of marriage: 1) *Preliminary marriage,* which would be legitimized cohabitation, entered into contractually for one year without the need for subsequent commitment, 2) *personal marriage,* similar to Margaret Mead's idea of individual marriage, which could be entered into only after a year's trial of preliminary marriage, and 3) *parental marriage,* the last step to be taken, but only after successful personal marriage.[1]

The seventy-four words in the original were effectively reduced to twenty-four. For an example of how one student eventually used this précis, see the sample research paper, p. 87.

PARAPHRASE

You will probably write many notes in the form of paraphrase—restating, in your own style, the thought or meaning expressed by someone else. In other words, you borrow an idea, opinion, interpretation, or statement of an authority and rewrite it in your own language. Furthermore, you write the note in about the same number of words as the original, hence the distinction between paraphrase and précis, the latter being a very *brief* condensation.

Obviously, you should choose only important materials for such treatment. Material of doubtful importance should be summarized, while bulky references should be condensed with a précis. Also, it is generally wiser to paraphrase material rather than to indiscriminately fill card after card with directly quoted matter. One danger of relying primarily on quoted materials is that they may lead you into plagiarism (see pp. 49–51). Of course, you are saved from plagiarism in the use of paraphrase only if you credit the thoughts you have borrowed with proper documentation. The point of view and the presentation may be yours, but the idea, you must always remember, belongs to the original author.

You will have success with paraphrasing if you:

1. Rewrite the original in your own style in about the same number of words.

2. Preserve the tone of the original by maintaining moods of satire, anger, humor, doubt, and so on.

3. Retain exceptional words and phrasing from the original.

4. In order to avoid any hint of plagiarism, provide documentation indicating the source of your material.

Provided below is a short extract from *The Future of Marriage* by Jessie Bernard, followed by a sample paraphrase note card restating the author's ideas.

"Renewable marriages" they have been called. A five-year commitment, or a ten-year commitment, or a three-year commitment would be made. The partners would promise to maintain the marriage at least for this limited period of time. If at the end of that period they felt that the relationship was not a good one, they could renege. Alternatively, if they felt that it was a good one, they could recommit themselves to it.[2]

[1]Michael Scriven as quoted in F. Phillip Rice, *The Adolescent* (Boston: Allyn and Bacon, 1978), p. 467.

[2]Jessie Bernard, *The Future of Marriage* (New York: Bantam, 1972), p. 106.

```
Renewable marriage                    Bernard, p. 106


     Jessie Bernard refers to three, five, or ten
year commitments by which the couple makes an
agreement to "maintain the marriage" for a set
number of years with the stipulation that each
person could renege at the end of the time period
or recommit to a union that continued to be
satisfactory and fulfilling.
```

The length of the note is nearly the same length as the original material. For an example of how the student eventually used this paraphrase, see the sample research paper, p. 86.

QUOTATION

Students frequently overuse direct quotation in taking notes, and as a result they overuse quotations in the final paper. Probably only about 10 percent of your final manuscript should appear as directly quoted matter. Therefore, you should strive to limit the amount of exact transcribing of source materials while taking notes. The overuse of quotation indicates either that you do not have a clear focus on your subject matter and are jotting down verbatim just about everything related to your subject, or that you have inadequate source materials and are using the quotations only as padding. Originality in research writing requires a personal presentation of thoroughly assimilated material. Accordingly, it should be you speaking in the major portion of your paper, giving, of course, proper credit where credit is due.

Direct quotation is most necessary with primary sources, especially when you are discussing matters of style or content in your primary source. For example, the study of Lorraine Hansberry's *A Raisin in the Sun* would demand several direct quotations from the drama itself. With secondary sources, direct quotation is useful as support for an assertion now and then, especially when you foresee its possible rejection by the reader. When quoting from secondary sources, therefore, look for material that is the best evidence on the subject, that is said with especially brilliant clarity, or that is subject to refutation.

You will have success with quotation note cards if you:

1.   Place quotation marks around material that is directly quoted to distinguish it from paraphrases and the like.

2.   Copy the exact words of the author, even to the retention of any errors in the original (see *sic* used on p. 64) or what might appear to be errors. *Sic* is a term

used within brackets to show that a quoted passage is reproduced precisely.

3. For special problems that you encounter, see "Handling Reference Material," pp. 59–70.

A sample note card that quotes a primary source follows:

**Fig. 32: Quotation
Note Card of
Primary Source**[*]

```
Walter's frustration                    Raisin, p. 61


"Walter: Sometimes it's like I can see the future
stretched out in front of me--just plain as day.
The future, Mama. Hanging over there at the edge
of my days. Just waiting for me--a big, looming
blank space--full of nothing."
```

A sample note card, quoting a secondary source, follows:[3]

**Fig. 33: Quotation
Note Card of
Secondary Source**

```
Importance of monogamy                    Gilder, p. 34



    "Monogamy is central to any democratic
social contract, designed to prevent a breakdown
of society into 'war of every man against every
other man.' "
```

For an example of how one student employed this quotation, see the sample research paper, p. 83.

---

[*]Instructors will find an example of how one student employed this note in the sample paper of the Instructor's Manual.

[3]George Gilder, "In Defense of Monogamy," *Commentary,* Nov. 1974, p. 34.

Avoiding Plagiarism

Fundamentally, plagiarism is the offering of the words or ideas of another person as one's own. While the most blatant violation is the use of another student's work, the most common is the intentional misuse of your reference sources. Since you will be working with the writings of others, it is important that you learn and adhere to certain ethical rules as to the use of reference material. One of the chief reasons for following these rules is that you want to avoid being falsely accused of plagiarism when your only error was unintentionally failing to acknowledge a source.

An obvious form of plagiarism is copying any direct quotation from your source material without providing quotation marks and without crediting the source. A more subtle form, but equally improper, is the paraphrasing of material or use of an original idea if that paraphrase or borrowed idea is not properly introduced and documented. Remember that another author's ideas, interpretations, and words are his or her property; they are protected by law and must be acknowledged whenever you borrow them. Consequently, your use of source materials requires that you conform to a few rules of conduct:

1. Acknowledge borrowed material within the text by introducing the quotation or paraphrase with the name of the authority from whom it was taken.
2. Enclose within quotation marks all quoted materials.
3. Make certain that paraphrased material is written in your own style and language. The simple rearrangement of sentence patterns is unacceptable.
4. Provide documentation for each borrowed item.
5. Provide a bibliography entry for every book or magazine that is referred to in your paper.

The examples provided below should reveal the difference between genuine research writing and plagiarism. First, here is the original reference material; it is followed by four student versions, two of which would be called plagiarism, two of which would not.

Original Material

> Probably the long-distance marriage works best when there are no minor-aged children to be considered. It probably also works better with those relatively rare men and women who are equipped by temperament and personality to spend a considerable amount of time alone and to function in a mature, highly independent fashion.[4]

[4]William C. Nichols, "Long-Distance Marriage," *Parents Magazine,* Oct. 1978, p. 54.

Student Version A (Unacceptable)

> There are certain factors which facilitate the implementation of this living arrangement. Probably the long-distance marriage works best when there are no children to be considered. It probably also works better with those men and women who are equipped by temperament and personality to spend a considerable amount of time alone.

This piece of writing is plagiarism in a most deplorable form. The student has simply borrowed abundantly from the original source, even to the point of retaining the essential wording, and has provided no documentation whatever, which implies to the reader that these sentences are entirely his or her original creation.

Student Version B (Unacceptable)

> There are certain factors which facilitate the implementation of this living arrangement. The long-distance marriage works best when there are no young children to be considered and the man and woman have the temperament and personality to spend a great deal of time alone.[15]

The student's endnote follows:

[15] William C. Nichols, "Long-Distance Marriage," Parents Magazine, Oct. 1978, p. 54.

This student's version is also plagiarism, even though the citation is carefully documented. He or she has obviously copied almost directly from the source, changing only a few words and phrases. The student also fails to introduce the borrowed materials; thus, the reader is uncertain about the note number. Does it refer to the entire paragraph or only the final sentence? As a research writer, you may avoid these errors by introducing the material as direct quotation or, if you prefer, as a scholarly paraphrase that might include direct quotation of a few significant or well-worded phrases.

Student Version C (Acceptable)

> There are certain factors which facilitate the implementation of this living arrangement. William Nichols points out several conditions which would add to the success of a long-distance marriage. He states that it "works best when there are no minor-aged children to be considered," the two people are "equipped by temperament and personality to spend a considerable amount of time alone," and they are both able to "function in a mature, highly independent fashion."[15]

This student also had the proper endnote. This version represents a satisfactory handling of the source material. The authority is acknowledged at the outset, and the substance of the commentary is well expressed in the student's own language with key phrases directly quoted, so as to give full credit where the credit is due. The student has been wholly honest to the source material while effectively using that source for a particular purpose.

Student Version D (Acceptable)

> If no young children are involved, William Nichols suggests the possibility of success in the long-distance arrangement, but he also reserves it for those individuals who by their nature enjoy living alone for long periods and who have the independent maturity to handle it.[15]

The proper endnote was furnished at the end of this paper. This version also represents a satisfactory handling of the source material. In this case, no direct quotation is employed, the authority is acknowledged, and the substance of the commentary is well presented in the student's own language.

WRITING YOUR PAPER

● During the course of research, you have been making judgments and comparisons and putting details into order and completing them. You are now ready to synthesize all research materials into a paper that will give the greatest possible clarity, orderliness, and meaning to your findings. But before beginning the actual writing, you should first formulate a detailed, exact outline.

The Final Outline

Your rough preliminary outline should now be expanded into a clear, logical plan that will guide the writing of your paper, especially your overall arrangement and paragraph development. Remember that you are not bound by your original plan, which was only intended to guide research and note-taking. If you see possibilities in a new arrangement, you should, by all means, try it.

Since you will write your final outline for your instructor and other readers, you should follow recognized conventions. First, use the standard outline symbols:

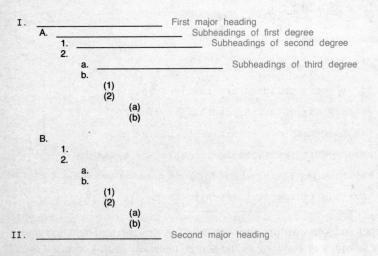

And so on. Your indentation of each heading will indicate the importance of the material; that is, you will progress from major concepts to minor ones. The degree to which you continue the subheads will depend, in part, upon the complexity of your subject; but, as a general rule, you should seldom find it necessary to carry the subheads beyond the first series of small letters.

In addition, headings of like rank on the same margin should have an equal importance. And if you establish ideas, give them parallel form. Note the mistake in the following:

```
I.  Spring sports
    A.  To play baseball
    B.  Tennis
    C.  Track
```

Obviously, the infinitive phrase "To play baseball" is not parallel with the nouns "Tennis" and "Track." If A is a noun, then make B and C nouns also, or if you prefer, make them all infinitives; but do not mix the grammatical forms.

When you indent outline headings, you are subordinating your ideas. Thus, if you find yourself attempting to enter a single subhead, you obviously have one major idea and not several subordinate ones. Note the following:

```
I.  Spring sports
    A.  Baseball
        1.  History
    B.  Tennis
        1.  History
    C.  Track
        1.  History
```

The writer probably intends to discuss the history of the sports and might rearrange the entries in the following manner:

```
Spring Sports
    I.  The History of Baseball
        A.  Origin
        B.  Growth
        C.  Maturity
   II.  The History of Tennis
        A.  Origin
        B.  Growth
        C.  Maturity
  III.  The History of Track
        A.  Origin
        B.  Growth
        C.  Maturity
```

Since your "introduction" is content and your "conclusion" is content, you need not label them as such in your outline. Instead, you should name specifically the contents of those sections, just as you do with the other parts of the outline. For example, the sample paper outline on pages 80–81 lists "The direction of marriage" in the introduction position and then in the conclusion spot the outline lists "Marriage: the relationship of the future."

Because the thesis is the main idea of the entire paper and no other idea can rank equally with it, you should not label your thesis sentence as item I in the outline. Otherwise, you may find yourself searching fruitlessly for a parallel idea to put in II, III, and IV. Instead, you should write your thesis sentence separately, placing it above the outline proper.

You may write your outline in topic, sentence, or paragraph form, remembering, of course, that you cannot alternate forms within a given outline. With the topic outline, every heading is a noun phrase or its equivalent, a gerund phrase or an infinitive phrase. In the sentence outline, either every heading is a sentence or the major headings are nouns and the subheads are sentences. With the paragraph outline, every section is a paragraph. However, you will seldom use the paragraph outline, although it is valuable for papers that require multiple, complex details.

Reproduced below is a portion of the outline from the sample research paper "Creative Marriage" (see pp. 80–81 for the complete topic outline) in topic, sentence, and paragraph forms.

Thesis sentence: While traditional marriages are having difficulty coping with society's pressures, couples today are developing styles of creative marriage within the boundaries of monogamy instead of disposing of marriage.

TOPIC OUTLINE

    I. The direction of marriage

       A. Divorce rates

       B. Alternatives

       C. Creative marriages

    II. The importance of monogamy

       A. Social necessity

       B. Personal preference

   III. Creative marriage

       A. Individual freedom

       B. Intellectual growth

   IV. Patterns of creative marriage

       A. Contract marriage
          1. History of contract marriage
          2. Personal and emotional growth
          3. Legality of contracts
          4. Renewable marriage

SENTENCE OUTLINE

    I. Modern marriage is taking on a new direction.

       A. Rising divorce rates seem to indicate that marriage is not meeting society's needs.

B. Some have rejected traditional marriage and adopted alternatives--including free relationships and extramarital relations.

C. Many others, though, want to develop alternatives within the institution of marriage and are forming creative marriages.

II. There is still a need for monogamy in today's changing world.

A. Society needs monogamy to prevent its own self-destruction.

B. Both men and women need a total commitment to another person.

III. The creative marriage is an agreement that allows a variety of options to traditional marriage.

A. The creative marriage offers opportunities for individual freedom.

B. The creative marriage safeguards the intellectual growth of the couple.

PARAGRAPH OUTLINE

I. The direction of marriage

A. Rising divorce rates would seem to indicate that traditional marriage is not meeting the needs of our society. Some couples have rejected traditional marriage and turned to free relationships. Others have found alternatives in extramarital relations.

B. Many, though, still believe in commitment to one person--an ideal that runs deep in our society. These couples are forming new types of marriages-- creative marriages--instead of rejecting the institution altogether.

II. The importance of monogamy

A. Monogamy serves as the foundation of the creative marriage. It is essential in order to prevent the breakdown of social order. Without monogamy every man will find himself fighting every other man, says critic Gilder.

B. A person's emotional balance is determined in part by his or her relations with others. Both men and women possess the need for a total emotional and physical commitment to another person. Consequently, the custom of marriage has continued throughout our history.

III. Creative marriage

A. A creative marriage is an agreement by a couple that allows a variety of options to traditional marriage. These options are usually addendums to the vows or articles of agreement written by the couple. It is important that the couple have faith in each other and make a commitment to the relationship.

Various outline forms that deviate from these classic models with respect to indenting, spacing, numbering, and so on are possible. The most popular deviation, especially in business and the sciences, is the decimal outline (also known as the industrial numerical outline):

DECIMAL OUTLINE

```
 1.  The direction of marriage

     1.1  Divorce rates

     1.2  Alternatives

     1.3  Creative marriages

 2.  The importance of monogamy

     2.1  Social necessity

     2.2  Personal preference

 3.  Creative marriage

     3.1  Individual freedom

     3.2  Intellectual growth

 4.  Patterns of creative marriage

     4.1  Contract marriage
          4.1.1  History of contract marriage
          4.1.2  Personal and emotional growth
          4.1.3  Legality
          4.1.4  Renewable marriage
```

Although many scientific and business reports use the decimal system, you should avoid it when doing conventional research papers. Because it is so precise and thorough, it breaks the material down into multiple, fragmented parts so that almost every sentence becomes a numerical subpart. A continuous numbering system tends to break down the organic relations found in the classic outline form.

Preparing to Write

If you begin writing your paper at least one full week before it is due, you should have sufficient time for writing, revising, and rewriting. However, you should not rush into the writing; instead, you should (1) examine your thesis sentence and outline to see that they provide you with a well-rounded, logically organized plan of procedure; (2) examine your tone to see that it suits your topic, purpose, and audience; and (3) examine your note cards to see that support for your ideas is abundantly supplied.

Ask yourself, "Do I know my main idea and supporting ideas?" If in doubt, you must read your thesis sentence and your outline again. With an objective eye you should examine your ideas and their logical progression through the outline. At this point you cannot afford ambiguity because each of your paragraphs must develop and expand your thesis sentence.

Next ask yourself, "Do I know my purpose?" To answer this question, you must consider both the intellectual framework (what you want the reader to understand) and the emotional framework (what you feel and what you want the reader to feel). Thus, you will have to present your material from a selected perspective that will influence your handling of the subject and your audience's reaction to it.

For example, suppose your topic deals with the world energy crisis. Obviously, you face an intellectual choice: you may defend or condemn the energy policies of various governments or governmental agencies. Complete objectivity is unlikely in a research paper which is, in fact, a form of argument. Moreover, you will determine your emotional framework by assuming either a detached or an involved position. For example, if you should select a detached approach, you would gain a degree of objectivity by giving an accurate, well-ordered presentation of both sides of the issue and by declaring your position with formal, controlled logic. If, on the other hand, you should assume an involved position, either pro or con, your presentation should be more persuasive, more demanding. You would need to avoid bias and prejudice, but you could be more subjective by condemning falsehoods, by destroying misconceptions, by rallying your audience to your cause, and by supporting your ideas with examples and comparisons that vividly portray the circumstances.

Moreover, with some topics you might consider the possibility of a humorous or a satiric approach, by which you relate, with tongue in cheek, the absurdity of a situation or you hold up to ridicule the foolishness of a condition, intending, thereby, to bring a new awareness of a problem to your reader. However, such papers are rare in scholarly writing, and you will need your instructor's approval before launching such a venture.

Finally, ask yourself, "Do I have sufficient support from several sources for my contentions?" Since many undergraduates attempt to rely upon one major source, this question is a vital one. Remember, reliance upon the frequent use of one source is an all too apparent confession that your research has been too restricted in its scope. The presence of almost endless strings of citations to the same work in your notes reflects a lack of industry and initiative on your part. The notes of your text, as well as the text itself, will reflect the quality of your research. Your instructor expects that you will put labor into collecting and assimilating adequate material from many sources and that you will then blend these sources into a readable and effective whole.

WRITING WITH UNITY, COHERENCE, AND CLARITY

After many hours of considerable effort, you are ready to give expression to your ideas, to share them with others, and to convince your readers of the validity of your findings. In order for your paper to reflect the care and time you have devoted to it, you must write it in the best possible language. In most instances, readers will see only the finished product, upon which they will base their judgment of your findings and writing ability. Therefore, you should carefully construct your paper, always seeking unity, coherence, and clarity. Your paper will have *unity* if it explores one topic in depth, with each paragraph carefully expanding upon a single aspect of the topic. Your paper will have *coherence* if your controlling ideas and your research details and evidence all flow together and function as an interrelated whole. Coherence requires that quotations and paraphrases be logical extensions of your writing, not intrusions or mere padding. Coherence also demands the logical progression of your ideas by the repetition of key words, the exact usage of pronouns and synonyms, and the application of transitional words and phrases (for example, the use of such words as *also, furthermore, nevertheless, in addition,* and *thus*). Your paper will have *clarity* if you use precise prose that avoids excessive rhetorical splendor. Research writing is exact writing, employing concrete, specific words and featuring well-balanced sentences with proper subordination of minor elements.

WRITING IN THE PROPER TENSE

When you are dealing with an event or concept of the past, your overall approach to the material should be in the past tense, as in the following example:

```
         This is quite similar to the marriage

    style that was suggested by Margaret Mead

    years ago.  Known as the two-step marriage, her

    plan is described by Phillip Rice: "The form

    was individual marriage, which was a business

    union between two individuals who would be

    committed to each other for as long as they

    wanted to remain together, but not as

    parents. . . ."18  Several advantages of this

    suggested style were given by Margaret Mead.
```

Clearly, the use of the past tense is required with the material concerning Margaret Mead's ideas—suggested years ago. But note the use of present tense in the same paper:

> Monogamy, viewed as old-fashioned by
> some, <u>remains</u> the foundation for the creative
> marriage. Possibly this is because it <u>pro-</u>
> <u>vides</u> a biological balance. George Gilder <u>be-</u>
> <u>lieves</u> that "monogamy is central to any demo-
> cratic social contract, designed to prevent
> a breakdown of society into 'war of every man
> against every other man.' "[2] He also <u>stipu-</u>
> <u>lates</u> that "monogamy is designed to minimize
> the effect of . . . inequalities--to prevent
> the powerful of either sex from disrupting
> the familial order."[3]

The writer of these lines is concerned with an article of the past, but since it continues in print, it continues into the present. Therefore, the writer uses the verbs *remains, believes, stipulates,* and *provides* rather than the past tense forms *remained, believed, stipulated, provided,* and so on. That is, the writer uses the historical present tense to indicate what is true at the present time and will remain true in the future.

In the same way, you should use the present tense for most comments or observations by authorities about a text under examination. Thus, use the present tense in referring to a view expressed by some quoted or paraphrased author, for the criticism is still in print and continues to be true in the present. Good usage demands "Richard Ellmann argues," "Professor Thompson writes," or "T. S. Eliot stipulates," rather than "Richard Ellman argued," "Professor Thompson wrote," or "T. S. Eliot stipulated."

Handling Reference Material

As you begin transferring your note material into your written text, you will have questions about the proper use of your references. For example, you will often ask yourself, "How should I use this note—as paraphrase or quotation?"

Obviously, you cannot just copy all your notes directly into the text. The trick is to skillfully incorporate a paraphrase or short quotation into your own writing so that the outside source is not obtrusive and at the same time illuminates and supports your own conclusions. You will find that this task is vital to the success of your manuscript.

SHORT PROSE QUOTATIONS AND PARAPHRASES

There are two basic forms for incorporating quoted matter into the text. First, if the quotation will take up no more than four lines in your paper, you may place it within the body of the text and enclose it within quotation marks. (The second form, for quotations that will exceed four lines in your paper, is discussed on pages 66–67.)

Suppose, for example, that you have the following material on a note card:

```
Long-distance marriage            Nichols, p. 54


     "Probably the long-distance marriage
works best when there are no minor-aged
children to be considered.  It probably also
works better with those relatively rare men
and women who are equipped by temperament and
personality to spend a considerable amount of
time alone and to function in a mature, highly
independent fashion."
```

There are several ways you could incorporate this material into your paper, but not all of them would be considered acceptable. Consider the following example:

Unacceptable

```
The long-distance marriage works best with

"no minor-aged children" and with persons who

have the temperament "to spend a considerable

amount of time alone and to function in a ma-

ture, highly independent fashion."15
```

This style is not *wrong* but would be *unacceptable* to most instructors because the writer provides no introduction for the quotation. Use the names of your authorities in order to move smoothly from your own material to quoted matter. Also try to assimilate the expert commentary into *your* writing.

Acceptable

```
        William Nichols points out several favorable
        conditions of a long-distance marriage,
        stating that it "works best when there are no
        minor-aged children to be considered," the two
        people are "equipped by temperament and
        personality to spend a considerable amount of
        time alone," and both are able to "function in
        a mature, highly independent fashion."15
```

To see how one student eventually used this quoted material in context, see the sample research paper, p. 89. Other examples of acceptable incorporation of source materials are as follows:

```
            Another variation on the theory of mar-
        riage by steps is presented by Vance Packard
        in his book The Sexual Wilderness in which
        he proposes "a two-year conformation period,
        after which marriage would become final or
        be dissolved."22  All of these. . . .
```

```
        Time also points out that "the well-to-do
        have long used marriage contracts to pro-
        tect their wealth from the caprices of di-
        vorce courts."9  Today, however, the. . . .
```

INTRODUCING SHORT QUOTATIONS AND PARAPHRASES

When introducing short reference material (four lines or less), you should avoid repetition of a stereotyped phrase—for example, "Professor Jones says." Rather, you should vary the method of formal introduction as shown in the following:

> Gilder believes that "monogamy is central to any democratic. . . ."
>
> Hopefully in a creative marriage "each will safeguard the emotional vulnerability of the other," suggests one author.
>
> An article in <u>Parents Magazine</u> discusses this arrangement and makes several observations. The author concludes that. . . .
>
> The difficulties associated with the relationship, according to one critic, are probably. . . .
>
> Many communes support group marriages or polygamy but Bernard reports that "some communes do include married couples who. . . ."
>
> Concerning this seeming paradox, McCary comments that "the changes taking place in marriage forms. . . ."
>
> In a critical article, William Nichols makes this conclusion, "Whether long–distance marriage will facilitate or. . . ."
>
> In this sense Dr. Clifford Sager proposes that the marriage contract becomes "a therapeutic and educational concept that . . . ."
>
> He also stipulates that "monogamy is designed to minimize. . . ."

Other words that will give variety to your introductions are *accept, add, admit, affirm, believe, confirm, declare, mention, propose, rely, reveal, state, submit, think,* and *verify.* However, you should avoid the monotony of such introductions by alternating them with your own contentions and with a few long indented quotations (see below, "Longer Quotations," p. 66).

COMBINING PARAPHRASE AND QUOTATION

As shown above, it is a good practice to introduce your material by citing the name of the authority from which it is drawn. However, you must place a note index numeral at the end of paraphrased and quoted matter whether the name of the author appears in the text or not. In the following example the writer of the research paper about "Creative Marriage" has obeyed these two rules. Additionally, this student has molded into one unified whole both paraphrase and quotation:

> The main problem with marriage contracts,
> if one discounts the effects of seeming dis-
> trust between marriage partners, concerns le-
> gality. "If a couple wants to make sure that
> their agreement has legal force," advises New
> York lawyer Brenda Feigen-Fasteau, "they
> should stay unmarried, in which case their
> contract is like any other private agreement
> between individuals."[11]
>
> This trend toward contract marriages ex-
> pands into a variation called the renewable
> marriage, which Jessie Bernard describes. The
> couple makes a commitment to "maintain the
> marriage" for a set number of years with the
> stipulation that each person could renege at
> the end of the time period or recommit to a
> union that continued to be satisfactory and
> fulfilling.[12]

You cannot paraphrase and synthesize such material into the desired context without intelligent, thoughtful effort.

REPRODUCING QUOTED MATERIAL

In general, you should reproduce quoted material exactly; but one exception is permitted for logical reasons: if the quotation forms a grammatical part of the sentence in which it occurs, you need not capitalize the first word of the quotation, even though it is capitalized in the original, as in:

> The opinion of this new group of couples is ex-
> pressed by Joan Barthel who argues that "when you make
> the exclusive commitment of a man and a woman each to
> the other a throwaway thing, desirable but disposable,
> you have effectively dissolved the grounds for
> marriage."[1]

However, if the quotation follows a formal introduction set off by a comma or colon, you should capitalize the first word as in the original:

> The opinion of this new group of couples is ex-
> pressed in this statement by Joan Barthel, "When you
> make the exclusive commitment of a man and a woman
> each to the other a throwaway thing, desirable but
> disposable, you have effectively dissolved the grounds
> for marriage."[1]

Other possible methods are as follows:

> The opinion of this new group of couples is ex-
> pressed by Joan Barthel, who states: "When you make
> the exclusive. . . ."

> Joan Barthel, expressing the opinion of this new
> group of couples, states that "when you make the
> exclusive. . . ."

Thus, a few rules for quoted material of four lines or less are:

1.   Reproduce the quotation exactly as it appears in the original with the one exception noted above.

2.   Place the material within quotation marks.

3.   Insert a note numeral after the last word of the material.

4.   Use the name of the authority, usually, to introduce the material. Items 3 and 4 apply with equal force to your paraphrases.

Should your original source contain an error, or what might appear on first reading to be an error, you are permitted to insert the term "sic" within brackets, as in the following:

> Mama: I wish you say something, son . . . I wish
>
> you'd say how deep inside you you [sic] think I
>
> done the right thing--(p. 87).

Placed in brackets in this manner, "sic" indicates two things: first, an error or apparent error has be made in the quoted passage and second, you are quoting accurately.

DOCUMENTING FREQUENT REFERENCES TO THE SAME NOVEL OR LONG WORK

If your paper is based solely on a single work (novel, drama, short story, or long poem) and if there is an initial note identifying the edition, you may employ a simpler method of documentation for citations of the primary source; that is, place the page numbers in parentheses after the prose quotations, followed by the terminal mark of punctuation, as in the examples that follow:

```
Hansberry describes Mama as a "full-bodied and
strong" woman who "has adjusted to many things
in life and overcome many more. . . ."10  We
can assume that for years she has been the
dominant figure in the lives of her children.
```

Note ten should read:

```
10 Lorraine Hansberry, A Raisin in the Sun (New York:
Random House, 1959), p. 15.  All further references
to this work appear in the text.
```

After such a note identifies your primary source, you may document page numbers in the following manner:

```
When Beneatha denies the existence of God,
Mama slaps her in the face and forces her to
repeat after her, "In my mother's house there
is still God" (p. 37).  Then Mama adds, "There
are some ideas we ain't going to have in this
house.  Not long as I am at the head of this
family" (p. 37, underlining is mine).  Thus
Mama meets Beneatha's challenge head on.
```

Note that the parenthetical documentation is part of the sentence and is placed inside the period. Such is not the case, however, with the documentation of long, indented quotations, as follows.

LONGER QUOTATIONS

Quotations that will exceed four lines in your paper should be indented and no quotation marks should be used. But do not overuse long quotations. The obvious fact is that most readers tend to skip over long, indented material unless it is strongly introduced and unless such quotations occur infrequently. The proper method for such quotations is shown below:

> long—distance nature of their marriage as
> temporary and not a fixed lifestyle, according
> to one source.[16] In his critical article
> Nichols makes this conclusion:
>
> > Whether long—distance marriage will
> > facilitate or retard growth and deepening
> > of the relationship between husband and
> > wife is an unknown, and probably depends
> > a great deal on the individuals, their
> > maturity, and on the degree of their
> > commitment to their careers——and to each
> > other.[17]
>
> Another creative marriage alternative evolving
> in our society is the idea of sharing roles.

As indicated in this example, you should observe the following rules:

1. Make certain that the quotation is properly introduced. Use a colon or comma to link the quotation with its introduction.

2. Do not employ quotation marks with a long quotation that is indented, unless there is a quote within the quotation.

3. Place the note index numeral or documentation, as always, after the last word of the quotation. With long, indented materials the documentation follows the terminal mark of punctuation. In all other cases the documentation precedes the period.

4. Indent the material at least five spaces (10 spaces is permissible) from the left margin and set it off from the text by triple-spacing.

5. If quoted matter begins with the opening of a paragraph, indent the first line at least ten spaces from the left margin; the quotation, that is, carries its own

paragraph indentation (see the sample research paper, p. 90). Otherwise there is no extra indentation of the first line.

   6.   Separate the quotation from the text by triple-spacing.

POETRY QUOTATIONS

Short passages of quoted poetry (three lines or less) are included in the text in the following manner:

```
In Antony and Cleopatra Shakespeare states

his theme at once through the indignant,

hard-natured Roman soldier Philo, who labels

Antony "the triple pillar of the world trans-

formed / Into a strumpet's fool" (Ant. I.i.12-

13). Philo thereby heralds the traditional

attitude of the Roman mind as opposed by the

sensuous nature of Egypt and its queen.
```

As this example indicates, you should again follow certain rules:

   1.   Set off the quotation by quotation marks.

   2.   Indicate separate lines of the poetry text by the use of a virgule (/) with a space before and after the slash mark.

   3.   Place the documentation in parentheses immediately following the quotation.

   4.   Insert the documentation inside the period because the reference, like the quotation, is a part of the larger context of the sentence.

   5.   Omit the note. But be certain that the quotation is properly introduced.

   6.   Good scholarship requires that the edition of Shakespeare's plays, or any similar anthology, be listed in an early note, for example:

[1] Citations from Shakespeare in the text are to Shakespeare: Twenty-Three Plays and the Sonnets, ed. Thomas M. Parrott (New York: Scribner's, 1953).

Longer passages of poetry (more than three lines) are handled differently, as shown by the following passage from Shakespeare's *Hamlet*.

In a famous soliloquy Hamlet declares:

> To be, or not to be: that is the question:
> Whether 't is nobler in the mind to suffer
> The slings and arrows of outrageous fortune,
> Or to take arms against a sea of troubles,
> And by opposing end them? To die, to sleep--
> No more; and by a sleep to say we end
> The heart-ache and the thousand natural shocks
> That flesh is heir to. . . . (<u>Ham</u>. III.i.56-63)

Also notice the form of documentation for the following:

In his poem "Among School Children," W. B. Yeats asks two profound questions:

> Are you the leaf, the blossom or the
>   bole?
> O body swayed to music, O brightening
>   glance,
> How can we know the dancer from the
>   dance?   (11. 62-64)

Again, you should follow certain rules:

1. Center the quotation on the page and type with double-spacing and with quotation marks omitted. Separate the quotation from the text by triple-spacing.

2. Use this method whenever poetry quotations run longer than three lines.

3. Place the documentation outside the final period because the reference is not a contextual part of the quoted sentence of poetry.

4. Use a colon to link the quotation with its introduction.

5. Omit the note. But, again, good scholarship requires an early note that lists the edition or anthology in which the poem is found (see item 6, p. 67).

ELLIPSIS

In a situation where less than an entire sentence of the quoted material is needed, you should use ellipsis dots to indicate omissions in the quoted material. This mark is three spaced periods, as (. . .). When the ellipsis ends a quoted passage, you should add a fourth period (with no space before the first) to indicate the termination of thought. Note the following:

```
R. W. B. Lewis declares that "if Hester has sinned, she
has done so as an affirmation of life, and her sin is
the source of life. . . ."1

One critic insists that it is possible for us "to read
The Scarlet Letter . . . as an endorsement of hope-
fulness. . . ."1

Mama says to Ruth, "He finally come into his manhood
today, didn't he?  Kind of like a rainbow after the
rain . . ." (p. 141).
```

Note that the parenthetical documentation in the last example is placed inside the fourth period because it is part of the context of the sentence. If the omission is significant (one or more lines of verse or one or more paragraphs of prose), indicate the ellipsis by a single typed line of spaced periods. Use introductions to avoid opening with ellipsis periods.

BRACKETS

You may find it necessary, on occasion, to insert personal comment within a quotation. You should enclose such an interpolation within brackets. Note the following:

```
"The black flower [of society] is shown in striking
contrast to the wild rose of Nature."

One critic indicates that "we must avoid the temptation
to read it [The Scarlet Letter] heretically."

"John F. Kennedy, assassinated in November of 1964 [sic],
became overnight an immortal figure of courage and
dignity in the hearts of most Americans."

"John F. Kennedy . . . [was] an immortal figure of courage
and dignity in the hearts of most Americans."
```

PUNCTUATION OF QUOTATIONS

In every instance, place commas and periods *inside* the quotation marks but semicolons and colons *outside* the quotation marks. Place the question mark and the exclamation mark inside the quotation marks if the mark is part of the quoted material; otherwise, place it outside the quotation marks:

```
The philosopher asks, "How should we order our lives?"

How should we order our lives when we face "hostility
from every quarter"?
```

For quotations within quotations use the following form:

```
George Gilder believes that "monogamy is central to any
democratic social contract, designed to prevent a
breakdown of society into a 'war of every man against
every other man.' "2
```

Note, if the quotation ends with both single and then double quotation marks, the period or comma is placed inside both.

Handling Problems of Format

In its basic organization the research paper consists of the following parts:
1. One blank sheet (optional)
2. Title page or Opening page (see below)
3. Outline (if required)
4. The text of the paper
5. Notes
6. Bibliography
7. One blank sheet (optional)

TITLE PAGE OR OPENING PAGE

The title page contains three main divisions: the title of the work, the author, and the course information. Note the following guidelines for title pages (see the title page of the sample research paper, p. 79, for an example):
1. If the title requires two or more lines, position the extra line(s) in such a manner as to form an inverted pyramid.
2. Do not underline your title or capitalize it in full. Underline only published works if they appear in your title. Also, do not use a period after a centered heading.
3. Enter your own name with the word ''by'' centered above it.
4. Provide the class and section information and the date. Entry of the instructor's name is usually optional.

5. Employ separate lines for each item.
6. Provide balanced, two-inch margins for all sides of the title page.
7. You may omit the title page and simply provide information on your opening page. In that case, place information in the upper right corner as in the following:

```
                                                    ↓ 1″
                                   Pamela Howell

                                   Professor Rimsky

                                   English 102c

                                   May 17, 1979

Quadruple-space
         →
                          Creative Marriages
Quadruple-space
         →

              Judging by recent divorce rates, it would

          seem that traditional marriage is not meeting

          the needs of our society. . . .
```

OUTLINE

The outline follows the title page in the finished manuscript, its pages being numbered with small Roman numerals (for example, ''iii,'' ''iv,'' ''v'') at the top right-hand corner of the page. For full information on outlining, see pp. 36–38 as well as 52–56.

THE TEXT OF THE PAPER

The heart of your paper, of course, is the text itself. Three dominant parts of the text are the opening, body, and conclusion. Each is discussed below.

The Opening

The opening of a research paper should clearly establish your subject and set limits upon the scope of your examination. The conventional opening for a research paper has two parts: identification or definition of the subject and the expression of your thesis. The opening of the sample research paper (see p. 82) follows this form. A brief history of the subject is often part of the opening.

Certain papers, especially those in the sciences, may require additional information in the opening, such as methods of investigation, tools and instruments employed, special problems encountered, or a list of prior work in this area.

Every paper has its own character and calls for a distinctive opening. However, a few standard ingredients are provided in the following (though not all would be necessary in the same paper):

1. Identify the subject clearly.
2. Define your terms, especially what *you* mean.
3. Give a brief history of the subject.
4. Offer a description of scholarship in this specific area and explain how your topic adds to that body of scholarship.
5. State your position or express your thesis without proclaiming "The purpose of my paper is to. . . ."
6. Offer a timely or well-expressed quotation.
7. Offer a challenge to a general belief or common assumption, for example, that too much television is harmful.
8. Examine a paradox, for example, that our civilized society condemns violence yet supports a variety of violent sporting events.
9. Cite statistics in the opening to awaken the reader to the magnitude of a situation.
10. Avoid cute artwork, repetition of the title, questions, dictionary definitions, and jokes.

The Body of Your Paper

The body of your paper should feature a logical development of the subdivisions of your thesis. These subdivisions will be suggested by your outline. Your primary concern should be clarification and amplification of your topic as you defend your thesis with well-reasoned statements, documented wherever necessary. See especially pages 56–70.

Normal paragraphing for the body is adequate. You need not label separate sections of your text with subtitles, centered headings, or Roman numerals. Such division markers are reserved for much longer works.

The Closing

Sometimes a final summarizing paragraph of text will be sufficient for the end of the paper, but usually circumstances will demand a separate conclusion. You will have expressed your thesis early and then presented your findings, properly documented. A conclusion that affirms something demonstrable about the subject would now be in order. For example, a research paper about the drama *A Raisin in the Sun* has this thesis: "Hansberry uses the sociological concept of black matriarchy to create dramatic conflict among the members of the Younger family." The conclusion should reaffirm that thesis as shown on the next page:

```
        By her characterization of Walter,

    Lorraine Hansberry has raised the black male

    above the typical stereotype.  Walter is not

    a social problem, a mere victim of matriarchy.

    Rather, Hansberry creates a character who

    breaks out of the traditional sociological

    image that dehumanizes the black male.  Cre-

    ating a character who struggles with his

    fate and rises above it, Hansberry has el-

    evated the black male.  As James Baldwin puts

    it, "Time has made some changes in the Negro

    face."15
```

For the way another writer closes the paper, see the final two paragraphs of the sample research paper, pp. 91–92.

A few standard elements of good closings are the following:

1.   Affirm something about the topic, especially a demonstrable statement in support of your thesis.

2.   Use a well-known piece of expert testimony in the form of statistics or quotation.

3.   Explain how you have proved your theory, disproved an assumption, or added in some way to the general body of knowledge on this topic.

4.   Mention additional areas worthy of further study that were either related to your work or that you did not adequately explore because of space limitations.

5.   Avoid questions, mere summary of or restatement of the opening, cute artwork, jokes, or entirely new ideas that cannot be explored at this point.

THE ENDNOTE PAGE

Your endnotes should appear on a separately typed page at the end of the paper. The first page of endnotes should not have a number on the page, although it is counted in the total pagination of the note pages. If the notes run onto more than one page, number all succeeding pages counting the first page as number one. See the endnote pages of the sample research paper, pp. 93–94, for an example. Also study Chapter 5, ''Endnotes and Footnotes'' for details about form and style of the endnotes. However, your professor may require you to use footnotes, discussed on page 75 and in Chapter 5.

THE BIBLIOGRAPHY PAGE

Your bibliography should appear on a separately typed sheet after the endnote page. See the bibliography pages of the sample research paper, pp. 95–96, for an example. Also study Chapter 6, "The Bibliography," for details about form and style of the bibliographical entries.

Handling Technicalities of Preparing the Manuscript

As you write your first draft (and even when typing the final version), you will have questions about such diverse matters as margins, numbering, type of paper, and so on. The following material, in alphabetical order, explains many of the immediate problems facing you. Other matters of a more specialized nature are explained in the "Glossary of Additional Research Terms," pp. 157–67.

ARABIC NUMERALS

Generally, write as numerals only those numbers that *cannot* be spelled out in one or two words (such as thirteen, twenty-one, three hundred *but* 3½, 154, or 1,269). Use figures for *all* numbers in a paragraph that contains both types. Use the small "1," not a capital "I" when typing the numeral "one." Samples of correct usage:

```
A.D. 200 but 200 B.C.
Art. 3
Col. 5
Fig. 6
in 1974-75 or from 1974 to 1975, but not from 1974-75
ll. 32-34
March 5, 1935 or 5 March 1935, but not both styles
1960's but the sixties
one-fifth but 153½ (for numbers that cannot be spelled
in one or two words)
pp. 121-22
pp. 1151-53 but pp. 1193-1215
Sec. 3
6 percent
six o'clock or 6:00 p.m.
6.213
twentieth century but 20th century in notes
page 45, but not the forty-fifth page
```

DATES

You should follow these examples:

```
14 March or March 14, not the fourteenth of March
14 March 1975 or March 14, 1975, but consistently use
one style
```

```
March 1975 or March, 1975, but consistently use one
style
1970's or the seventies
in 1974-75 or from 1974 to 1975, but not from 1974-75
150 B.C. but A.D. 150
fourteenth century but 14th century in notes
```

FOOTNOTES

Although endnotes (discussed on p. 73 and in Chapter 5) are commonly used in undergraduate papers, your instructor may prefer that you use footnotes. Footnotes appear on the same page as do the note index numerals in your text. Separate the footnotes from the text by triple spacing (that is, leave two lines of space). Single space the footnotes, indent each as a paragraph, and double space between each note. See especially Chapter 5, "Endnotes and Footnotes."

ITALICS

Indicate italics in a typed manuscript by underlining, see p. 78.

LENGTH OF THE RESEARCH PAPER

Generally speaking, plan a paper of 2000 or 3000 words, about ten typewritten pages, excluding the title page, outline, endnotes, and bibliography. However, your instructor may set definite restrictions concerning the length of the paper. Various factors make it difficult to set an arbitrary length, which may well vary with the topic, the reference material available, the time allotted to the project, and the initiative of the student.

MARGINS

A basic one inch margin on all sides is recommended. Place your page number one inch down from the top edge of the paper and one inch in from the right edge. You should then triple-space (leave two spaces) between the page number and the text. For pages with a major heading (such as the Bibliography page) use a two inch margin at the top of the page.

NOTE NUMERALS IN THE TEXT

Place note numerals within the text of the paper by turning the roller of the typewriter so that the Arabic numeral strikes about half a space above the line. Each numeral immediately follows the quotation or material to which it refers with no space between a word or a mark of punctuation. (See also "Placing Note Numbers Within the Text," p. 99.)

NUMBERING

Assign a number to each page of the text of the paper, except blank pages. Number the pages in Arabic numerals in the upper right-hand corner of the page, one inch down from the top edge of the paper and one inch from the right edge. Number these pages consecutively from the first page of the text through the last page of the text. However, do not place a number on your first page—though this page is of course counted. Number the pages before the first page of the text, except the title page, with small Roman numerals, e.g., iii, iv, v, and so on, at the top, right side of the page.

PAPER

Type on one side of white bond paper, sixteen- or twenty-pound weight, eight and one-half by eleven inches. If your final manuscript is in longhand, use ruled theme paper.

REVISING AND PROOFREADING

After you complete your first draft, begin revising and rewriting in a critical and exacting mood—there is no place for any complacent pride of accomplishment at this point. Conscientiously delete unnecessary material, add supporting statements and evidence, relate facts to one another, rearrange data, and rewrite for clarity. Follow this cycle until the paper meets your full approval. Check for errors in sentence structure, spelling, and punctuation; read each quotation for accuracy. Finally, check each note and bibliographic entry for correctness of content and form.

After your final copy is finished, you should proofread carefully, remembering that you, and you alone, are responsible for everything within the paper. Failure to proofread is an act of carelessness that may seriously lower your final grade. Typing a paper, of course, does not remove the requirement of proofreading; if anything, it doubles your responsibility, whether you have done the typing yourself or had it done. Typographical errors will often count against the paper just as heavily as other shortcomings. Should you find errors but have no time for retyping, you should make the necessary corrections neatly in ink. It is far better to mar a page with a few handwritten corrections than to leave damaging errors in the paper.

SHORT TITLES IN THE TEXT

Shorten titles of books and articles mentioned often in the text after a first, full reference. For example, *English as Language: Backgrounds, Developments, Usage* should be shortened, after initial usage, to *English as Language* both in the text and notes (see pp. 124–25). The title *A Raisin in the Sun* could be shortened to *Raisin* except for the fact that a musical adaptation of the play has been produced using *Raisin* as its title.

SPACING

Double-space the body of the paper, indented quotations, and both the end-note and bibliography entries. Triple-space between your text and indented quotations. Quadruple-space between major headings and the text. (If your instructor requests footnotes, they should be single-spaced and set off from the text by triple-spacing.) Note the following:

2″ ↓

The Theme of Black Matriarchy

Double-space →   in A Raisin in the Sun

Quadruple-space →

Indent
5 spaces →   Lorraine Hansberry's popular and successful A

Raisin in the Sun, which first appeared on Broadway in

1959, is a problem play that tells the story of a black

family's determination to move out of the ghetto to a

1″
→ better life. Most critics have said that this escape

theme explains the drama's forceful dramatic conflict 1″
←

and its importance to the black movement in general. As

Grier and Cobbs point out, the black family is often in

serious trouble:

Triple-space →
    It is coming apart and it is failing to provide the

nurturing that black children need. In its failure

the resulting isolated men and women fail generally

Indent 5
spaces → to make a whole life for themselves in a nation

designed for families. . . .[1]

Triple-space →

Thus another issue lies at the heart of the drama.

Hansberry develops a modern view of the sociological

aspects of black matriarchy in order to examine the

cohesive and, more importantly, the conflict—producing

effects it has on the individual members of the Younger

family.

1″ ↑

SPELLING

Spell accurately. When in doubt, always consult a dictionary. If the dictionary says a word may be spelled in two separate ways, be consistent in the form employed, as with *theater* and *theatre,* unless the variant form occurs in quoted materials. Use American (as opposed to English) spelling throughout. In addition, proofread carefully for errors of hyphenation.

TYPING

Preferably, you should submit the paper in typed form, although some instructors will accept handwritten manuscripts, if neat and legible. Also, use pica type, though the small elite face may be used if necessary. Clean the type carefully and insert a new ribbon if necessary before starting the final copy.

UNDERLINING

Underlining takes the place of italics in a typed manuscript. Use a continuous line. Always underline the title of a book, journal, or periodical, whether it appears in the text, in a note, or in the bibliography. Also underline the titles of pamphlets, newspapers, plays, movies, radio and television programs, long poems, and operas. In addition, underline foreign words (except proper names, quotations in a foreign language, titles of articles in a foreign language, and other foreign words anglicized through usage). However, enclose within quotation marks titles of articles, essays, chapters, sections, short poems, stories, and songs.

On occasion underlining is also used to emphasize certain words or phrases in a typed paper, such as in this sentence:

```
Yet Beneatha, unlike her sister-in-law Ruth, is a
rivaling matriarch.
```

There may be occasions when you wish to emphasize certain words within quoted materials. Handle such underlining as in the following example:

```
Then Mama adds, "There are some ideas we ain't going to
have in this house.  Not long as I am at the head of
this family" (p. 37, underlining is mine).
```

Follow this rule: You may underline another person's words only if you stipulate within parentheses that you have done so.

Remember that a little underlining goes a long way. Like too many neon signs, too much underlining for emphasis (and too many exclamation marks, for that matter) distracts your reader and gives the impression that nearly everything in your paper is of the utmost importance, a practice the reader will quickly grow tired of.

SAMPLE RESEARCH PAPER

Creative Marriage

The comments which follow in the margins will serve to clarify the form of the research paper and to explain specific problems you may encounter.

by

Pamela Howell

English 102c

Dr. Rimsky

May 17, 1979

Creative Marriage

The title is repeated at the beginning of the outline.

Preferably, the thesis sentence should be placed at the beginning of the outline, though it may take a different form in the paper itself.

Thesis sentence: While traditional marriages are having difficulty coping with society's pressures, couples today are developing styles of creative marriage within the boundaries of monogamy instead of disposing of marriage.

I. The direction of marriage

   A. Divorce rates

   B. Alternatives

   C. Creative marriages

II. The importance of monogamy

   A. Social necessity

   B. Personal preference

III. Creative marriage

   A. Individual freedom

   B. Intellectual growth

IV. Patterns of creative marriage

   A. Contract marriage
      1. History of contract marriage
      2. Personal and emotional growth
      3. Legality of contracts
      4. Renewable marriage

   B. Marriage by steps
      1. Margaret Mead's 2-step version
      2. Michael Scriven's 3-step version
      3. Vance Packard's conformation period

C. Long—distance marriage
   1. Reasons for development
   2. Associated problems
      a. Loneliness
      b. Difficulties with child rearing
      c. Financial burden
      d. Emotional strain
   3. Factors that help make the long—distance marriage work
   4. Temporary nature of this arrangement

D. Role sharing
   1. Sharing responsibilities and rewards
   2. Sharing in communal life

V. Marriage: the relationship of the future

A. Need for growth and change

B. Continuing need for the foundations of traditional marriage

The introduction and conclusion should be treated as the other parts of the outline. They should not be labeled.

Creative Marriage

Judging by rising divorce rates, it would seem that traditional marriage is not meeting the needs of our society. While many people have totally rejected the idea of such a strict commitment and turned to free relationships, others have adopted new styles or alternatives to traditional marriage. Although some such alternative styles may be found in extramarital relations, many others reflect the desire for commitment to one person that runs deep in our culture. This desire forms the basis for the new types of marriage frequently seen today, the creative marriages.

So the men and women of today are refusing to make commitment a "throwaway thing." While traditional marriages may be having difficulty coping with society's pressures, these couples are developing styles of creative marriage within the boundaries of monogamy instead of disposing of marriage. As Joan Barthel exclaims, "When you make the exclusive commitment of a man and woman each to the other a throwaway thing, desirable but disposable, you have effectively dissolved the grounds for marriage."[1]

The title is repeated on the first page of the body of the paper.

The opening sentence is attention-getting and challenges beliefs.

The thesis is stated early, letting the reader know the exact purpose of the study.

The length of the introduction ought to be at least two full paragraphs.

The raised numeral signals the reader to the presence of an endnote.

Monogamy, viewed as old—fashioned by some, remains the foundation for the creative marriage. Possibly this is because it provides a biological balance. George Gilder believes that "monogamy is central to any democratic social contract, designed to prevent a breakdown of society into 'war of every man against every other man.' "[2] He also stipulates that "monogamy is designed to minimize the effect of . . . inequalities—to prevent the powerful of either sex from disrupting the familial order."[3]

Use single quotation marks for quotations within a quotation.

While monogamy may provide a necessary biological balance for society, it also reflects the needs of both men and women for a total emotional and physical commitment to another person. Perhaps that is why the custom of marriage has continued throughout our history. As author James McCary argues,

> Marriage is the best solution developed to this date to the dilemma of aloneness. Because most people do marry and spend most of their lives in the married state, the hope for satisfying the goals of personal maturity and emotional fulfillment would seem to lie within marriage.[4]

A long quotation is set off from the text, indented, and double-spaced. No quotation marks are placed around the quoted passage. Use either a comma or a colon to introduce.

What is a creative marriage actually? Basically, it is an agreement by a couple that allows a variety of

Creative marriage is defined.

options to traditional marriage. These options may be expressed in the form of addendums to the marriage vows or articles of agreement written by the couple. Or they may simply be agreed upon principles that the couple adheres to. However the agreements are made, what is most important is that the couple have faith and trust in one another and make a commitment to the success of the relationship.

The creative marriage offers opportunities for individual freedom and safeguards the intellectual growth of both the husband and wife. James McCary emphasizes this in his book <u>Freedom and Growth in Marriage</u> in which he says that:

> A creative marriage . . . is an adventure shared by two people who believe that individual freedom and growth are possible within a marriage, and that it is possible for that marriage to grow as a third entity that spins off greater satisfaction to the individuals in it, who in turn strengthen the marriage by their greater resources, strength, and courage.[5]

Naturally, each creative marriage is unique since it reflects the individual characteristics of the partners. Yet even though no two creative marriages are

Three spaced ellipsis marks are used to indicate an omission within a single sentence.

exactly alike, basic styles around which most creative marriages are built have developed. One such style that has been gaining in popularity in recent years bears the businesslike title of contract marriage. In essence, it requires that each participant agree in principle or in writing to preconceived conditions. These may be financial, personal, or emotional. In this sense, according to Dr. Clifford Sager, the marriage contract becomes "a therapeutic and educational concept that tries to spell out the vague and intuitive."[6]

Actually, marriage contracts have existed since earliest times; consider the old agreement reviewed in Psychology Today "that a husband bear economic responsibility for his wife in return for the virginity she brought to him."[7] Time also points out that "the well-to-do have long used marriage contracts to protect their wealth from the caprices of divorce courts."[8] Today, however, the contract in a creative marriage does not basically concern itself with financial affairs but with each individual's personal and emotional growth. When a person marries, he or she brings expectations into the marriage and offers promises whether they are consciously acknowledged or not. If these promises are made through a contract and the couple understands the concepts of the commitment, a meaningful relationship can be established.

Short quotations should be introduced smoothly and a variety of introductions should be used.

The writer expresses her own conclusions based on her research.

The main problem with marriage contracts, if one discounts the effects of seeming distrust between marriage partners, concerns legality. "If a couple wants to make sure that their agreement has legal force," advises New York lawyer Brenda Feigen-Fasteau, "they should stay unmarried, in which case their contract is like any other private agreement between individuals."[9]

This trend toward contract marriages expands into a variation called the renewable marriage, which Jessie Bernard describes. The couple makes a commitment to "maintain the marriage" for a set number of years with the stipulation that each person could renege at the end of the time period or recommit to a union that continued to be satisfactory and fulfilling.[10]

This is quite similar to the marriage style that was suggested by anthropologist Margaret Mead years ago. Known as the two-step marriage, her plan is described by Phillip Rice:

> The form was individual marriage, which was a business union between two individuals who would be committed to each other for as long as they wanted to remain together, but not as parents. . . . If their relationship deepened and was compatible, they could agree to move on to the second step of marriage, parental marriage.[11]

A quoted sentence can be broken up for variety in presentation. Thus, the quoted material is part of the paper's natural flow.

Use of the past tense is necessitated by the quotation. Later, the writer returns to the historical present tense.

Several advantages of this style were given by Margaret Mead. Within this structure, couples could become acquainted before having children and could take the time to be sure that they wanted a family. It would also provide young adults with a legal sex life instead of having them trapped in early parental marriages.[12] Results from this two-step plan would include, declares Phillip Rice, individual marriages without final commitments and, if the individual marriage should break up "the husband would not be responsible for the continued financial support of his wife, so there would be no alimony."[13] A popular professor of philosophy, Michael Scriven, extends Mead's idea into a three-step marriage: preliminary, a legitimized cohabitation; personal, like Mead's individual marriage; and parental, entered into only after success with the previous levels.[14]

Another variation on the theory of marriage by steps is presented by Vance Packard in his book The Sexual Wilderness in which he proposes "a two-year conformation period, after which marriage would become final or be dissolved."[15] All of these plans for step-type marriages incorporate some of the characteristics of contract marriage, but they differ in that the couples are advancing through levels of intimacy, en-

The student effectively uses both paraphrase and quotation.

The student's précis can easily be inserted into the paper because it was written in formal English on the note card.

Again, the student draws her own conclusions based on her research.

abling them to be sure of their feelings before making
the final decision of a complete contractual commitment.
While these marriages do sound businesslike and slightly
cool, Bernard describes the concept as it should be
understood:

> The form of the commitment is less important than
> the emotional context it underlines. It may be a
> written contract or simply vows and promises made
> before witnesses or even simply an "understanding"
> or consensual agreement. Merely fly-by-night,
> touch-and-go relationships do not qualify.[16]

While contract and step-type marriages are
concerned with the problems which arise from living
together, the long-distance marriage confronts the
problems which arise from a married couple living a-
part. A fairly new development, this variation of the
creative marriage results from large numbers of women

entering the work force as professionals with important
careers. Husbands and wives live separately while pur-
suing their independent courses of business and see
one another when possible. If absence makes the heart
grow fonder, this style of marriage should improve the
quality of marriage and lower the divorce rate among
couples participating in long-distance marriages, or

commuter marriages as they are sometimes called.

But, serious problems are inevitable in this type of marriage. For example, in an article in <u>Parents Magazine</u> discussing this arrangement, the author concludes that the partners in a long–distance marriage must not only cope with the loneliness of separation but deal with child rearing difficulties and face the challenges surely to arise in this situation.[17]

Obviously the couple needs to adapt habits and attitudes to the new lifestyle, but another factor to consider involves finances. The cost of maintaining two homes and traveling between them is a heavy financial burden to bear. Besides the expenses in this arrangement, a long–distance marriage, according to <u>U.S. News & World Report,</u> "can create emotional strains . . . and lead to psychological barriers between husband and wife."[18] Yet there are certain factors that help to make the arrangement work. The long–distance marriage, according to William Nichols, "works best when there are no minor–aged children to be considered," the two people are "equipped by temperament and personality to spend a considerable amount of time alone," and both are able to "function in a mature, highly independent fashion."[19]

A couple must develop a strong bond before attempting to negotiate such an obstacle–ridden course

Paraphrase must be carefully introduced and properly documented.

Many quoted phrases from the same passage in one source have one documentation to cover them all.

like a long—distance marriage. The difficulties asso—
ciated with the relationship are probably the reason
why most couples in commuter marriages see the long—
distance nature of their marriage as temporary and not a
fixed lifestyle, according to one source.[20] In his crit—
ical article Nichols makes this conclusion:

> Whether long—distance marriage will facilitate or
> retard growth and deepening of the relationship
> between husband and wife is an unknown, and
> probably depends a great deal on the individuals,
> their maturity, and on the degree of their com—
> mitment to their careers——and to each other.[21]

Another creative marriage alternative evolving in
our society is the idea of sharing roles. Who does the
dishes or takes out the trash are not the crucial is—
sues, although they might assume importance in role re—
versal. Role sharing, though, consists of exactly what
the name implies——sharing the responsibilities and bene—
fits of a relationship. One author's argument con—
tends that role sharing is based on the ideas "that
children should have the care of both parents, that all
who benefit from the services supplied in the household
should contribute to them, and that both partners should
share in supporting the household."[22] In actuality, role

The first line of the quotation is flush left because it was not the beginning of a new paragraph in the original.

sharing has existed for years between couples who have established cooperative and committed marriages. When that type of relationship is formed, the individuals instinctively strive toward the sharing of problems and responsibilities, as well as rewards.

Communal life, a system torn by conflict, has become associated with the concept of role sharing. Many communes support group marriages or polygamy, but Bernard reports that "some communes do include married couples who retain their conventional monogamous relationship."[23] Basically, the theory is identical with role sharing except the duties are delegated to several couples or families instead of one. If a person possesses the ability to cope with group living, his or her life within the commune (while remaining monogamous) will probably be productive and rewarding. However, because of the roles which have been ingrained into our society, Bernard suggests that "it takes a considerable amount of sophistication to understand, let alone accept, the logic and the justice of the shared-role ideology, and a considerable amount of goodwill to implement it."[24]

Marriage, accompanied by its many modern variations, has grown into a target of heated criticism and controversy in recent years. Yet couples continue to

fall in love, get married, and aim for a happy life together. At the same time, divorce rates are rising to
astonishing levels. Concerning this seeming paradox,
McCary comments that "the changes taking place in
marriage forms do not reflect simply a restless impul-
siveness on the part of married people, but instead
reflect genuine needs for growth that are as inevitable
as are the needs of a child to move from one stage of
growth to another."[25] So, in a sense, today's marriages
are undergoing growing pains. Changes must occur if
marriage is to remain a viable institution; otherwise
stagnation will eventually destroy marriage.

It should be noted that the terms "commitment" and
"relationship" are evident in all the marriage forms
discussed thus far. This reflects our society's un-
willingness to discard, even in the new marriages of
today, the foundations of traditional marriage. On the
contrary, "this institution . . . is here to stay,"[26]
according to James DeBurger. Another critic's proposal
creates a fitting conclusion to a discussion of the
creative marriages of the future: "It is fallacious,
then, even to speak of 'the future of marriage.' We
should rather speak of the 'marriage in the future.' "[27]

Student reaffirms the topic, explains how she has proved her thesis, and uses a quotation from an expert as a final support of her point.

<u>Notes</u>

[1] "Old Fashioned Marriage Is Back in Style," <u>Ladies' Home Journal</u>, Jan. 1976, p. 136.

[2] "In Defense of Monogamy," <u>Commentary</u>, Nov. 1974, p. 34.

[3] Gilder, "In Defense of Monogamy," p. 36.

[4] <u>Freedom and Growth in Marriage</u> (Santa Barbara, Cal.: Hamilton, 1975), p. ii.

[5] McCary, <u>Freedom and Growth in Marriage</u>, p. 120.

[6] <u>Marriage Contracts and Couple Therapy</u> (New York: Brunner/Mazel, 1976), p. 48.

[7] Pam Moore, "Marriage Contract—New Twists on Old Ideas," <u>Psychology Today</u>, Aug. 1975, p. 29.

[8] "Ties That Bind," <u>Time</u>, 1 Sep. 1975, p. 62.

[9] As quoted in Moore, p. 62.

[10] <u>The Future of Marriage</u> (New York: Bantam, 1972), p. 106.

[11] <u>The Adolescent</u> (Boston: Allyn and Bacon, 1975), p. 466.

[12] Rice, <u>The Adolescent</u>, pp. 466–67.

[13] Rice, p. 466.

This student uses endnotes for her documentation. Your professor may prefer you to use footnotes.

Use this form if the author's name was given in the text.

The second reference to Gilder must connect him with his work.

Standard monthly magazine reference.

Use this form rather than Ibid.

[14] As reported in Rice, p. 464.

[15] The Sexual Wilderness (New York: D. McKay, 1968), p. 467.

Use this form even though both author and title are given in the text.

[16] Bernard, The Future of Marriage, pp. 87–88.

[17] William C. Nichols, "Long–Distance Marriage," Parents Magazine, Oct. 1978, p. 54.

[18] " 'Commuter Marriages'––Latest Product of Women's Changing Status," U.S. News & World Report, 24 Oct. 1977, p. 109.

Use this form for articles with an unknown author.

[19] Nichols, p. 54.

[20] "Commuter Marriages," p. 110.

[21] Nichols, p. 54.

[22] Bernard, p. 279.

[23] Bernard, p. 216.

[24] Bernard, p. 282.

[25] McCary, p. 382.

[26] James E. DeBurger, ed. Marriage Today (New York: Halsted, 1977), p. 272.

Even though DeBurger's name was given in the text, it is given again here to indicate that he is the editor, not the author, of the work.

[27] Bernard, p. 302.

A Selected Bibliography

Barthel, Joan. "Old Fashioned Marriage Is Back in
    Style." Ladies' Home Journal, Jan. 1976, pp.
    93, 132f.

Bernard, Jessie. The Future of Marriage. New York:
    Bantam Books, 1972.

" 'Commuter Marriages'--Latest Product of Women's Chang-
    ing Status." U.S. News & World Report, 24 Oct. 1977,
    pp. 109-10.

DeBurger, James E., ed. Marriage Today. New York: Hal-
    sted, 1977.

Gilder, George. "In Defense of Monogamy." Commentary,
    Nov. 1974, pp. 31-36.

McCary, James Leslie. Freedom and Growth in Marriage.
    Santa Barbara, Cal.: Hamilton, 1975.

Moore, Pam. "Marriage Contracts--New Twists on Old
    Ideas." Psychology Today, Aug. 1975, p. 29.

Nichols, William C. "Long-Distance Marriage." Parents
    Magazine, Oct. 1978, p. 54.

132f means page 132 and the following page.

Alphabetize anonymous works according to the title.

Standard book form.

Standard monthly magazine form.

Packard, Vance. _The Sexual Wilderness_. New York: D.
    McKay, 1968.

Rice, F. Phillip. _The Adolescent_. Boston: Allyn and
    Bacon, 1975.

Sager, Clifford J., M.D. _Marriage Contracts and Couple
    Therapy_. New York: Brunner/Mazel, 1976.

"Ties That Bind." _Time_, 1 Sep. 1975, p. 62.

ENDNOTES AND FOOTNOTES

● With as much effort as you have already exercised in organizing the body of your paper, you will now want to document your sources with complete accuracy. Consequently, you must credit in a note the source of every quotation, paraphrase, fact, or idea, specifying the exact location of each item so that the reader may investigate further if he or she so desires. Therefore, you should fully understand, perhaps even memorize, the basic forms of documentation—that is, both note and bibliography entries for a book and for a periodical article.

The note examples below show the form for *endnotes,* which are collected together on a separate page at the end of the paper. They differ from *footnotes,* which are placed at the bottom of the page on which the citations appear. For further discussions of the differences between endnotes and footnotes, see pp. 100-103.

The basic forms for a book are:

Endnote

1 John Baxter, <u>The Bidders</u> (New York: Lippincott, 1979), p. 38.

Bibliography

Baxter, John. <u>The Bidders</u>. New York: Lippincott, 1979.

In other words, a note to a book differs from the bibliography entry for that book in six ways: (1) indentation of the first line; (2) raised index numeral, (3) author's given name first, (4) a comma following the author's name, (5) publication data within parentheses, and (6) a specific page reference. (For a fuller discussion of bibliography entries, see pp. 128-148.)

The basic forms for periodical articles are:

Endnote

> 2 B. J. Shade, "Social-Psychological Traits of Achieving
> Black Children," Education Digest, 44 (Oct. 1978), 38.

Bibliography

> Shade, B. J. "Social-Psychological Traits of Achieving Black
> Children." Education Digest, 44 (Oct. 1978), 38–47.

That is, a note to a periodical article differs from the bibliography entry for that article in six ways: (1) indentation of the first line, (2) raised index numeral, (3) author's given name first, (4) a comma following the author's name, (5) a comma rather than a period following the title of the article, and (6) a specific page reference rather than complete pagination.

You must keep your notes correct, clear, and concise. By recording data *carefully* and by double-checking each entry *before* typing the final manuscript, you can ensure accuracy. (Imagine the reaction of your reader, or instructor, if your reference directs him or her to page 568 of a book that contains only 465 pages!) Also, you must maintain clarity. Remember, for example, that "Ibid." should not appear as a note when "Thompson, p. 216." serves the same purpose with greater clarity. Also, "Smith, op. cit., p. 16" may confuse the reader more than a simple reference to "Smith, p. 16." More information on these forms is provided on pp. 124-25. Finally, you should not interrupt the reader with an overabundance of notes. In fact, when you are citing a primary source many times in the paper, you can insert a brief note, within parentheses, in the text itself. Clearly, you will not seriously interrupt the reader's attention with such references in your text as (p. 35), (XI.357), or (*Ham*.III.i.56-63). Remember, however, in such cases to write a first full reference to a work that you cite often, putting it in a correct note and informing your reader that subsequent references to this edition appear in your text (see pp. 64-65).

When to Note a Source

Sometimes the decision to document or not to document certain information with a note becomes troublesome. If in doubt, you should ask yourself, "Would a mature reader be likely to know this information?" If you believe he or she would not, you should provide documentation that locates the source for the reader. For example, the fact that Richard M. Nixon was president of the United States would not usually require a note entry. Nor would you probably need to indicate a source for the fact that Nixon's foreign policy resulted in détente with Russia and the renewal of diplomatic relations with China. For that matter, his decision to resign as a result of the Watergate scandal is common knowledge. However, you should credit, by means of a note, the source of specific decisions and statements by Nixon—for example, his communications with Russian and Chinese leaders, his cabinet decisions, or his public proclamations and statements.

Do *not* document a common dictionary definition, but *do* note a special or extended definition from, for example, the *Oxford English Dictionary* or an encyclopedia. Do *not* document an item of common knowledge, such as "Faulkner created a mythic community within his novels that he labeled Yoknapatawpha county"; "Faulkner wrote *The Sound and the Fury*"; Faulkner was preoccupied with the South's heritage." But *do* note any paraphrase of highly specific information or commentary so original that it goes beyond what an average young scholar might know. Do *not* document an idea of your own, though the idea may result from your reading and the combination of ideas suggested by your sources, but *do* document any idea that you can credit to a specific source.

Therefore, a good rule of thumb might well be the following: You should document when borrowing directly from your notes, but you may omit the note when you compose sentences not directly derived from reference material. Of course, you must always note a quotation, précis, summary, or paraphrased sentence. (See pp. 43-48, and the discussion of plagiarism, pp. 49-51.)

In addition, resist the tendency to construct each paragraph so that a note at the end of it would blanket the entire unit. This method often results in ambiguous references. Rather, you should consider as one unit each sentence or group of sentences from the same source. You should seldom find it necessary to document a complete paragraph if you synthesize and develop all the material as your own. (See "Handling Reference Material," pp. 59-70.)

Placing Note Numbers Within the Text

The rules for inserting note numbers into your text are:

1. Use Arabic numerals typed slightly above the line.
2. Always place the number at the *end* of your quotation, paraphrase, idea, and so on—not after introductory words or punctuation.
3. The note number comes immediately after the final word or punctuation—there is no space between a word or a mark of punctuation and the index numeral:

tionship deepened and was compatible, they
could agree to move on to the second step of
marriage, parental marriage."[18] Several reasons for this suggested style were given by
Margaret Mead. Within this structure, couples
could take the time to be sure they wanted a
family. It would also provide young adults
with a legal sex life instead of having them
trapped in early parental marriages.[19] Results from this. . . .

Arranging the Endnotes or Footnotes

As mentioned earlier, there are two ways to arrange your notes: as endnotes or as footnotes.

Endnotes appear on a separate page following the body of your paper, not at the bottom of the pages of your text. Footnotes are placed at the bottoms of the text pages where their corresponding citations appear. Footnotes are traditional with a thesis or dissertation in which the work should show a finished look. As often happens, though, a practical form wins wide acceptance. Such is the case with endnotes. Because endnotes are less confusing and easier to handle than footnotes, they have become an often practiced and widely accepted form of documentation for the undergraduate research paper. Rather than struggle with spacing problems, you merely number your text correctly and then collect all notes at the end of the text.

The endnote form is the one that will be employed in the examples found later in this chapter and is also the form used in the sample research paper in Chapter 4. However, examples of both forms are included here. Ask your professor which he or she prefers and act accordingly. And remember, never use both endnotes and footnotes in the same paper.

ENDNOTES

When writing endnotes be sure to:
1. Begin notes on a new page at the end of your text.
2. Entitle the page ''Notes,'' centered and placed two inches from top of the page. This page is unnumbered, but number all other pages of endnotes.

3. Indent the first line of each note five spaces, type the note number slightly above the line, skip a space, begin the note, and use the left margin for succeeding lines.

4. When typing, double-space the notes and double-space between the notes:

Notes

[1] "Old Fashioned Marriage Is Back in Style," <u>Ladies' Home Journal</u>, Jan. 1976, p. 136.

[2] "In Defense of Monogamy," <u>Commentary</u>, Nov. 1974, p. 34.

[3] Gilder, "In Defense of Monogamy," p. 36.

[4] <u>Freedom and Growth in Marriage</u> (Santa Barbara, Cal.: Hamilton, 1975), p. ii.

FOOTNOTES

Unlike the endnote, the footnote is single spaced and there is no space between the note number and the first word of the note. However, you do double space between footnotes.

When writing your footnotes, be sure to:

1. Number the footnotes consecutively throughout the entire paper (but by chapters in longer works such as a graduate thesis).

2. Collect at the bottom of each page all footnotes for citations made on that page.

3. Separate the footnotes from your text by triple spacing (that is, leave two lines of space). Also, single space each footnote, but double space between the notes:

and freedom calling for separate rooms and

nights out."[10] This type of provision does

not seem to promote a loving and creative

marriage.

[8]Pam Moore, "Marriage Contracts--New
Twists on Old Ideas," Psychology Today, Aug.
1975, p. 29.

[9]"Ties That Bind," Time, 1 Sept. 1975, p.
62.

[10]Jessie Bernard, The Future of Marriage
(New York: Bantam Books, 1972), p. 106.

4.   Do not start a footnote on one page and complete it on the next. In order to
prevent your footnotes from running over to the next page or descending below
your bottom margin, you can estimate the amount of space you will need by
inserting each footnote, with the proper spacing, etc., in the *rough* draft of the text
in this fashion:

. . . . and lead to psychological barriers between

husband and wife."[14]

---

[14]" 'Commuter Marriages'--Latest Product of Women's Changing Status," U.S. News &
World Report, 24 Oct. 1977, p. 109.

There are certain factors which facilitate the

implementation . . .

This is done in the rough draft only. At the retyping stage, then, the exact number
of lines and spaces needed can be calculated and enough room left at the bottom
for footnotes.

5. Employ a separate line for each footnote unless you have numerous short notes. The following form is acceptable:

> [4]Johnson, p. 3.   [6]Thomas, p. 456.
>
> [5]Johnson, p. 9.   [7]Johnson, p. 9.

Also acceptable:

> [4]Johnson, p. 3.
>
> [5]Johnson, p. 9.
>
> [6]Thomas, p. 456.
>
> [7]Johnson, p. 9.

Note Form—Books

You should use the following order when placing data for books within the first, full note, omitting any unnecessary items:

1. The author's or authors' name(s), in normal order, followed by a comma:

> [1] Azriel Rosenfeld, Picture Languages: Formal Models for Picture Recognition (New York: Academic Press, 1979), p. 10.

Avoid abbreviations by providing the name in the fullest form known to you. Imagine the dilemma of a reader searching the card catalog for ''L. Lewis'' or ''J. H. Smith''! However, if you supply missing ingredients—that is, ones not given on the title page of the book—place them within square brackets (for example, ''L[awrence] Lewis''). In the case of well-known authors, give the name in its most usual form (for example, ''T. S. Eliot'' and ''Dante'').

2. The title of the chapter or part of the book, within quotation marks, followed by a comma inside the final quotes:

2 Dante, "Purgatorio," in his <u>The Divine Comedy</u>, trans. Lawrence Grant White (New York: Pantheon, 1948), p. 74.

This entry is only necessary for specific chapters or parts of long works. See sample notes 23 through 26 (pp. 108–9) for examples of cases where the chapter or part of a book is in a collection of pieces by different authors or in an anthology by an editor. Words that refer to a Preface or Introduction or any other untitled section of a book are capitalized but *not* placed within quotation marks nor underlined. See "Foreword," p. 110.

3. The title of the book, underlined, followed by a comma unless the next item is enclosed within parentheses. Use the full title as shown on the title page of the book, including any subtitle (which you distinguish by a colon):

3 Arthur O. Lovejoy, <u>The Great Chain of Being: A Study in the History of an Idea</u> (Cambridge, Mass.: Harvard Univ. Press, 1936), p. 118.

4. The name of the editor, translator, or compiler, in normal order, preceded by "ed.," "trans.," or "comp.," followed by a comma unless the next item is enclosed within parentheses:

4 Aleksandr Solzhenitsyn, <u>August 1914</u>, trans. Michael Glenny (New York: Farrar, Straus and Giroux, 1972), p. 17.

5 N. Scott Momaday, "A Vision Beyond Time and Place," in <u>Speaking for Ourselves: American Ethnic Writing</u>, ed. Lillian Faderman and Barbara Bradshaw, 2nd ed. (Glenview, Ill.: Scott, Foresman, 1975), p. 15.

Note that this text is *edited* by the two authors (compare with note 6 below).

If you are discussing the editor's or translator's work rather than the text, provide his or her name first, followed by a comma, followed by "ed.," eds.," or "trans.," and another comma. Place the author's name, if any, preceded with a comma and "by," after the title:

6 Lillian Faderman and Barbara Bradshaw, eds., <u>Speaking for Ourselves: American Ethnic Writing</u>, 2nd ed. (Glenview, Ill.: Scott, Foresman, 1975), p. iv.

7 Hugh Shelley, trans., <u>Nightmare Rally</u>, by Pierre Castex (New York: Abelard-Schuman Ltd., 1965), p. 16.

5. The edition number, if it is not the first, in Arabic numerals, followed by a comma unless the next item is enclosed within parentheses:

> [8] Weston A. Price, <u>Nutrition and Physical Degeneration</u>, 9th ed. (La Mesa, Cal.: Price-Pottenger, 1977), p. 56.

Reprints of old editions, paperback reprints especially, require notation of the original date and edition as well as publication facts of the reprint:

> [9] Frank N. Egerton, ed., <u>Natural History of the European Seas</u>, by Edward Forbes and Robert Godwin-Austen, 3rd ed. (1859; rpt. New York: Arno, 1978), p. 63.

6. The series name, without quotation marks and not underlined, followed by a comma, followed by the number of this book in the series, followed by a comma unless the next item is enclosed within parentheses:

> [10] David Fowler, <u>Piers the Plowman</u>, Univ. of Washington Publications in Lang. and Lit., 16 (Seattle: Univ. of Washington Press, 1961), p. 89.

7. The number of volumes with this title, in Arabic numerals (for example, "5 vols."). Use only if there is more than one volume and the information is pertinent—that is, if your reference is to the work as a whole, not to a specific passage:

> [11] Vernon L. Parrington, <u>Main Currents in American Thought</u>, 3 vols. (New York: Harcourt, 1927–32).
>
> Note that the page number is omitted in this note because the reference is to the entire work.

8. The place, publisher, and date of publication within parentheses and with a colon between the place and publisher and commas after the publisher and the second parenthesis:

> [12] Andrew Wright, <u>A Reader's Guide to English and American Literature</u> (Glenview, Ill.: Scott, Foresman, 1970), p. xix.

If more than one city appears on the title page, use only the first. Include the name of the state if necessary for clarity (for example, "Springfield, Mass." or "Springfield, Ill."). Provide the publisher's name in an abbreviated form (for example, "Macmillan," "Norton," McGraw-Hill," etc.). But list university presses in full to distinguish between a publication of the university and that of a university press (for example, "Louisiana State Univ." or "Univ. of Oklahoma Press"). If the title page does not carry the publication date, use the most recent copyright date as shown on the reverse side of the title page.

9.   The volume number, if the book is one of two or more volumes with the same title, in Roman numerals, followed by a comma:

> 13 Ivan Turgenev, <u>Virgin Soil</u>, trans. Constance Garnett
>
> (New York: Macmillan, 1951), I, 81.

If the volumes were published in different years, show this fact by placing the volume number *before* the place and date of publication:

> 14 Vernon L. Parrington, "Roger Williams," <u>Main Cur-</u>
>
> <u>rents in American Thought</u>, I (New York: Harcourt, 1927), 62.

10.   Page number(s), preceded by a comma, in Arabic numerals unless the text has small Roman numerals (for example, "p. iv."). Use "p." and "pp." only for works of a single volume. Also note the following common usage: "pp. 92-93," not "pp. 92-3"; but "pp. 215-18," not "pp. 215-8" or "pp. 215-218." Page numbers are followed by a period unless some additional information must be included (for example, "p. 12, n. 2.").

SPECIMEN NOTES—BOOKS

These note samples follow the form for endnotes—they are double-spaced and a space is left between the note numeral and the first word of the note. Footnotes should be single-spaced with no space following the note numeral.

Author, *first full reference*

> 1 David C. McClelland, <u>Power: The Inner Experience</u> (New
>
> York: Halsted, 1975), pp. 92–94.

Subsequent reference:

> 2 McClelland, p. 75.
>
> Here and elsewhere below, the inclusion of "subsequent references" will indicate how to set up notes for sources that have been cited previously in the text of the paper.

Author's name already given in text

> 3 <u>Pillar of Salt</u> (New York: Manor Books, 1978), p. 43.
>
> Use this form even if both author and title are given in your text.

Subsequent reference:

⁴ Vincent, <u>Pillar of Salt</u>, p. 40.

Since you did not name Vincent in the first note, you must connect him with the title in the second note. Thereafter, "Vincent, p. 7." will suffice.

Author, *anonymous*

⁵ <u>The Song of Roland</u>, trans. Frederick Bliss Luquines (New York: Macmillan, 1960), p. 22.

Subsequent reference:

⁶ <u>Roland</u>, p. 23.

Author, *anonymous but name supplied*

⁷ [James Madison], <u>All Impressments Unlawful and Inadmissible</u> (Boston: William Pelham, 1804), p. 10.

Subsequent reference:

⁸ [Madison], p. 12.

Author, *pseudonymous but name supplied*

⁹ Robert Slender [Philip Freneau], <u>Letters on Various and Important Subjects</u> (Philadelphia: D. Hogan, 1799), p. 140.

Subsequent reference:

¹⁰ Slender [Freneau], p. 141.

Authors, *two*

¹¹ Henry O. Hooper and Peter Gwynne, <u>Physics and the Physical Perspective</u> (New York: Harper & Row, 1977), p. 61.

Subsequent reference:

¹² Hooper and Gwynne, p. 79.

Authors, *three*

¹³ Wilbur O. Sypherd, A. M. Fountain, and V. E. Gibbens, <u>Manual of Technical Writing</u> (Glenview, Ill.: Scott, Foresman, 1957), p. 60.

Subsequent reference:

¹⁴ Sypherd et al., p. 61.

Authors, *more than three*

¹⁵ Laurel J. Lewis et al., <u>Linear Systems Analysis</u> (New York: McGraw-Hill, 1969), p. 153.

The use of "and others" is also acceptable (see p. 127).

Subsequent reference:

16 Lewis et al., p. 153.

Biblical references

17 Psalms 14:4–5.

18 II Peter 2:17 (The Interpreter's Bible, XII).

Editions of the Bible other than the King James version should be noted within parentheses.

Classical works

19 Homer, <u>The Iliad</u>, trans. Richmond Lattimore (Chicago: Univ. of Chicago Press, 1951), p. 101 (Bk. III, ll. 38–45).

20 Plato, <u>The Republic</u>, trans. Paul Shorey (Cambridge, Mass.: Harvard Univ. Press, 1937), p. 225 (III, vi).

You should give the reader more information than the page number for classics that appear in several editions. However, do not use this form if you make numerous citations to one work. Rather, you should provide an initial full reference and thereafter place the documentation in your text (see pp. 64-65).

Component part of a book

21 Lewis Thomas, "The Music of This Sphere," in his <u>The Lives of a Cell</u> (New York: Viking, 1974), pp. 20–25.

22 Dante, "Purgatorio," in his <u>The Divine Comedy</u>, trans. Lawrence Grant White (New York: Pantheon, 1948), p. 74.

Use this form (notes 21 and 22) for citation to one chapter or section of a complete work by an author.

23 Robert Penn Warren, "Holly and Hickory," in his <u>You Emperors, and Others: Poems 1957–1960</u> (New York: Random House, 1960), p. 38.

24 Flannery O'Connor, "The Nature and Aim of Fiction," in her <u>Mystery and Manner</u>, ed. Sally and Robert Fitzgerald (New York: Noonday, 1970), pp. 76–77.

Use this form (notes 23 and 24) for citation to one piece in a collection of different pieces all by the same author.

25 Nathan Scott, Jr., "Society and Self in Recent American Literature," in his <u>The Broken Center</u> (New Haven: Yale Univ. Press, 1966), pp. 539–54; rpt. in <u>Dark Symphony: Negro Literature in America</u>, ed. James A. Emanuel and Theodore L. Gross (New York: Free Press, 1968), p. 540.

Collections of articles are highly useful, but you must take care that you inform your reader about the original source as well as the collection from which you quote or paraphrase. You cannot usually check a reprint against the original, so caution dictates that citations be made to the text actually in hand.

26 Robert Browning, "My Last Duchess," in Better Reading Two: Literature, ed. Walter Blair, John Gerber, and Eugene Garber, 4th ed. (Glenview, Ill.: Scott, Foresman, 1966), pp. 55–56.

Use this form (note 26) for a festschrift or collection of many pieces by different authors.

Subsequent reference:

27 Browning, pp. 55–56.

Consolidation of several references in one note

28 For additional commentary on this point see Lionel Trilling, "F. Scott Fitzgerald," in his The Liberal Imagination: Essays on Literature and Society (New York: Viking, 1951); William Troy, "Scott Fitzgerald, the Authority of Failure," Accent (Autumn 1945); and John Aldridge, "Fitzgerald: The Horror and the Vision of Paradise," in his After the Lost Generation (New York: McGraw–Hill, 1951).

Corporate authorship

29 Committee on Telecommunications, Reports on Selected Topics in Telecommunications (New York: National Academy of Sciences, National Research Council, 1970), p. 4.

Subsequent reference:

30 Committee on Telecommunications, p. 5.

Double reference

31 Stuart Symington as quoted in Victor Marchetti and John D. Marks, The CIA and the Cult of Intelligence (New York: Knopf, 1974), p. 321.

Subsequent reference:

32 Symington, p. 321.

Edition

33 Oscar Thompson, The International Cyclopedia of Music and Musicians, rev. Robert Sabin, 9th ed. (New York: Dodd, Mead, 1964), p. 81.

Editor

[34] Hugh Henry Brackenridge, <u>Modern Chivalry</u>, ed.
Claude M. Newlin (New York: American Book, 1962), p. 18.
The writer is citing Brackenridge, the author.

[35] Hardin Craig and David Bevington, eds., <u>The Com-
plete Works of Shakespeare</u>, rev. ed. (Glenview, Ill.: Scott,
Foresman, 1973),p. 22.
The writer is citing Craig and Bevington, the editors.

Encyclopedia

[36] Robert E. Dickinson, "Norman Conquest," <u>The World
Book Encyclopedia</u>, 1976.
References alphabetically arranged need not be identified by volume and
page. Notes to unsigned articles begin with the title of the article.

Subsequent reference:

[37] Dickinson.

[38] A[rne] D. N[aess], "Martin Heidegger," <u>Encyclopaedia
Britannica: Macropaedia</u>, 8, 1974.
Authors of articles in the 15th edition of the *New Encyclopaedia Britannica*
are identified by initials at the end of the article, and their full names are
given in a separate volume called the "Propaedia." Brackets are required
because you are adding full information to the "A.D.N."

Subsequent reference:

[39] N[aess].

Footnote citation

[40] Fawn M. Brodie, <u>Thomas Jefferson: An Intimate His-
tory</u> (New York: Norton, 1974), p. 543, n. 61.

Foreword, *or introduction*

[41] Robert Lowell, Foreword, <u>Ariel</u>, by Sylvia Plath (New
York: Harper & Row, 1966), pp. ix–xi.

Manuscript collections

[42] British Museum, <u>Cotton Vitellius</u>, A. XV.

Subsequent reference:

[43] <u>Cotton Vitellius</u>.

[44] Corpus Christi College, Cambridge, MS CCCC 201.

Play, *classical*

45 William Shakespeare, <u>Macbeth</u>, in <u>Shakespeare:</u>
<u>Twenty—Three Plays and the Sonnets</u>, ed. T. M. Parrott
(New York: Scribner's, 1953), p. 835 (II.i.33—34).

> Since your reader may not have the same edition of Shakespeare's plays, you offer a courtesy by providing act, scene, and lines within parentheses at the end of the note.

Subsequent reference

> Should be placed within the text (see pp. 64–65).

Play, *modern*

46 Tom Stoppard, <u>Rosencrantz and Guildenstern Are Dead</u>
(New York: Grove, 1967), p. 16.

Poem, *classical*

47 Dante, "Purgatorio," in his <u>The Divine Comedy</u>,
trans. Lawrence Grant White (New York: Pantheon, 1948),
p. 74 (vii.1—12).

> Again, your reader may not have the same edition as you, therefore you offer a courtesy by providing the canto and lines within parentheses at the end of the note.

48 Edmund Spenser, <u>The Faerie Queene</u>, ed. Ernest Rhys
(London: Dutton, 1910), I, 58—59 (I.iv.21).

> Note that this edition of *The Faerie Queene* is published in two volumes.

Poem, *modern*

49 Gary Snyder, "Burning the Small Dead," in his <u>The</u>
<u>Back Country</u>, (New York: New Directions, 1968), p. 13.

50 John Keats, "Ode to a Nightingale," in <u>Begin-</u>
<u>nings in Poetry</u>, ed. William J. Martz, 2nd ed. (Glen-
view, Ill.: Scott, Foresman, 1973), pp. 302—4.

Reprint

51 Raymond M. Weaver, Introduction, <u>The Shorter Novels</u>
<u>of Herman Melville</u> (1928; rpt. New York: Premier—Fawcett,
1960), p. 56.

Series, *numbered*

52 David Fowler, <u>Piers the Plowman</u>, Univ. of Washington

Publications in Lang. and Lit., 16 (Seattle: Univ. of Washington Press, 1961), p. 89.

> Since a series number rather than a volume number is given, use the abbreviation "p." with the page number.

Series, *unnumbered*

53 Lawrence Henry Gibson, The Coming of the Revolution: 1762–1775, ed. Henry Steele Commager and Richard B. Morris, The New American Nation Series (New York: Harper & Row, 1954), pp. 1–10.

54 Howard E. Wilson, "Education, Foreign Policy, and International Affairs," in Cultural Affairs and Foreign Relations, ed. Robert Blum, The American Assembly Series (Englewood Cliffs, N.J.: Prentice-Hall, 1963), p. 22.

Source books

55 Cleanth Brooks, "The Formalist Critics," Kenyon Review, 13 (1951), 73; rpt. in H. G. Duffield and Manuel Bilsky, eds., Tolstoy and the Critics: Literature and Aesthetics (Glenview, Ill.: Scott, Foresman, 1965), p. 13.

> Source books contain articles gathered from other publications and compiled into one book. If possible, always cite an original source, but in this case, use the method demonstrated above and below, that is, provide an exact reference to both sources, including page numbers if available.

56 Richard Ellmann, "Reality," in his Yeats: The Man and the Masks (New York: Macmillan, 1948); rpt. in John Unterecker, ed., Yeats: A Collection of Critical Essays, Twentieth Century Views (Englewood Cliffs, N.J.: Prentice-Hall, 1963), p. 165.

Translator

57 Yukio Mishima, The Decay of the Angel, Part 4 of The Sea of Fertility, trans. Edward G. Seidensticker (New York: Knopf, 1974), p. 7.

58 Benedictus de Spinoza, Spinoza's Short Treatise on God, Man and His Well Being, trans. and ed. A. Wolf (New York: Russell and Russell, 1963), p. 3.

> In instances where the author's name is included in the title, you must show the name twice, as above.

Volumes, *one of several*

[59] Edgar Allan Poe, "MS. Found in a Bottle," in The
Works of Edgar Allan Poe (New York: Crowell, 1902), II, 1–
15. Hereafter cited as Works.

> When all volumes are published in the same year, place the volume number after the facts of publication. Cf. note 63 below.

Subsequent reference:

[60] Poe, Works, p. 13.

[61] Constance Garnett, trans., Introduction, Virgin Soil,
by Ivan Turgenev (New York: Macmillan, 1951), I, v.

[62] Aleksandr Pushkin, Eugene Onegin, trans. Vladimir
Nabokov, Bollingen Series 72 (New York: Bollingen, 1964),
I, 186.

[63] Harold Child, "Jane Austen," in The Cambridge History of English Literature, ed. A. W. Ward and A. R. Waller,
XII (London: Cambridge Univ. Press, 1914), 231–33. Hereafter
cited as CHEL.

> When the separate volumes of a work are published in different years, the volume number precedes the facts of publication. Cf. note 59 above.

Subsequent reference:

[64] Child, CHEL, 232.

[65] Christopher Marlowe, The Tragical History of Doctor
Faustus, in The Literature of England, ed. George K. Anderson
and William E. Buckler, 5th ed. (Glenview, Ill.: Scott,
Foresman, 1968), I, 711.

[66] Bliss Perry, The American Spirit in Literature, The
Chronicles of America Series, ed. Allen Johnson, XXXIV (New
Haven: Yale Univ. Press, 1918), 35.

Works alphabetically arranged

[67] E[dmund] K. A[lden], "Alden, John," DAB (1928).

> There is no need to give publishing data on the *Dictionary of American Biography* in an ordinary note. However, give that data in the bibliography entry.

Subsequent reference:

[68] A[lden].

Note Form—Periodicals

You should use the following order when placing data within the first, full note, omitting any items that are unnecessary:

1. The author's name in normal order, followed by a comma:

> ¹ Herbert Aptheker, "The History of Anti-Racism in the United States," The Black Scholar, 6 (1975), 17.

2. The complete title of the article, enclosed within quotation marks, followed by a comma inside the second quotation mark (see note 1 above).
3. The name of the periodical, underlined, followed by a comma (see note 1 above).
4. The volume number (without the abbreviation "Vol." preceding), in Arabic numerals, followed by a comma unless the next item is enclosed within parentheses (see note 1 above). However, omit the volume number for weekly or monthly periodicals which are paged anew in each issue. Give instead the complete data, set off by commas, not parentheses:

> ² "Labor's Grand Old Godfather," Time, 3 March 1975, p. 11.

5. The issue number when pagination of the issue is separate and the month of publication is not given:

> ³ William R. Elkins, "Thoreau's Cape Cod: The Violent Pond," Oklahoma English Bulletin, 2, No. 2 (1965), 15.
>
> Without the issue number the reader could find the article only by looking on page 15 of every issue of 1965.

6. The month (if needed) and year, enclosed in parentheses, followed by a comma. If you can quickly determine that all issues of a journal fall within a calendar year, use only the year. However, you must always precede the year with the month or season (Spring 1970) when pagination is separate in the issue of a periodical, as with weekly and monthly magazines. When in doubt, include the month.

> ⁴ Hans Joachim Marx, "Some Corelli Attributions Assessed," Musical Quarterly, 56 (1970), 89.
>
> Because all 1970 issues are bound together in one volume that is paged continuously, there is no need to include the month.

5 Jerrald Ranta, "Palindromes, Poems, and Geometric Form," College English, 36 (Oct. 1974), 161–72.

> This journal has a volume number that does not coincide with the calendar year (i.e., its first issue is published in October of each year). Adding the month is an aid to a reader who may wish to locate this article.

7. The page number(s), in Arabic numerals, followed by a period, except when additional information follows (for example, ''17, n. 3.''). Use abbreviations ''p.'' or ''pp.'' only when a volume number is *not* included in the reference:

6 Curtis J. Sitomer, "Baby Black Market Charged in California," Christian Science Monitor, 5 March 1975, p. 1.

> Since a volume number is *not* included, use the abbreviation "p."

7 Robert M. Jordan, "The Non–Dramatic Disunity of the Merchant's Tale," PMLA, 78 (1963), 293–94.

> Since a volume number is provided, do *not* use the abbreviation "pp."

SPECIMEN NOTES—PERIODICALS

Address

1 U.S. President, "Address to Veterans of Foreign Wars," 19 Aug. 1974; rpt. in Weekly Compilation of Presidential Documents, 10 (26 Aug. 1974), 1045–46.

Author, *anonymous*

2 "Commodities: Sweet and Sour," Time, 16 Dec. 1974, p. 32.

Subsequent reference:

3 "Commodities," p. 32.

Authors, *multiple*

4 Roger W. Libby, Alan C. Acock, and David C. Payne, "Configurations of Parental Preferences Concerning Sources of Sex Education of Adolescents," Adolescence, 9 (Spring 1974), 76–77.

Subsequent reference:

5 Libby et al., p. 77.

Bulletin

6 "Spotlight on Crime," World of Politics Monthly, Nov. 1974, pp. 10–11.

Monthly bulletin for subscribers to *Taylor's Encyclopedia of Government Officials.*

Subsequent reference:

7 "Spotlight on Crime," p. 10.

8 Economic Research Service, Demand and Price Situation (Washington, D.C.: U.S. Dept. of Agriculture, Aug. 1974), DPS–141, p. 7.

Critical review

9 John Gardner, rev. of Falconer, by John Cheever, Saturday Review, 2 April 1977, p. 20.

Information above is sufficient, but if additional publication information is readily available include it also, as in notes 10 and 12.

10 Rev. of Sexual Suicide, by George F. Gilder (New York: Quadrangle, 1973), Adolescence, 9 (Spring 1974), 151.

Subsequent reference:

11 Rev. of Sexual Suicide, p. 151.

12 Remi Clignet, rev. of Urban Poverty in a Cross-cultural Context, by Edwin Eames and Judith Granich Goode (New York: Free Press, 1973), American Journal of Sociology, 80 (Sept. 1974), 589–90.

Subsequent reference:

13 Clignet, p. 590.

14 Irving Dolodin, "Verdi for Openers," rev. of Simone Boccanegra, Saturday Review World, 2 Nov. 1974, pp. 54–55.

Interview

15 "For an 'Uncultured' America, World Leadership in Arts," Interview with Nancy Hanks, Chairman, National Endowment for the Arts, U.S. News and World Report, 7 Oct. 1974, p. 59.

Journal, *with continuous pagination*

16 Vernon Van Dyke, "Human Rights and the Rights of Groups," <u>American Journal of Political Science</u>, 81 (1974), 729.

> There will be only one page "729" in a volume numbered consecutively through all issues.

17 John A. Dussinger, "Conscience and the Pattern of Christian Perfection in <u>Clarissa</u>," <u>PMLA</u>, 81 (1966), 238–39.

> Adding the month is not necessary.

Journal, *with separate pagination*

18 Doreen Mangan, "Henry Casselli: Superb Contradic-tions," <u>American Artist</u>, 38 (Dec. 1974), 39.

> Because each issue of this journal is paged separately, you should include the month; i.e., page "39" will prove inadequate because a researcher will find a page "39" in each of the twelve issues of volume 38.

19 Jesse Stuart, "Love Affair at the Pasture Gate," <u>Ball State University Forum</u>, 15 (Winter 1974), 3–6.

> Adding the season, rather than month or issue number is sometimes necessary.

20 Raven I. McDavid, "Sense and Nonsense About American Dialects," <u>PMLA</u>, 81, No. 2 (1966), 9–11.

> *PMLA* normally pages continuously, but this issue is paged separately, necessitating the issue number. Compare note 17 above.

Journal, *volume number embracing two years*

21 Douglas J. Kramer, "Protecting the Urban Environment from the Federal Government," <u>Urban Affairs Quarterly</u>, 9 (March 1974), 359–60.

> Again, adding the month will locate the article more specifically for your reader. Any time you have doubts, put the month into your note.

Letter

22 Mary D. Cole, Letter to the Editor, <u>Cumberland</u>, 3 (Fall 1979), 7.

Magazine, *monthly*

23 Alex Poinsett, "The 'Whys' Behind the Black Lawyer Shortage," <u>Ebony</u>, Dec. 1974, p. 95.

> The volume number is now omitted and "p." is added before the page number.

24 Leonard Cottrell, "How Egypt Lived and Died," <u>Réalités</u>, March 1970, pp. 52–53.

[25] Karen Lingo, "The Merchants of Veracruz," Southern Living, Feb. 1975, pp. 38 and 42.

This page reference is necessary with magazine articles that often skip from an opening page or two to the back of the magazine where the article is finished.

Magazine, weekly

[26] "Chaos in Television," Time, 12 March 1979, pp. 60–61.

Use the above form for those articles that do not list an author.

[27] Harry T. Moore, "Motes in the Eye of a Mountainous Man," Saturday Review, 7 March 1970, pp. 23–24.

[28] "Carter vs. Brezhnev: A Contrast in Styles," U.S. News and World Report, 18 June 1979, p. 20.

Quotation, within the article's title

[29] Warren Bennett, "Character, Irony, and Resolution in 'A Clean, Well-Lighted Place,'" American Literature, 62 (March 1970), 70–71, 74.

This page reference is clearer to the reader than "70 et passim."

Note Form—Public Documents

Since the nature of public documents is so varied, the form of the entry cannot be standardized. Therefore, you should provide sufficient information so that the reader can easily locate the reference. As a general rule, arrange information in the note in this order: government, body, subsidiary body, title of document, identifying numbers.

Congressional papers

[1] Cong. Rec., 6 March 1974, pp. S2916–17.

[2] U.S. Cong., Senate, Transportation System for Alaskan Natural Gas, 95th Cong., 1st sess., S. 2411 (Washington, D.C.: GPO, 1977), p. 3.

[3] U.S. Cong., House, Committee on Interstate and Foreign Commerce, Federal Cigarette Labeling and Advertising Act, 89th Cong., 1st sess., H. Rept. 449 to accompany H.R. 3014 (Washington, D.C.: GPO, 1965), pp. 9–12.

4 U.S. Cong., Senate, The Constitution of the United
States of America: Analysis and Interpretation, 82nd Cong.,
2nd sess., S. Doc. 170 (Washington, D.C.: GPO, 1952),
pp. 512–13.

Executive branch documents

5 U.S. President, "Jimmy Carter: 1977," Public Papers
of the Presidents of the United States (Washington, D.C.:
Office of the Federal Registrar, 1978), p. 1563.

6 U.S. President, Alternative to Drugs: A New Approach
to Drug Education, Pr Ex 13.2:D84/3/1972 (Washington, D.C.:
GPO, 1972), p. 3

"Pr Ex" is a code for Executive Office of the President.

7 U.S. Dept. of State, Foreign Relations of the United
States: Diplomatic Papers, 1943, II, 175–77.

Since the date is part of the title above, it precedes the volume number.
Compare with note below.

8 U.S. Dept. of State, United States Treaties and Other
International Agreements, XV, Part 1, 1964, 556.

Legal citations

9 U.S. Const., art. II, sec. 1.

10 California, Const., art. II, sec. 4.

11 15 U.S. Code, sec. 78h (1964).

Note that a title number must be included for references to U.S.C.

12 Noise Control Act of 1972, Statutes at Large, LXXXVI,
Public Law 92–574, 1234–35 (1972).

Laws enacted by Congress are printed in Statutes at Large as public laws,
private laws, and proclamations. Later they are printed in the U.S. Code.
See above and below.

13 Gold Coin and Gold Bullion Act, 31 U.S. Code, Supp.
III, sec. 442 (1970).

14 Environmental Protection Agency et al. v. Mink et
al., U.S. Reports, CDX (1972).

A standard form for law cases.

Note Form—Other Sources

The sample entries below will enable you to formulate a suitable note for miscellaneous types of reference material:

Art work

[1] Raphael, <u>School of Athens</u>, The Vatican, Rome; Illus. in <u>The World Book Encyclopedia</u>, 1976 ed.

> Use this form for art works reproduced in other books or journals, citing the artist, work, location of the artwork and then the source of the illustration. If you actually view the work itself, use the following form.

[2] Frederic Remington, <u>Mountain Man</u>, sculpture, Metropolitan Museum of Art, New York.

> Naming the type of art is not required, but it does add valuable information for your reader.

Bulletin

[3] "Financial Operation of Government Agencies and Funds," <u>Treasury Bulletin</u> (Washington, D.C.: Dept. of Treasury, June 1974), p. 135.

[4] Earl French, <u>Personal Problems in Industrial Research and Development</u>, Bulletin of N.Y. State School of Industrial and Labor Relations, No. 51 (Oct. 1963), p. 22.

Dissertation, *published*

[5] Per Nykrog, <u>Les Fabliaux: Etude d'histoire littéraire et de stylistique médiévale</u>, Diss. Aarhus 1956 (Copenhagen: Munksgaard, 1957), p. 62.

Dissertation, *unpublished*

[6] Emmett Loy Phillips, "A Study of Aesthetic Distance in Thoreau's <u>Walden</u>," Diss. Univ. of Oklahoma 1970, p. 42.

[7] Emmett Loy Phillips, "A Study of Aesthetic Distance in Thoreau's <u>Walden</u>," <u>DAI</u>, 30 (1970), 3953A (Univ. of Oklahoma).

> This note refers to the abstract, not the dissertation itself, as published in <u>Dissertation Abstracts International</u>.

Film

[8] <u>Last Tango in Paris</u>, United Artists, 1972.

[9] <u>The World of the Weed</u>, Bloomington, Ind.: National

Educational TV, Inc. (16 mm., 21 min., black/white).

[10] Bernard Wilets, _Environment_, Santa Monica, Calif.:
BFA Educational Media, 1971 (16 mm., 29 min., color).

Interview

[11] Personal interview with Robert Turrentine, President,
Acme Boot Co., Clarksville, Tenn., 11 Feb. 1979.

Letter, _personal_

[12] Letter received from Professor Winston Weathers of
the University of Tulsa, 5 March 1975.

Manuscript (MS) and typescript (TS), _unpublished_

[13] Journal 3, MS, p. 32. This journal is in the private
collection of Malcolm Glass, Clarksville, Tennessee.

[14] The Hardlanders, TS, p. 193. This and other materials cited are in the Malcolm Glass papers, Clarksville,
Tennessee.

Microfilm or microfiche

[15] H. T. Tuckerman, "James Fenimore Cooper," _North American Review_, 89 (1859), 298, Microfilm.

Indicate at the end of your entry that your source is on microfilm or micro-
fiche.

Mimeographed material

[16] Jane L. Smith, "Terms for the Study of Fiction"
(mimeographed paper, Cleveland, 1975), p. 2.

Monograph

[17] NEA Research Division, _Kindergarten Practices, 1961_
(monograph 1962–M2, Washington, D.C., 1962), p. 3.

[18] William R. Veeder, _W. B. Yeats: The Rhetoric of
Repetition_, Univ. of California English Studies, 34 (Berkeley: Univ. of California Press, 1968), p. 12.

Musical composition

[19] Mozart, _Jupiter_, Symphony No. 41.

[20] Beethoven, Symphony No. 7 in A, op. 92.

Compositions should be cited in the text if at all possible.

Newspaper

21 Jane E. Brody, "Harvard Backs Genetic Study," New York Times, Late City Ed., 14 Dec. 1974, Sec. B, p. 20, col. 1.

Locate the article on the page whenever possible with notations such as "col. 1," "Sec. B," "Late City Ed."

22 Richard Holbrooke, "Kissinger: A Study in Contradictions," Editorial, Washington Post, 15 Sept. 1974, pp. B1–B2.

Use this form for special newspaper articles, such as editorials, letters to the editor, cartoons, and so on.

23 Alice Franklin Bryant, "U.N. Role," Letter to the Editor, Chattanooga Times, 15 Dec. 1974, p. B7.

24 "How to Measure Justice," Editorial, The Tennessean [Nashville], 18 Aug. 1979, p. 8.

25 Elizabeth Mooney, "The Unreal Real Estate Game," Potomac, Washington Post magazine, 15 Sept. 1974, p. 12.

Most newspapers publish a magazine with their Sunday edition. This citation requires the name of the magazine as well as the newspaper.

26 "Egypt Demands That Israel Put Limit on Population Growth," Los Angeles Times, 14 Dec. 1974, p. 1, col. 4.

When an item is unsigned, the title comes first and all the subsequent information remains the same.

Subsequent reference:

27 "Egypt Demands," p. 1.

Pamphlet

28 U.S. Civil Service Commission, The Human Equation: Working in Personnel for the Federal Government, Pamphlet 76 (Washington, D.C.: GPO, May 1970), pp. 2–4.

Public address or lecture

29 David Sarnoff, "Television: A Channel for Freedom," Address presented at the University of Detroit Academic Convocation, Detroit, May 16, 1961.

Recording on record or tape

30 Chaucer, "The Nun's Priest's Tale," in his Canterbury Tales, narrated in Middle English by Robert Ross, Caedmon recording TC 1008, 1971.

31 Elton John, "This Song Has No Title," in his Goodbye Yellow Brick Road, MCA Records, MCA2–10003, 1974.

[32] The Statler Brothers, Jacket Notes, The Originals,
Mercury, SRM-1-5016, 1979.

> Jacket notes and libretto may be designated in the note in order to distinguish between the recording and the accompanying materials.

Report

[33] Fabian Linden, "Women: A Demographic, Social and
Economic Presentation," Report by The Conference Board (New
York: CBS/Broadcast Group, 1973), pp. 24-25.

[34] Panama Canal Company, Annual Report: Fiscal Year
Ended June 30, 1968 (Panama: Canal Zone Government, 1968),
pp. 7-9.

[35] Womanpower (Brookline, Mass.: Betsy Hogan Asso-
ciates, Nov. 1974), p. 1.

> If you cannot quickly determine the author of the report, begin with the title.
> Reports in book or pamphlet form require underlining.

Reproductions and photographs

[36] Blake's Comus, Plate 4, photograph as reproduced in
Irene Tayler, "Blake's Comus Designs," Blake Studies, 4
(Spring 1972), 61.

[37] James A. Michener, "Structure of Earth at Centennial,
Colorado," line drawing in Centennial (New York: Random
House, 1974), p. 26.

Table or illustration

[38] Donald L. Helmich, "Organizational Growth and Succession Patterns," Academy of Management Journal, 17 (Dec. 1974),
773, Table 2.

[39] Edward P. J. Corbett, Syllogism graph, Classical
Rhetoric for the Modern Student (New York: Oxford Univ.
Press, 1965), p. 46.

> Because the graph has no title, the descriptive heading should not be placed within quotation marks.

Television or radio program

[40] Eric Sevareid, CBS News (New York: CBS-TV, 11
March 1975).

41 William Shakespeare, <u>As You Like It</u> (Nashville: Nashville Theatre Academy, 11 March 1975), WDCN–TV.

Local productions should include the local broadcasting station; national programs require only the network.

42 The Commanders: Douglas MacArthur (New York: NBC–TV, 13 March 1975).

Theater

43 Neil Simon, <u>They're Playing Our Song</u>, with Robert Klein and Lucy Arnaz, Imperial, New York, 18 Aug. 1979.

Emphasis may be placed on others, as shown below.

44 Marvin Hamlisch, comp., <u>They're Playing Our Song</u>, by Neil Simon, Imperial, New York, 18 Aug. 1979.

Thesis, *published*

See "Dissertation, published," p. 120.

Thesis, *unpublished*

See "Dissertation, unpublished," p. 120.

Transparency

45 La Vaughn Sharp and William E. Loeche, <u>The Patient and Circulatory Disorders: A Guide for Instructors</u> (Philadelphia: Lippincott, 1969), Transparency 15.

Unpublished paper

46 William R. Elkins, "The Dream World and the Dream Vision: Meaning and Structure in Poe's Art," an unpublished paper.

Subsequent References

To repeat, after you once provide full reference data for a primary citation, your subsequent notes for the same source should be brief but clear. Normally, the author's last name and the page number will suffice (for example, "Johnson, p. 12."). However, if the first full reference is not found in a recent note or if you are citing more than one book by this author, you should add the title, preferably in the shortest possible form (for example, "Johnson, *Experiences*, p. 12."). If another author has an identical surname, you must add the given name to each reference (for example, "James Johnson, p. 12.").

You should find it unnecessary to employ the Latinate abbreviations "ibid.," "op. cit.," and "loc. cit." "Ibid.," an abbreviation for *ibidem* ("in the same place"), refers to the source in the immediately preceding note, but a reference to "Johnson, p. 12" serves the same purpose. "Op. cit." is an abbreviation for *opere citato*, which means "in the work cited." It is sometimes employed in a nonconsecutive reference to a different page of the same work (for example, "Jones, op. cit., p. 65."). But a simple reference to "Jones, p. 65" serves the same purpose and is less confusing. "Loc. cit." is an abbreviation for *loco citato*, which means "in the place cited." Since this note names the exact passage from a source as listed in a preceding note, the author's name and a page reference may be omitted (for example, "Loc. cit." or "Johnson, loc. cit."). But the use of "Johnson, p. 12" serves the same purpose.

Note the following sequence of specimen notes:

1 Lionel Stevenson, " 'My Last Duchess' and Parisina," Modern Language Notes, 74 (1959), 490.

2 Stevenson, p. 491.

3 William C. DeVane, A Browning Handbook (New York: Appleton, 1955), pp. 98–99.

4 Robert F. Fleissner, "Browning's Last Lost Duchess: A Purview," Victorian Poetry, 5 (1967), 218.

5 Stevenson, p. 492.

6 DeVane, p. 98.

7 DeVane, p. 98.

8 DeVane, p. 99.

9 Robert F. Fleissner, "My Last Duchess," Times Literary Supplement, No. 3536 (4 Dec. 1959), p. 1405.

Although it has continuous pagination, this journal does not employ a volume number; therefore you do the reader a service by providing issue number and exact date.

10 Stevenson, p. 492.

11 Fleissner, "My Last Duchess," p. 1405.

Since two separate articles by Fleissner appear above, you must add a title to this note.

12 "Browning's Shrewd Duke," PMLA, 74 (1959), 157–59.

Use this form when the author's name and even the title have been given in the text.

13 DeVane, p. 98; cf. B. E. Jerman, "Browning's Witless Duke," PMLA, 72 (1957), 488–93.

14 Laurence Perrine, "Browning's Shrewd Duke," p. 158.

15 Fleissner, "My Last Duchess," p. 1405.

Content Notes

As shown in the preceding pages, references notes perform the basic function of documenting the original source. But you may have occasion to write other types of notes, classified as content notes, offering further information that the average reader might need or profit by. Rather than distract the reader with an incidentally related item within the text, you should place it within a note, using the following as a guide:

Definition

1 Briefly, existentialism expounds the theory that man lives in a purposeless universe in which he must exercise freedom of will to combat his environment.

This type of note defines or amplifies a term or phrase you have used in the text.

Explanation and elaboration

2 Jean-Paul Sartre became the chief spokesman for existentialism in France after World War II. (Smith, p. 6.)

This note offers additional information that is not pertinent to textual matters. The entry at the end is necessary if the information is borrowed from an authority.

Evaluation and comparison of authorities

3 Cf. Edmund Wilson, Axel's Castle, p. 114: "As a critic, Eliot occupies today a position of distinction and influence equal in importance to his position as a poet."

The writer is asking the reader to compare textual analysis with Wilson's statement.

Cross reference to another part of the paper

4 The importance of Emerson as a poet, however, is questioned by some authorities. See above, p. 3.

The writer is asking the reader to refer to an earlier portion of the paper for the discussion of Emerson.

Reference to a special source

5 A thorough analysis of anomie as it relates to Durkheim may be found in Stephen R. Marks, "Durkheim's Theory of Anomie," American Journal of Sociology, 80 (Sept. 1974), 329-63.

Abbreviations in Notes

You should employ abbreviations often and consistently in your notes, though in your text you should avoid them (except "Dr.," "Esq.," "Hon.," "Jr.," "Mr.," "Ms.," "Rev.," and "St.,"). In notes you should abbreviate dates (for example, "Jan.," "Feb.") and institutions (for example "Univ.," "Assn."). Finally, you may use or encounter the following common abbreviations and reference words:

A.D. *anno Domini* 'in the year of the Lord'; *precedes* numerals with no space between letters, as in "A.D. 350"

anon. anonymous

art., arts. article(s)

B.C. 'Before Christ'; *follows* numerals with no space between letters, as in "500 B.C."

bk., bks. book(s)

ca. (or c.) *circa* 'about,' used to indicate an approximate date, as in "ca. 1812"

cf. *confer* 'compare' (one source with another); not, however, to be used in place of "see"

ch., chs. (or chap., chaps.) chapter(s)

col., cols. column(s)

comp. compiled (by) or compiler

diss. dissertation

ed., eds. editor(s), edition, or edited (by)

e.g. *exempli gratia* 'for example,' preceded and followed by a comma

enl. enlarged, as in "enl. ed."

esp. especially, as in "pp. 312-15, esp. p. 313"

et al. *et alii* 'and others'; "John Smith et al." means John Smith and other authors

et pas. *et passim* 'and here and there' (see "passim")

et seq. *et sequens* 'and the following'; "pp. 9 et seq." means page nine and the following page; compare "f." and "ff."

f., ff. page or pages following a given page; "pp. 8f." means page eight and the following page; but exact references are preferable, for example, "pp. 45-51, 55, 58" instead of "pp. 45 ff."

ibid. *ibidem* 'in the same place,' i.e., in the immediately preceding title (see p. 124–25)

i.e. *id est* 'that is,' preceded and followed by a comma

illus. illustrated by, illustrations, or illustrator

infra 'below,' refers to a succeeding portion of the text; compare "supra." Generally, it is best to write "see below"

intro. (or introd.) introduction (by)

l., ll. line(s)

loc. cit. *loco citato* 'in the place (passage) cited' (see p. 124–25)

MS, MSS manuscript(s); but followed by a period ("MS.") when referring to a specific manuscript

n., nn. note(s), as "p. 23, n. 2" or "p. 51 n."

n.d. no date (in a book's title or copyright pages)

no., nos. number(s)

n.p. no place (of publication)

op. cit. *opere citato* 'in the work cited' (see pp. 124–25)

p., pp. page(s); use "Pages" instead of "Pp."

passim 'here and there throughout the work,' e.g., "pp. 67, 72, et passim"

pseud. pseudonym

pt., pts. part(s)

rev. revised (by), revision, review, or reviewed (by)

rpt. reprint, reprinted

sec., secs. section(s)

sic 'thus,' placed in brackets to indicate an error has been made in the quoted passage and the writer is quoting accurately

st., sts. stanza(s)

sup. (or supra) 'above,' refers to a preceding portion of the text; it is just as easy to write "above"

s.v. *sub voce (verbo)* 'under the word or heading'

trans. (or tr.) translator, translated (by), or translation

vol., vols. volume(s), as in "Vol. III"

THE BIBLIOGRAPHY

● After writing your paper, you should prepare a selected bibliography, listing the source material actually used in the writing of your manuscript. That is, you should provide publication data for each reference. Some instructors may request that you label the bibliography "List of References Cited" or "Selected Bibliography" because the bibliography will offer the reader a limited indication of the scholarship related to your subject, not a comprehensive or exhaustive list.

If you have carefully developed your working bibliography (pp. 11–15), you will find that preparation of the final one is a relatively simple process. The final bibliography is really not a new assignment at all because your bibliography cards, arranged alphabetically, already provide the necessary information. However, this will be true only if you have kept the bibliography cards up-to-date during note-taking by adding new sources and by disposing of cards that you have found to be irrelevant.

To repeat: you should include in the bibliography all works actually used in your study. And you must, without exception, include a bibliography entry for all first references in the notes. You may also insert other works pertinent to the paper, such as an article that strongly influenced your thinking, although you did not quote or paraphrase it and therefore had no note reference to it.

Bibliography Form

You should arrange the items of the bibliography in alphabetical order by the surname of the author. Place the first line of each entry flush with the left margin and indent succeeding lines approximately five spaces. Double space each entry and also double space between entries. Study carefully the examples given in the following sample "Selected Bibliography":

↓ 2″

A Selected Bibliography

Quadruple-space
←

1″→ The Bible. Revised Standard Version.   ←1″

Bulfinch, Thomas. _Bulfinch's Mythology_. 2 vols. New
      York: Mentor, 1962.

Campbell, Joseph. _The Hero with a Thousand Faces_.
      Cleveland: Meridian Books, 1956.

----------. _The Masks of God_. 4 vols. New York:
      Viking-Compass, 1970.

Henderson, Joseph L., and Maud Oakes. _The Wisdom of
      the Serpent: The Myths of Death, Rebirth, and
      Resurrection_. New York: Collier, 1971.

Homer. _The Iliad_. Trans. Richmond Lattimore.
      Chicago: Univ. of Chicago Press, 1951.

Laird, Charlton. "A Nonhuman Being Can Learn Lan-
      guage." _College Composition and Communication_,
      23 (May 1972), 142-54.

Levi-Strauss, Claude. "The Structural Study of Myth."
      In _Myth: A Symposium_. Ed. A. Sebeok. Bloomington:
      Indiana Univ. Press, 1958.

McFadden, George. " 'Life Studies'--Robert Lowell's
      Comic Breakthrough." _PMLA_, 90 (1975), 96-106.

Robinson, Lillian S. "Criticism--and Self-Criticism."
      College English, 36 (Dec. 1974), 436-45.

Note: Enter anonymous works alphabetically by the first important word of the
title. Imagine lettered spelling for unusual items, such as ''#2 Red Dye & Can-
cer'' (entered as though ''Number 2 Red Dye'') or ''6 Million Die in Earthquake''
(entered as ''Six Million'').

BIBLIOGRAPHY FORM—BOOKS

When entering references to books, you should use the following order, omitting unnecessary items:

1. The author's name, surname first, followed by given name or initials, followed by a period:

> Baxter, John. <u>The Bidders</u>. New York: Lippincott, 1979.

Always give authors' names in the fullest possible form: for example, "Cosbey, Robert C." rather than "Cosbey, R. C." unless, as indicated on the title page of the book, the author's preference is for initials.

However, if an author has two or more works in the bibliography, do not repeat his or her name with each work. Rather, insert a continuous, ten-dash line flush with the left margin, followed by a period:

> Hansberry, Lorraine. <u>A Raisin in the Sun</u>. New York: Random
>
> House, 1959.
>
> —————————. <u>To Be Young, Gifted and Black</u>. Ed. Robert
>
> Nemiroff, Englewood Cliffs, N.J.: Prentice-Hall, 1969.
> An alternative is that of extending the line of dashes the length of the author's name.

Use the following when an author has two or more works in the bibliography, including one written in collaboration with someone else.

> Healey, James. "Little Magazines: 'A Little Madness
>
> Helps.'" <u>Prairie Schooner</u>, 47 (Winter 1973/74), 335–42.
>
> —————————, and Walt Utroske. "Literature as Process, Not
>
> Product." <u>Arizona English Bulletin</u>, 21 (October 1978),
>
> 10–19.

2. A chapter or a part of a book, placed before the title, within quotation marks or underlined, followed by a period (the word "In" may follow this period to specify the anthology or collection in which this piece appears):

> Elder, Lonne. "Ceremonies in Dark Old Men." In <u>New Black</u>
>
> <u>Playwrights: An Anthology</u>. Ed. William Couch, Jr. Baton
>
> Rouge: Louisiana State Univ. Press, 1968.
>
> Aristophanes. <u>The Birds</u>. In <u>Five Comedies of Aristophanes</u>.
>
> Trans. Benjamin B. Rogers. Garden City, N.Y.: Double-
>
> day, 1955.

Usually the listing of chapter or part of a book is made in bibliographies only when the work is separately edited, translated, or written. For example, note the following:

```
Thomas, Lewis.  "The Music of This Sphere."  In his The Lives
     of a Cell. New York:  Viking, 1974.
```
but preferably

```
Thomas, Lewis.  The Lives of a Cell.  New York:  Viking,
     1974.
```

> Since "The Music of This Sphere" is a chapter in this book and is not
> separately published, it need not be mentioned in the bibliography (but the
> note should contain that information).

In some instances the name of the primary author of an article may be omitted:

```
Child, Harold.  "Jane Austen."  In The Cambridge History of
     English Literature.  Ed. A. W. Ward and A. R. Waller.
     London:  Cambridge Univ. Press, 1927, XII, 231-44.
```
but preferably

```
Ward, A. W., and A. R. Waller, eds.  The Cambridge History of
     English Literature.  15 vols.  London:  Cambridge Univ.
     Press, 1927.
```

3.   The title of the work, underlined, followed by a period:

```
Lagercrantz, Olof.  From Hell to Paradise:  Dante and His
     Comedy.  Trans. Alan Blair. New York:  Washington Square
     Press, 1966.
```

> Separate the subtitle from the primary title by a *colon,* even though the title
> page may have no mark of punctuation or the card catalog entry may have
> a semicolon.

4. The name of the editor or translator, preceded by "Ed." or "Trans.":

```
Mirandola, Giovanni Pico della.  On the Imagination.  Trans.
     and notes Harry Caplan.  1930; rpt. Westport, Conn.:
     Greenwood, n.d.
```

However, if the work is a collection or if the editor's or translator's work rather than the text is under discussion, place the editor's or translator's name first, followed by a comma, followed by "ed." or "eds." or "trans." without further punctuation:

Craig, Hardin, and David Bevington, eds. The Complete Works

of Shakespeare. Rev. ed. Glenview, Ill.: Scott,

Foresman, 1973.

Ciardi, John, trans. The Purgatorio. By Dante. New York:

New American Library, 1961.

5. Edition used, whenever it is not the first, in Arabic numerals (for example, "2nd ed."), without further punctuation:

Beyer, Robert, and Donald J. Trawicki. Profitability

Accounting: For Planning and Control. 2nd ed. New York:

Ronald, 1972.

6. The name of the series, without quotation marks and not underlined, followed by a comma, followed by the number of this work in the series in Arabic numerals (for example, "vol. 3," "No. 3," or simple "3"), followed by a period:

Fowler, David. Piers the Plowman. Univ. of Washington

Publications in Lang. and Lit., 16. Seattle: Univ. of

Washington Press, 1961.

7. The number of volumes with this particular title, if more than one, in Arabic numerals (for example, "6 vols."):

Horacek, Leo, and Gerald Lefkoff. Programmed Ear Training.

4 vols. New York: Harcourt, 1970.

8. The place, publisher, and date of publication, followed by a period (for example, "New York: Macmillan, 1967."). If more than one place of publication appears on the title page, the first city mentioned is usually sufficient. Also, if successive dates of copyright are given, the most recent is usually sufficient (unless your study is specifically concerned with an earlier, perhaps definitive, edition):

Steinbeck, John. The Grapes of Wrath. New York: Viking,

1939.

A new printing does not constitute a new edition nor demand usage of its corresponding date. If the text has a 1940 copyright date but a 1975 third printing, use 1940 unless you have other information, such as: "1975 Diamond Printing," "1975 third printing rev.," or "1975 reprint of original 1940 edition" (see immediately below).

Weaver, Raymond. Introduction. The Shorter Novels of Herman

Melville. 1928; rpt. New York: Premier-Fawcett, 1960.

Include the name of the state if necessary for clarity:

>   Forliti, John E. Program Planning for Youth Ministry. Wi-
>
>   nona, Minn.: St. Mary's College Press, 1975.

If the place, publisher, or date of publication is not provided, insert either "n.p." or "n.d.":

>   Bouret, Jean. The Life and Work of Toulouse Lautrec. Trans.
>
>   Daphne Woodward. New York: Abrams, n.d.
>
>   Lowell, James Russell. Democracy. N.p., 1886.

Provide the publisher's name in a slightly shortened form whenever possible, for example: Macmillan; Doubleday; Free Press; Scott, Foresman; Norton; Dell; Little, Brown; William Brown; Wiley; Knopf.

But list university presses in full to distinguish between a publication of the university and that of a university press: Harvard Univ. Press, Louisiana State Univ. Press, Yale Univ. Press, Oxford Univ. Press.

9. The volume number, in capital Roman numerals, preceded and followed by a comma, only if you find it necessary to specify such information (and the occasions are rare because you will normally insert only the total number of volumes, for example, "5 vols."). Remember that your note, not the bibliography, contains the specific location of the material:

>   Child, Harold. "Jane Austen." The Cambridge History of
>
>   English Literature. Ed. A. W. Ward and A. R. Waller.
>
>   London: Cambridge Univ. Press, 1927, XII, 231-44.

10. Page numbers of the entire selection, in Arabic numerals, preceded by a comma and followed by a period. Again, supply this information only upon rare occasions (see item 9 above and item 2, p. 130).

Sample Bibliography Entries—Books

Author

>   Baxter, John. The Bidders. New York: Lippincott, 1979.

Author, *anonymous*

>   The Song of Roland. Trans. Frederick Bliss Luquines. New
>
>   York: Macmillan, 1960.
>
>   You should alphabetize this entry by the "S" of the first important word of
>   the title.

Author, *anonymous but name supplied*

>   [Madison, James.] All Impressments Unlawful and Inadmissible.
>
>   Boston: William Pelham, 1804.

Author, *pseudonymous but name supplied*

Slender, Robert [Freneau, Philip]. <u>Letters on Various and</u>

<u>Important Subjects</u>. Philadelphia: D. Hogan, 1799.

Author, *more than one work by the same author*

Hansberry, Lorraine. <u>A Raisin in the Sun</u>. New York: Random

House, 1959.

——————. <u>To Be Young, Gifted and Black</u>. Ed. Robert

Nemiroff. Englewood Cliffs, N.J.: Prentice-Hall, 1969.

Rather than repeat the author's name in succeeding entries, insert ten
continuous typewriter dashes, or extend a line of dashes the length of the
author's name.

Authors, *two*

Hooper, Henry O., and Peter Gwynne. <u>Physics and the Physical</u>

<u>Perspective</u>. New York: Harper & Row, 1977.

Authors, *three*

Richardson, Charles E., Fred V. Hein, and Dana L. Farnsworth.

<u>Living: Health, Behavior, and Environment</u>. 6th ed.

Glenview, Ill.: Scott, Foresman, 1975.

Authors, *more than three*

Baugh, Albert C., Tucker Brooke, Samuel C. Chew, Kemp Malone,

and George Sherburn. <u>A Literary History of England</u>.

2nd ed. New York: Appleton, 1967.

An alternative to this form is the use of "et al." or "and others," as follows:

Lewis, Laurel J., et al. <u>Linear Systems Analysis</u>. New York:

McGraw-Hill, 1969.

Bibles

The Bible.

The Bible. Revised Standard Version.

The King James Version is assumed unless you specify another version.

Classical works

Homer. <u>The Iliad</u>. Trans. Richmond Lattimore. Chicago:

Univ. of Chicago Press, 1951.

Shorey, Paul, trans. The Republic. By Plato. Cambridge,

　　Mass.: Harvard Univ. Press, 1937.

Use the translator's name first only if his or her work rather than the text is
the focus of your study (see pp. 131–32).

Component part of a book

Thomas, Lewis. "The Music of This Sphere." In his The Lives

　　of a Cell. New York: Viking, 1974.

but preferably

Thomas, Lewis. The Lives of a Cell. New York: Viking,

　　1974.

Citation to a specific piece in a collection or a longer work is seldom necessary in bibliography entries. Remember that your note will offer specific
information.

Scott, Nathan, Jr. "Society and Self in Recent American

　　Literature." In his The Broken Center. New Haven:

　　Univ. Press, 1966. Rpt. in Dark Symphony: Negro

　　Literature in America. Ed. James A. Emanuel and

　　Theodore L. Gross. New York: Free Press, 1968.

but preferably

Emanuel, James A., and Theodore L. Gross, eds. Dark Sym-

　　phony: Negro Literature in America. New York: Free

　　Press, 1968.

Corporate authorship

Committee on Telecommunications. Reports on Selected Topics

　　in Telecommunications. New York: National Academy of

　　Sciences, National Research Council, 1970.

Double reference

Symington, Stuart. As quoted in Victor Marchetti and John D.

　　Marks. The CIA and the Cult of Intelligence. New York:

　　Knopf, 1974.

but preferably

Marchetti, Victor, and John D. Marks. The CIA and the Cult

　　of Intelligence. New York: Knopf, 1974.

As with the "Component part of a book" (above), you may offer specific
information, but the main purpose of a bibliography is the listing of books
used, not parts of books.

Edition

Keith, Harold. Sports and Games. 6th ed. Scranton, Penn.:
Crowell, 1976.

Nordloh, David J. et al. A Hazard of New Fortunes. Vol. XVI
of A Selected Edition of W. D. Howells. Gen ed. Don L.
Cook. Bloomington: Indiana Univ. Press, 1976.

Editor

Craig, Hardin, and David Bevington, eds. The Complete Works
of Shakespeare. Rev. ed. Glenview, Ill.: Scott,
Foresman, 1973.

If the work is a collection or if the editor's work rather than the text is under
discussion, place the editor's name first. Otherwise, place the editor's
name after the title, as follows:

Brackenridge, Hugh Henry. Modern Chivalry. Ed. Claude M.
Newlin. New York: American Book, 1962.

Encyclopedia

The World Book Encyclopedia. 1976 ed.

If you feel a necessity for specific information, which you should have
located within a note, employ the following form.

Dickinson, Robert E. "Norman Conquest." The World Book
Encyclopedia. 1976 ed.

N[aess], A[rne] D. "Martin Heidegger." Encyclopedia Britannica: Macropaedia. 1974 ed.

Illustrations

Venturi, Lionello. Botticelli. With 50 Plates. Greenwich,
Conn.: Fawcett, n.d.

Honoré Daumier: Drawings and Watercolors. Selected and with
introduction by Jean Adhemar. With 58 Illustrations.
New York: Macmillan, 1954.

Introduction

Webb, Walter Prescott. The Great Frontier. Introd. Arnold J. Toynbee. Austin, Texas: Univ. of Texas
Press, 1964.

Lowell, Robert. Foreword. <u>Ariel</u>. By Sylvia Plath. New

York: Harper & Row, 1966.

Use the above form only if your subject is Lowell's work, not the poetry of
Plath.

Manuscript collections

British Museum. <u>Cotton Vitellius</u>. A. XV.

Corpus Christi College, Cambridge. MS CCCC 201.

Play, *classical*

Parrott, T. M., ed. <u>Shakespeare: Twenty-Three Plays and the</u>

<u>Sonnets</u>. New York: Scribner's, 1953.

but also

Shakespeare, William. <u>Macbeth</u>. In <u>Shakespeare: Twenty-</u>

<u>Three Plays and the Sonnets</u>. Ed. T. M. Parrott.

New York: Scribner's, 1953.

See item 2, pp. 130–31, and item 4, pp. 131–32.

Play, *modern*

Greene, Graham. <u>The Complaisant Lover</u>. New York: Viking,

1959.

Poem, *classical*

Dante, <u>The Divine Comedy</u>. Trans. Lawrence Grant White. New

York: Pantheon, 1948.

Ciardi, John, trans. <u>The Purgatorio.</u> By Dante. New York:

New American Library, 1961.

Use the translator's or editor's name first only if his or her work rather than
the primary text is under discussion (see pp. 131–32).

Poem, *modern*

Warren, Robert Penn. <u>You, Emperors, and Others: Poems 1957–</u>

<u>1960</u>. New York: Random House, 1960.

Keats, John. "Ode to a Nightingale." In <u>Beginnings in Po-</u>

<u>etry</u>. Ed. William J. Martz. 2nd ed. Glenview, Ill.:

Scott, Foresman, 1973.

but preferably

Martz, William J., ed. <u>Beginnings in Poetry</u>. 2nd ed.

Glenview, Ill.: Scott, Foresman, 1973.

Reprint

> Lowes, John Livingston. The Road to Xanadu: A Study in the
> Ways of the Imagination. 2nd ed. 1930; rpt. New York:
> Vintage–Knopf, 1959.
>
> Fay, Bernard. Two Franklins, Fathers of American Democracy.
> 1933; rpt. New York: Scholarly, 1971.

Series, *numbered and unnumbered*

> Fowler, David. Piers the Plowman. Univ. of Washington
> Publications in Lang. and Lit., 16. Seattle: Univ.
> of Washington Press, 1961.
>
> Gibson, Lawrence Henry. The Coming of the Revolution:
> 1762–1775. Ed. Henry Steele Commager and Richard B.
> Morris. The New American Nation Series. New York:
> Harper & Row, 1954.

Series, *paperback*

> Commager, Henry Steele. The Nature and the Study of His-
> tory. Social Science Seminar Series. Columbus, Ohio:
> Merrill, 1965.
>
> Wilson, Howard E. "Education, Foreign Policy, and
> International Relations." In Cultural Affairs and
> Foreign Relations. Ed. Robert Blum. The American
> Assembly Series. Englewood Cliffs, N.J.: Prentice–
> Hall, 1963.
>
> but preferably
>
> Blum, Robert, ed. Cultural Affairs and Foreign Relations.
> The American Assembly Series. Englewood Cliffs, N.J.:
> Prentice–Hall, 1963.

Source books

> Unterecker, John, ed. Yeats: A Collection of Critical Es-
> says. Twentieth Century Views. Englewood Cliffs, N.J.:
> Prentice–Hall, 1963.
>
> Walker, Warren S., ed. Leatherstocking and the Critics.
> Glenview, Ill.: Scott, Foresman, 1965.

but also

Wasserstrom, William. "Cooper, Freud, and the Origins of
Culture." The American Image, 17 (Winter 1960), 423–37.
Rpt. in Leatherstocking and the Critics. Ed. Warren S.
Walker. Glenview, Ill.: Scott, Foresman, 1965.
Use this last form if the note does not include specific details of both
sources.

Translator

Lagercrantz, Olof. From Hell to Paradise: Dante and His
Comedy. Trans. Alan Blair. New York: Washington
Square Press, 1966.

Homer. Iliad. Trans. Robert Fitzgerald. Garden City,
N.Y.: Anchor, 1974.

Ciardi, John, trans. The Purgatorio. By Dante. New York:
New American Library, 1961.
If the translator's work rather than the text is under discussion, place the
translator's name first (see item 4, pp. 131–32).

Volumes, *a work of several volumes*

Parrington, Vernon L. Main Currents in American Thought. 3
vols. New York: Harcourt, Brace, 1927–32.

Volumes, *one of several volumes*

Daiches, David. A Critical History of English Literature.
2nd ed. New York: Ronald, 1970. Vol.I.
but

Wellek, Rene. A History of Modern Criticism, 1750–1950.
Vol. III. New Haven: Yale Univ. Press, 1965.
When volumes are published in different years, the volume number(s)
should precede the publication materials.

Perry, Bliss. The American Spirit in Literature. The
Chronicles of America Series. Ed. Allen Johnson. 48
vols. New Haven: Yale Univ. Press, 1918.
It is seldom necessary to include a specific volume number in the bibliography entry (see below).

Volumes, *component part of one of several volumes*

Child, Harold. "Jane Austen." In The Cambridge History of
English Literature. Ed. A. W. Ward and A. R. Waller.
London: Cambridge Univ. Press, 1927. XII, 231–44.

but also

> Ward, A. W., and A. R. Waller, eds. The Cambridge History
> of English Literature. 15 vols. London: Cambridge Univ.
> Press, 1927.
> For a discussion of these entries, see p. 133.

Works alphabetically arranged

> DAB (1928). Dumas Malone. 20 vols.
>
> but also
>
> A[lden], E[dmund] K. "Alden, John." DAB (1928).
> For a discussion of these entries, see p. 113 and item 2, 130–31.

BIBLIOGRAPHY FORM—PERIODICALS

As you recall, the note entry for a periodical article employs the following form:

> ¹ B. J. Shade, "Social-Psychological Traits of Achieving
> Black Children," Education Digest, 44 (Oct. 1978), 38.

The bibliography entry for this same reference differs in only three ways:

1. The author's name is flush with the left margin, without a numeral, and with succeeding lines indented approximately five spaces. Enter the surname first, followed by a comma, followed by a given name or initials, followed by a period:

> Shade, B. J. "Social-Psychological Traits of Achieving Black
> Children." Education Digest, 44 (Oct. 1978), 38–40.

2. Place a period after the title of the article (see example above).
3. Provide page numbers for the entire article, not for specific pages cited (see example above). If the article is paged here and there throughout the issue (for example, pages 46, 48, 50, and 81), the following are possible methods of page citation:

pp. 46 et passim.   which means page 46 and several pages here and there throughout the work

pp. 46, 48, 50, 81.   which designates each page; use this method if only three or four pages are involved

In other circumstances the following forms might be appropriate:

pp. 46ff.   which means page 46 and several
                                   immediately following pages

pp. 46 et seq.   which means page 46 and the fol-
                                   lowing page

pp. 46f.   which means page 46 and the fol-
                                   lowing page (same as ''pp. 46 et
                                   seq.'')

Sample Bibliography Entries—Periodicals

Address

U.S. President. "Address to Veterans of Foreign Wars." 19
Aug. 1974. Rpt. in Weekly Compilation of Presidential
Documents, 10 (26 Aug. 1974), 1045–50.

Author, anonymous

"Commodities: Sweet and Sour." Time, 16 Dec. 1974, p. 32.

Authors, multiple

Libby, Roger W., Alan C. Acock, and David C. Payne.
"Configurations of Parental Preferences Concerning
Sources of Sex Education of Adolescents." Adolescence,
9 (Spring 1974), 73–80.

Bulletin

"Financial Operations of Government Agencies and Funds."
Treasury Bulletin. Washington, D.C.: Dept. of
Treasury, June 1974, pp. 134–41.

"Spotlight on Crime." World of Politics Monthly, Nov.
1974, pp. 10–11.
For examples of bulletins published separately, see p. 145.

Critical review

Clignet, Remi. Rev. of Urban Poverty in a Cross–cultural
Context, by Edwin Eames and Judith Granich Goode (New
York: Free Press, 1973). American Journal of Sociol-
ogy, 80 (Sept. 1974), 589–90.

Kolodin, Irving. "Verdi for Openers." Rev. of <u>Simone</u>
  <u>Boccanegra</u>. <u>Saturday Review World</u>, 2 Nov. 1974,
  pp. 54–55.

Rev. of <u>Sexual Suicide</u>, by George F. Gilder (New York:
  Quadrangle, 1973). <u>Adolescence</u>, 9 (Spring 1974), 151.

Gardner, John. Rev. of <u>Falconer</u>, by John Cheever. <u>Saturday</u>
  <u>Review</u>, 2 April 1977, p. 20.

Interview

"For an 'Uncultured' America, World Leadership in Arts."
  Interview with Nancy Hanks, Chairman, National Endowment
  of the Arts. <u>U.S. News and World Report</u>, 7 Oct. 1974,
  pp. 58–60.

Journal, *with continuous pagination*

Dyke, Vernon Van. "Human Rights and the Rights of Groups."
  <u>American Journal of Political Science</u>, 18 (1974), 725–
  41.

Kilchenmann, Ruth. "Traum und Wirklichkeit in den Werken
  Friedrich Schnacks." <u>German Quarterly</u>, 34 (May 1961),
  257–63.
  The month may be added for clarity but is not necessary.

Journal, *with separate pagination*

Mangan, Doreen. "Henry Casselli: Superb Contradictions."
  <u>American Artist</u>, 38 (Dec. 1974), 39–43.
  Because each issue of the journal is paged separately, you should include
  the month, season, or issue number. Page numbers alone will not locate
  the article within a volume of twelve issues with each issue having separate
  pagination.

McDavid, Raven I. "Sense and Nonsense About American
  Dialects." <u>PMLA</u>, 81, No. 2 (1966), 9–11.
  PMLA normally pages continuously, but this issue is paged separately,
  necessitating the issue number.

Stuart, Jesse. "Love Affair at the Pasture Gate." <u>Ball</u>
  <u>State University Forum</u>, 15 (Winter 1974), 3–6.

Journal, *volume number embracing two years*

Ranta, Jerrald. "Palindromes, Poems, and Geometric Form."
  <u>College English</u>, 36 (Oct. 1974), 161–72.

Magazine, *monthly*

Morris, Philip. "Back to the Waterfront." Southern Living, April 1979, pp. 98–100.

Poinsett, Alex. "The 'Whys' Behind the Black Lawyer Shortage." Ebony, Dec. 1974, pp. 74 et passim.

Sontag, Susan. "Baby." Playboy, Feb. 1974, pp. 74 et passim.

> Note that monthly magazine citations often require the "et passim" designation for page numbers, which means page 74 and several following pages here and there throughout the issue.

Magazine, *weekly*

"Chaos in Television." Time, 12 March 1979, pp. 60–61.

DeMott, Benjamin. "Saul Bellow and the Dogmas of Possibility." Saturday Review, 7 Feb. 1970, pp. 25–29, 37.

Quotation, *within the article's title*

Morgan, William W. "Form, Tradition, and Consolation in Hardy's 'Poems of 1911–13.' " PMLA, 89 (1974), 496–505.

Skulsky, Harold. " 'I Know My Course': Hamlet's Confidence." PMLA, 89 (1974), 477–86.

BIBLIOGRAPHY FORM—PUBLIC DOCUMENTS

Since the nature of public documents is so varied, the form of the entry cannot be standardized. Therefore, you should provide sufficient information so that the reader can easily locate the reference. As a general rule, place information in the bibliography entry in this order: Government. Body. Subsidiary body. Title of document. Identifying numbers.

Congressional papers

Cong. Rec. 6 March 1974, pp. S2916–28.

U.S. Cong. Senate. Transportation System for Alaskan Natural Gas. 95th Cong., 1st sess. S. 2411. Washington, D.C.: GPO, 1977.

U.S. Cong. House. Committee on Interstate and Foreign Commerce. Federal Cigarette Labeling and Advertising Act. 89th Cong., 1st sess. H. Rept. 449 to accompany H.R. 3014. Washington, D.C.: GPO, 1965.

U.S. Cong. Senate. <u>The Constitution of the United States of</u>
<u>America: Analysis and Interpretation</u>. 82nd Cong., 2nd
sess. S. Doc. 170. Washington, D.C.: GPO, 1952.

Executive branch documents

U.S. President. <u>Public Papers of the Presidents of the</u>
<u>United States</u>. Washington, D.C.: Office of the
Federal Registrar, 1978.

U.S. President. <u>Alternative to Drugs: A New Approach to</u>
<u>Drug Education</u>. Pr Ex 13.2:D84/3/1972. Washington,
D.C.: GPO, 1972.

U.S. Dept. of State. <u>Foreign Relations of the United</u>
<u>States: Diplomatic Papers, 1943</u>. 5 vols. Washington,
D.C.: GPO, 1943–44.

Legal citations

U.S. Const. Art. II, sec. 1.

California, Const. Art. II, sec. 4.

15 U.S. Code. Sec. 78h (1964).

Noise Control Act of 1972. Statutes at Large. LXXXVI.
Public Law 92–574 (1972).

Gold Coin and Gold Bullion Act. 31 U.S. Code. Supp. III,
sec. 442 (1970).

Environmental Protection Agency et al. v. Mink et al. U.S.
Reports, CDX (1972).

BIBLIOGRAPHY FORM—OTHER SOURCES

Art Work

Raphael. <u>School of Athens</u>. The Vatican, Rome. Illus. in
<u>The World Book Encyclopedia</u>. 1976 ed.
Use this form for art works reproduced in other books or journals. If you
actually experience the work itself, use the following form.

Remington, Frederic. <u>Mountain Man</u>. Metropolitan Museum of
Art, New York.

Bulletin

Economic Research Service. Demand and Price Situation. Washington, D.C.: Dept. of Agriculture, Aug. 1974, DPS–141, 14 pp.

French, Earl. Personal Problems in Industrial Research and Development. Ithaca, N.Y., 1963. (Bulletin of the New York State School of Industrial and Labor Relations, No. 51.)

For examples of bulletins published within periodicals, see p. 141.

Dissertation, *published*

Nykrog, Per. Les Fabliaux: Etude d'histoire littéraire et de stylistique mediévale. Diss. Aarhus 1957. Copen–hagen: Munksgaard, 1957.

Dissertation, *unpublished*

Phillips, Emmett Loy. "A Study of Aesthetic Distance in Thoreau's Walden." Diss. Univ. of Oklahoma 1970.

Film

Last Tango in Paris. United Artists, 1972.

Wilets, Bernard. Environment. Santa Monica, Calif.: BFA Educational Media, 1971. (16 mm., 29 min., color.)

Interview

Personal interview with Robert Turrentine, President, Acme Boot Co. Clarksville, Tenn., 11 Feb. 1979.

Letter, *personal*

Weathers, Winston. Letter to author. 5 March 1979.

Manuscripts (MS) and typescripts (TS)

Glass, Malcolm. Journal 3, MS. M. Glass Private Papers. Clarksville, Tenn.

Glass, Malcolm. The Hardlanders, TS. M. Glass Private Papers. Clarksville, Tenn.

Microfilm or microfiche

Tuckerman, H. T. "James Fenimore Cooper." North American Review, 89 (1859), 298–316. (Microfilm.)

Indicate at the end of your entry that your source is on microfilm or micro-fiche.

Mimeographed material

Smith, Jane L. "Terms for the Study of Fiction." Cleveland,

1975. (Mimeographed.)

Monograph

NEA Research Division. Kindergarten Practices, 1961.

Washington, D.C., 1962. (Monograph 1962-M2.)

Veeder, William R. W. B. Yeats: The Rhetoric of Repetition.

Univ. of California English Studies, 34. Berkeley:

Univ. of California Press, 1968.

Musical composition

Mozart, Wolfgang A. Jupiter. Symphony No. 41.

Newspaper

Bryant, Alice Franklin. "U.N. Role." Letter to the Editor.

Chattanooga Times, 15 Dec. 1974, p. B7,cols. 6-7.

Use this form for special newspaper articles, such as editorials, letters to
the editor, cartoons, and so on.

"Egypt Demands That Israel Put Limit on Population Growth."

Los Angeles Times, 14 Dec. 1974, p. 1.

When an item is unsigned, the title comes first and all subsequent information remains the same.

Sperling, Godfrey, Jr. "Ford's Plan to Spur Republican

Revival." Christian Science Monitor, 29 Nov. 1974,

p. 20.

The basic form for signed newspaper articles.

"How to Measure Justice." Editorial. The Tennessean

[Nashville], 18 Aug. 1979, p. 8.

Pamphlet

U.S. Civil Service Commission. The Human Equation: Working

in Personnel for the Federal Government. Pamphlet 76.

Washington, D.C.: GPO, May 1970.

Public address or lecture

Sarnoff, David. "Television: A Channel for Freedom." De-

troit, 1961. Address presented at the University of

Detroit Academic Convocation.

Recording on record or tape

"Chaucer: The Nun's Priest's Tale." In his <u>Canterbury</u>
<u>Tales</u>. Narrated in Middle English by Robert Ross.
Caedmon recording, TC 1008, 1971.

John, Elton. "This Song Has No Title." In his <u>Goodbye Yel-</u>
<u>low Brick Road</u>. MCA Records, MCA 2-10003, 1974.

Statler Brothers. Jacket Notes. <u>The Originals</u>. Mercury,
SRM-1-5016, 1979.

Report

Linden, Fabian. "Women: A Demographic, Social and Economic
Presentation." Report by The Conference Board. New
York: CBS/Broadcast Group, 1973.

Panama Canal Company. <u>Annual Report: Fiscal Year Ended June</u>
<u>30, 1968</u>. Panama: Canal Zone Government, 1968.
Reports in the form of books or pamphlets require underlining.

<u>Womanpower</u>. Brookline, Mass.: Betsy Hogan Associates, 1974.

Reproductions and photographs

Blake's <u>Comus</u>, Plate 4. Photograph reproduced in Irene
Tayler. "Blake's <u>Comus</u> Designs." <u>Blake Studies</u>, 4
(Spring 1972), 61.

Michener, James A. "Structure of Earth at Centennial,
Colorado." Line drawing in <u>Centennial</u>. New York:
Random House, 1974.

Table or illustration

Corbett, Edward P. J. Syllogism graph. <u>Classical Rhetoric</u>
<u>for the Modern Student</u>. New York: Oxford Univ. Press,
1965.
Because the graph has no title, the descriptive heading should not be
placed within quotation marks.

Helmich, Donald L. "Organizational Growth and Succession
Patterns." <u>Academy of Management Journal</u>. 17 (Dec.
1974), 773, Table 2.

Television or radio program

> The Commanders: Douglas MacArthur. New York: NBC–TV, 17
>
> > March 1975.

> Sevareid, Eric. CBS News. New York: CBS–TV, 11 March 1975.
> > There is a tendency in documentation to omit periods in abbreviations of
> > well-known societies and associations.

> Shakespeare, William. As You Like It. Nashville: Nashville
>
> > Theatre Academy, WDCN–TV, 11 March 1975.

Thesis

> See "Dissertation, unpublished," p. 145.

Transparency

> Sharp, La Vaughn and William E. Loeche. The Patient and
>
> > Circulatory Disorders: A Guide for Instructors. 54
> >
> > Transparencies, 99 overlays. Philadelphia: Lippincott,
> >
> > 1969.

Unpublished paper

> Elkins, William R. "The Dream World and the Dream Vision:
>
> > Meaning and Structure in Poe's Art." (Unpublished
> >
> > paper.)

DOCUMENTATION OF SCIENCE PAPERS

You may discover that your science instructor requires a system of documentation quite different from that described in the preceding two chapters. Accordingly, when you write a research paper in the fields of biological science, physical science, mathematics, or psychology, you should consult this chapter, which is intended to supply a brief but adequate description of science-paper documentation. However, you should keep in mind at the start that modifications of style exist from field to field, and agreement does not always exist within a given field. Nevertheless, after consultation with your instructor, you should find one of the two systems outlined below satisfactory for your needs.

As a general rule, science papers, excluding those dealing with physics (see p. 155), require no notes except content footnotes (see p. 126). Instead you insert within your text reference numbers (1) or reference dates (1975). Then at the end of your paper you list, numerically or alphabetically, only those references actually mentioned in your text. You may label the list as "List of References" or "Literature Cited." The title "Bibliography" seldom appears in science papers.

In addition, you should be aware of other characteristics of the scientific reference entries. First, you will usually capitalize only the first word of titles of books and articles (for example, "The biology of the algae"). But some fields (for example, chemistry and physics) omit completely the title of a periodical article. Second, you will usually abbreviate and seldom underline the name of the periodical (for example, "Amer. J. Bot."; see pp. 168–73, 175–76 for listings of science journals and their standard abbreviations). But you should note that the field of psychology, since 1963, spells in full the names of periodicals. Third, you will usually write the volume numbers in Arabic numerals, although placement and form will vary (for example, "vol. 70 or "70").

Name and Year System

When employing the name and year system, you should place within your text, in parentheses or brackets, the year of publication of the authority's book or journal article. Furthermore, note the following:

1. Place the entry immediately after the authority's name:

> ```
> Smith (1977) ascribes no species-specific
> behavior to man.  However, Adams (1979) pre-
> sents data that tend to be contradictory.
> ```

2. If your sentence construction does not require the use of the authority's name, insert both the name and date in parentheses:

> ```
> Hopkins (1979) found some supporting evidence
> for a portion of the Marr data (Marr and
> Brown, 1979) through point bi-serial cor-
> relation techniques.
> ```

3. For two authors, employ both names: "(Torgerson and Andrews, 1979)." For three authors, name them all in the first entry, as "(Torgerson, Andrews, and Dunlap, 1979)," but thereafter use "(Torgerson et al., 1979)." For four or more authors, employ "(Fredericks et al., 1979)" in the first and all subsequent instances.

4. Use small letters (a, b, c) to identify two or more works published in the same year by the same author, for example, "Thompson (1966a)" and "Thompson (1966b)."

5. If necessary, specify additional information; for example, "Thompson (1967, III)," "(Wallace, 1948, 1967)," and "White and Thurston (1979, 211-14)":

> ```
> Horton (1966; cf. Thomas, 1962, p. 89) sug-
> gests an intercorrelation of these testing
> devices.  But after multiple-group analysis,
> Welston (1979, p. 211) reached an opposite
> conclusion.
> ```

6. Alphabetize the "List of References" at the end of your paper. List chronologically two or more works by the same author (for example, Fitzgerald's 1977 publication would precede his 1979 publication). Main parts for a periodical reference entry are: name(s) of author(s); year of publication; title of the article; name of the journal; volume number; and inclusive page numbers. Main parts for a book reference entry are: name(s) of author(s); year of publication; title of the book; name and city of publisher; number of pages in the book.

A sample "List of References"[1] follows:

```
              List of References


Klein, R. M., and D. T. Klein.  1970.
   Research methods in plant science. Natural
   History Press, Garden City, New York.  796
   p.

Muller, W. H.  1974.  Botany:  A functional
   discharge.  Macmillan, Riverside, N.J.
   601 p.

Olive, L. S.  1962.  The genus Protostelium.
   Amer. J. Bot. 49:  297-303.

------.  1964a.  Spore discharge mechanism in
   basidiomycetes.  Science 146:  542-543.

------.  1964b. A new member of the Mycetozoa.
   Mycologia 61:  885-896.

Thomson, W. W., and R. DeTournett.  1970.
   Studies on the ultrastructure of the
   guard cells of Opuntia.  Amer. J. Bot.
   57:  309-316.
```

**Fig. 34: Sample
List of References**

The Number System

After completing your "List of References," you should assign a number to each entry. Then, to designate your source of information, you should employ the appropriate number within your text. Furthermore, note the following:

1. Place the entry, enclosed within parentheses (or brackets), immediately after the authority's name:

---

[1]The form of these botany entries conforms to the *CBE Style Manual,* 3rd ed. (Washington, D.C.: American Institute of Biological Sciences, 1972).

> In particular the recent paper by Hershel,
> Hobbs, and Thomason (1) raises many interesting
> questions related to photosynthesis, some of
> which were answered by Skelton (2), (3).

2. If the sentence construction does not require the use of the authority's name, employ one of the following three methods:

● Insert both name and number within parentheses:

> Additional observations include alterations in
> carbohydrate metabolism (Evans, 3), changes in
> ascorbic acid incorporation into the cell (Dodd
> and Williams, 11) and adjoining membranes (Holt
> and Zimmer, 7).

● Insert both name and number within parentheses and enclose the number within brackets (few journals, however, use this method):

> The subject of the cytochrome oxidase system
> in cell metabolism has received a great deal
> of attention (Singleton [4]).

● Insert the number only, enclosing it within parentheses (or brackets):

> It is known (1) that the DNA concentration of
> a nucleus doubles during interphase.

3. If necessary, add specific data to the entry (for example, "[3, Proposition 8]" or "[6, p. 76]"):

```
The results of the respiration experiment
published by Jones (3, p. 412) had been
predicted earlier by Smith (5).
```

Arrange your references in alphabetical order and number them consecutively (in which case, of course, the numbers will not appear in consecutive order in your text), *or* forego an alphabetical arrangement and number the references consecutively as they appear in the text, interrupting that order in your text when entering an earlier reference. An entry for the number system is usually similar to that for the name-and-year system (see p. 149) except that it is preceded by a numeral on the line and a period.

A numbered, alphabetized list follows:[2]

Literature Cited

1. Baldwin, K. M. 1979. Cardiac gap junction configuration after an uncoupling treatment as a function of time. J. Cell. Biol. 82: 66–75.

2. Hodson, P. H., and J. W. Foster. 1966. Dipicolinic acid synthesis in Penicillium citreoviride. J. Bacteriol. 91: 562–569.

3. Kaminskas, Edvardas, and B. Magasanik. 1970. Sequential synthesis of histidine-degrading enzymes in Bacillus sybtilis. J. Biol. Chem. 245: 3549–3555.

4. McClintic, J. Robert. 1975. Basic anatomy and physiology of the human body. John Wiley and Sons, New York. 528 p.

5. Meister, A. 1965. Biochemistry of the amino acids, 2nd ed., vol. 2. Academic Press, Inc., New York.

6. Smith, I. [ed.] 1976. Chromatographic and electrophoretic techniques, 4th ed., vol. 1. Chromatography. Year Book Medical Publishers, Chicago.

Fig. 35: Literature Cited

[2]The form of these biology entries conforms to the *CBE Style Manual*, 3rd ed. (Washington, D.C.: American Institute of Biological Sciences, 1972). See also "List of References" p. 151.

SAMPLE FORMS OF ENTRIES FOR THE VARIOUS SCIENCE DISCIPLINES

Biology

See "Literature Cited," p. 153.

Botany

See "List of References," p. 151.

Chemistry[3]

(1) L. W. Fine, "Chemistry Decoded," Oxford Univ. Press, Oxford, England, 1976, pp. 23–41

(2) J. D. Corbett in "Fused Salts," B. R. Sundheim, Ed., McGraw-Hill Book Co., Inc., New York, 1964, p. 341.

(3) W. H. Baddley, Ph.D. Dissertation, Northwestern University, Evanston, Ill., 1964.

(4) P. J. Lewi and W. W. Braet, J. Chem. Doc., 10, 95-97 (1970).

(5) G. C. Berry and T. G. Fox, J. Am. Chem. Soc., 86, 3540 (1964).

(6) J. R. Morton, Chem. Rev., 64, 452 (1964).

Geology[4]

Donath, F. A., 1963, Strength variation and deformational behavior in anisotropic rock, p. 281–297 in Judd, Wm. R., Editor, State of stress in the earth's crust: New York, American Elsevier Publishing Co., Inc., 732 p.

Friedlander, G., Kennedy, J. W., and Miller, J. M., 1964, Nuclear and radiochemistry: New York, John Wiley and Sons, 585 p.

Heard, H. C., Turner, F. J., and Weiss, L. E., 1965, Studies of heterogeneous strain in experimentally deformed calcite, marble, and phyllite: Univ. Calif. Pub. Geol. Sci., v. 46, p. 81–152.

Hill, M. L., and Troxel, B. W., 1966, Tectonics of Death Valley region, California: Geol. Soc. America Bull., v. 77, p. 435–438.

Mattson, Peter H., 1979, Subduction, buoyant braking, flipping, and strike–slip faulting in the northern Caribbean: J. of Geology, v. 87, p. 293–304.

Thorpe, R. S., 1974, Aspects of magmatism and plate tectonics in the precambrian of England and Wales: Geol. J., v. 9, p. 115–136.

[3]The form of these chemistry entries conforms to the *Handbook for Authors* (Washington, D.C.: American Chemical Society, 1978).

[4]The form of these geology entries conforms to *Suggestions to Authors of the Reports of the United States Geological Survey*, 6th ed. (Washington, D.C.: Dept of the Interior, 1978).

Mathematics[5]

1. R. Artzy, Linear geometry, Addison—Wesley, Reading, Mass., 1965.

2. H. Helpern, Quasi—Equivalence classes of normal representations for a separable C*—algebra, Trans. Am. Math. Soc. 203 (1975), 129—140.

3. I. M. Isaacs and D. S. Passman, Groups with representations of bounded degree, Canad. J. Math. 16 (1964), 299—309.

4. ------, Characterization of groups in terms of the degrees of their characters, Pacific J. Math. 15 (1965), 877—903.

5. A. Scarselli, On a class of inseparable finite groups, J. Algebra 58 (1979), 94—99.

6. O. Solbrig, Evolution and systematics, The Macmillan Co., New York, 1966.

Physics[6]

[1]F. Riesz and Bela Nagy, Functional Analysis (Frederick Ungar Publishing Company, New York, 1955), Secs. 121 and 123.

[2]S. Bergia and L. Brown, in Proceedings of the International Conference on Nucleon Structure, edited by R. Hofstadter and L. I. Schiff (Stanford University Press, Stanford, California, 1963), p. 320.

[3]Oswald H. Blackwood, William C. Kelly, Raymond M. Bell, General Physics (John Wiley and Sons, Inc., New York, 1963), p. 510.

[4]S. Hess, Phys. Rev. A 11, 1086 (1975).

[5]K. Gottfried and J. D. Jackson, Nuova Cimento 22, 309 (1964).

[6]L. Monchick, S. Chem. Phys. 71, 576 (1979).

Psychology[7]

Anderson, J. R., and Bower, G. H. Recognition and retrieval processes in free recall. Psychological Review, 1972, 79, 97—123.

Gaito, John (Ed.). Macromolecules and behavior. New York: Appleton—Century—Crofts, 1966.

Hall, Calvin S. A primer of Freudian psychology. Phoenix: NAL, 1973.

---

[5]The form of these math entries conforms to *A Manual for Authors of Mathematical Papers*, 4th ed. (Providence: American Mathematical Society, 1971).

[6]The form of these entries conforms to *Style Manual for Guidance in the Preparation of Journals Published by the American Institute of Physics*, rev. ed. (New York: American Institute of Physics, 1970).

[7]The form of these psychology entries conforms generally to *Publication Manual of the American Psychological Association*, 2nd ed. (Washington D.C.: American Psychological Association, 1974).

Herman, Louis M. Information encoding and decision time as variables in human choice behavior. <u>Journal of Experimental Psychology</u>, 1966, <u>71</u> (5), 718–724.

Keniston, Kenneth. <u>The uncommitted: Alienated youth in American society</u>. New York: Harcourt Brace Jovanovich, Inc., 1966.

Winett, Richard A. Attribution of attitude and behavior change and its relevance to behavior therapy. <u>The Psychological Record</u>, 1970, <u>20</u>, 17–32.

Zoology

See forms on biology, p. 153, and for botany, p. 151.

APPENDIX I
A Glossary of Additional
Research Terms

Acknowledgments Place necessary acknowledgments or explanations in a note to your first sentence:

> ¹ I wish here to express my thanks to Mrs. Horace
>
> A. Humphrey for permission to examine the manuscripts of
>
> her late husband.

Usually there is no need for a preface in a research paper.

Ampersand Avoid using the ampersand symbol "&." Instead, spell out the "and" in the name of a company or organization, unless custom demands it, as in, "A & P."

Annotated Bibliography Write descriptive notes for each entry.

Appendix Place additional material in an appendix at the end of your paper. It is a logical location for numerous tables and illustrations or other accumulated data.

Apostrophe Add an apostrophe and *s* to form the possessive of one-syllable proper names that end in *s* or another sibilant (for example, "Keats's poem," "Rice's story," "Bates's *The Kinds of Man*"). In words of more than one syllable ending in a sibilant, add the apostrophe only (for example, "Rawlings' novel," "Evans' essay," "Daiches' criticism"), except for names ending in a sibilant and a final *e* (for example, "Lovelace's enduring appeal").

Asterisks Use Arabic numerals for note numbers and asterisks only for notes to illustrations or tables (see Fig. 41, p. 164).

Bible Use parenthetical documentation for biblical references in your text—that is, place the entry within parentheses immediately after the quotation, for example, "(II Kings xviii.13)." Do not underline titles of books of the Bible. Abbreviations of most books of the Bible follow (but do not abbreviate one-syllable titles, for example, "Mark" or "Acts"):

I and II Chron.	I and II Chronicles	Lev.	Leviticus
Col.	Colossians	Mal.	Malachi
I and II Cor.	I and II Corinthians	Matt.	Matthew
Dan.	Daniel	Mic.	Micah
Deut.	Deuteronomy	Nah.	Nahum
Eccles.	Ecclesiastes	Neh.	Nehemiah
Eph.	Ephesians	Num.	Numbers
Exod.	Exodus	Obad.	Obadiah
Ezek.	Ezekiel	I and II Pet.	I and II Peter
Gal.	Galatians	Phil.	Philippians
Gen.	Genesis	Prov.	Proverbs
Hab.	Habakkuk	Ps. (Pss.)	Psalm (s)
Hag.	Haggai	Rev.	Revelation
Heb.	Hebrews	Rom.	Romans
Hos.	Hosea	I and II Sam.	I and II Samuel
Isa.	Isaiah	Song of Sol.	Song of Solomon
Jas.	James	I and II Thess.	I and II Thessalonians
Jer.	Jeremiah	I and II Tim.	I and II Timothy
Josh.	Joshua	Zech.	Zechariah
Judg.	Judges	Zeph.	Zephaniah
Lam.	Lamentations		

Capitalization   Titles of books: capitalize the first word and all principal words, but not articles, prepositions, and conjunctions (for example, *The Last of the Mohicans*).

Titles of magazines and newspapers: as above, except do not treat an initial definite article as part of the title except when the title is entered separately in a list:

```
"He was referring to the Kansas City Star and. . . ."
     10 Editorial, Kansas City Star, March 18, 1978, p.
   43D.
```

Titles of parts of a specific work: capitalize as for books (for example, "Thompson's Appendix II," "Jones's Preface," "Writing the Final Draft").

Abbreviations: capitalize a noun followed by a numeral indicating place in a sequence (for example, "Ch. iv," "No. 14," "Vol. III"). Do not capitalize "l.," "n.," "p.," or "sig."

Titles of French, Italian, and Spanish works: capitalize the first word, the proper nouns, but not adjectives derived from proper nouns.

Titles of German works: capitalize the first word, all nouns, and all adjectives derived from names of persons.

Definitions For definitions within your text, use single quotation marks without intervening punctuation (for example, *et alii* 'and others').

Enumeration of Items Incorporate short items into the text, as follows:

```
College instructors are usually divided into four ranks:
(1) instructors, (2) assistant professors, (3) associate
professors, and (4) full professors.
```

Present longer items in a tabular form, as follows:

```
College instructors are usually divided into four ranks:
    1.  Instructors, at the bottom of the scale, are usually
        beginning teachers with little or no experience.
    2.  Assistant professors. . . .
```

Etc. *Et cetera* 'and so forth': avoid using in the text by listing at least four items, as follows:

```
Images of color occur frequently in Crane's writing,
especially blue, gold, red, and grey.
```

Foreign Languages Underline foreign words used in an English text:

```
Like his friend Olaf, he is aut Caesar, aut nihil,
either overpowering perfection or ruin and destruction.
```

Do not underline quotations:

```
Obviously, he uses it to exploit, in the words of Jean
Laumon, "une admirable mine de themes poetiques."
```

Do not underline titles of magazine articles:

```
3 Von Thomas O. Brandt, "Brecht und die Bibel,"
PMLA, 79 (March 1964), 171.
```

Do not underline places, institutions, proper names, or titles that precede proper names:

```
Of course, Racine became extremely fond of Mlle
Champmeslé, who interpreted his works at the Hotel
de Bourgogne.
```

Illustrations and Tables A table is a systematic arrangement of statistical materials, usually in columns. An illustration is any item that is not a table: blueprint, chart, diagram, drawing, graph, photograph, photostat, map, and so on. Note the samples on the following page.

Fig. 36: Illustration

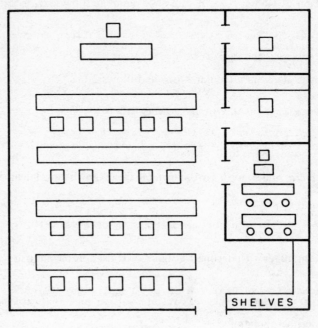

Fig. 36

Audio Laboratory with Private Listening Rooms and a
Small Group Room

Fig. 37: Table

TABLE I

RESPONSE BY CLASS ON NUCLEAR ENERGY POLICY

	Freshmen	Sophomores	Juniors	Seniors
1. More nuclear power	150	301	75	120
2. Less nuclear power	195	137	111	203
3. Present policy is acceptable	87	104	229	37

When presenting an illustration or table in your research paper, conform to the following stipulations:

1. Present only one kind of information in each illustration, making it as simple and as brief as possible; frills and fancy artwork may distract rather than attract the reader.

2. Place small illustrations within your text. Large illustrations should go on a separate page. If you have numerous illustrations or long, complex tables, these should be placed in an appendix at the end of your paper.

3. Place the illustration as near to your textual discussion as possible, although the illustration should not precede your first mention of it.

4. Make certain that your textual discussion adequately explains the significance of the illustration. Follow two rules: (1) write the illustration so that your reader can understand it without reference to your discussion; and (2) write your discussion of the illustration so that your reader may understand your observations without reference to the illustration. But avoid giving too many numbers and figures in your text.

5. In your textual discussion refer to illustrations by number (for example, "Figure 5" or "Table IV, p. 16"), not by a vague reference (for example, "the table above," "the following illustration," or "the chart below").

6. Number illustrations consecutively throughout the paper with Arabic numbers, preceded by "Fig." or "Figure" (for example, "Figure 4"), placed one double space above the caption and centered on the page *below* the illustration.

7. Number tables consecutively throughout the paper with capital Roman numerals, preceded by "Table" (for example, "Table II"), placed one double space above the caption and centered on the page *above* the table.

8. Always insert a caption that explains the illustration, placed *above* the table and *below* the illustration, centered, in full capital letters or in capitals and lower case, but do not mix forms in the same paper. An alternative is to place the caption on the same line with the number (see Fig. 38 below).

9. Insert a caption or number for each column of a table, centered above the column or, if necessary, inserted diagonally or vertically above it.

10. When inserting an explanatory or reference note, place it below both a table and an illustration; then use an asterisk as the identifying superscript, not an Arabic numeral (for example, see Figs. 40 and 41, p. 164).

The charts and illustrations on the following pages are examples of what you might use in a research paper.

Fig. 38: Illustration

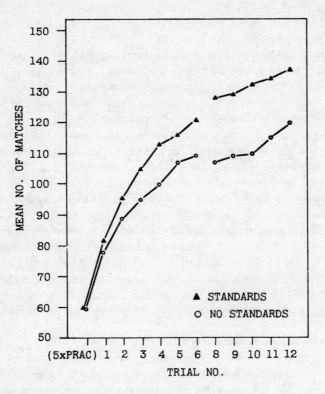

Fig. 38: Mean Number of Matches by Subjects with and without Standards (By Trial). From Edwin A. Locke and Judith F. Bryan. Cognitive Aspects of Psychomotor Performance. Journal of Applied Psychology, 1966, 50, 289.

Fig. 39: Illustration

SUPRASEGMENTAL

STRESS ╱   ⋀   ╲   ⋃

(primary)   (secondary)   (tertiary)   (weak)

PITCH

1   2   3   4 (relatively rare)

(low)   (average)   (high)   (exceptionally high)

Juncture

    open

╶┼╴ at minor break, usually between words

    terminal

    │   or ⟶   "level"

    at greater break within sentence, also in

      apposition;

                     level pitch

‖   or ╱   "rising"

    in "yes-no" questions, series;

                  pitch-rise before the pause

╪   or ╲   "falling"

    at end of most sentences;

               pitch-drop, voice fades off

Fig. 39: Phonemes of English. Generally, this figure follows the Trager-Smith system, used widely in American linguistics. From Anna H. Live, "Pattern in Language," The Journal of General Education, 18 (July 1966), 94.

Fig. 40: Table

TABLE II*

Mean Scores of Six Values Held by College

Students According to Sex

All Students		Men		Women	
Pol.	40.61	Pol.	43.22	Aesth.	43.86
Rel.	40.51	Theor.	43.09	Rel.	43.13
Aesth.	40.29	Econ.	42.05	Soc.	41.62
Theor.	39.80	Rel.	37.88	Pol.	38.00
Econ.	39.45	Soc.	37.05	Econ.	36.85
Soc.	39.34	Aesth.	36.72	Theor.	36.50

*From Carmen J. Finley, Jack M. Thompson, and Albert Cognata, "Stability of the California Short Form Test of Mental Maturity: Grades 3, 5, and 7," California Journal of Educational Research, 17 (Sept. 1966), 165.

Fig. 41: Table

TABLE III. Inhibitory effects of sugars on the growth of Clostridium histolyticum (11 strains) on nutrient agar*

Sugar added (2%)	Aerobic incubation (hr)		Anaerobic incubation (hr)	
	24	48	24	48
None	11**	11	11	11
Glucose	0	0	11	11
Maltose	0	0	11	11
Lactose	1	1	11	11
Sucrose	3	6	11	11
Arabinose.	0	0	0	0
Inositol	0	0	11	11
Xylose.	0	0	0	0
Sorbitol	2	7	11	11
Mamnitol	9	10	11	11
Rhamnose	0	0	11	11

*From Shoki Nishida and Masaaki Imaizumi. 1966. Toxigencity of Clostridium histolyticum. J. Bacteriol. 91: 481.

**No. of strains which gave rise to colonies in the presence of the sugar.

Names of Persons   Formal titles (Mr., Mrs., Ms., Dr., Hon.) are usually omitted in textual and note references to distinguished persons, living or dead. As a
general rule, first mention of a person requires the full name (for example, Ernest
Hemingway or Margaret Mead) and thereafter requires only usage of the surname
(Hemingway or Mead).

Convention suggests that certain prominent figures (Lord Byron, Dr. Johnson, Dame Edith Sitwell) require the title while others, for no apparent reason, do
not (for example, use Tennyson, Browne, and Hillary rather than Lord Tennyson,
Sir Thomas Browne, or Sir Edmund Hillary). Where custom dictates, you may
employ simplified names of famous authors (for example, use ''Dante'' rather
than his surname ''Alighieri'' and use ''Michelangelo'' rather than ''Michelangelo Buonarroti''). You may also use pseudonyms where custom dictates (for
example, George Eliot, Maxim Gorkey, Mark Twain).

Parenthetical Documentation   Handle references within sentences in one of
the following ways:

```
According to William C. DeVane, A Browning Handbook (New
York:  Appleton, 1955), p. 37, Browning's liberalism
follows the doctrine of Victorian laissez-faire.
```

or

```
According to William C. DeVane--A Browning Handbook (New
York:  Appleton, 1955), p. 37--Browning's liberalism
follows the doctrine of Victorian laissez-faire.
```

If these forms prove awkward, recast the sentence so that the documentation
comes at the end:

```
Browning's laissez-faire liberalism is stressed by
William C. DeVane, A Browning Handbook (New York:
Appleton, 1955), p. 37.
```

Punctuation   Consistency is a key to punctuation for research writing. A careful
proofreading of your paper for punctuation errors will generally improve the
clarity and accuracy of your writing.

1. *Commas* are used in a series of three or more before ''and'' and ''or.''
Never use a comma and a dash together. The comma follows a parenthesis (such
as this), if your text requires the comma. The comma goes inside single quotation
marks as well as double quotation marks (for example, ''The Sources of Franklin's 'The Ephemera,' '').

2. *Dashes* are formed with your typewriter by typing two hyphens with no
blank space before or after.

3. *Exclamation marks* are seldom used in research writing. A forceful declarative sentence is preferable.

4. *Hyphens* to separate words at the end of a typed line are acceptable in research papers. However, you should always double-check word division by consulting a dictionary. If possible, do not separate by a hyphen two letters at the end or beginning of a line (for example, use "depend-able," not "de-pendable"). If possible, avoid the hyphenation of proper names.

5. *Periods* end complete sentences of the text, endnotes or footnotes, and all bibliography entries. The period normally follows the parenthesis. (The period is placed within the parenthesis only when the parenthetical statement is independent, as in this instance.) See also "Ellipsis," p. 69, for explanation of the period in conjunction with ellipsis dots.

6. *Brackets* should be inserted by hand if these figures are not on your typewriter. Brackets are used to enclose a parenthesis within a parenthesis, to enclose phonetic transcription, and to enclose interpolations in a quotation (See "Brackets," p. 69).

7. *Words discussed,* such as slang, words cited as words, or words purposely misused, should be enclosed within quotation marks. Also use quotation marks for English translations of foreign words. However, linguistic studies require that you underline all linguistic forms (letters, words, phrases) that are subjects of discussion and also require that you employ single quotation marks for definitions, without intervening punctuation (for example, nosu 'nose').

8. *Quotation marks* should enclose all quotations run on as part of your text. For quotations within quotations, use single marks. You should put all commas or periods inside quotation marks, whether double or single, unless a parenthetical reference intervenes. Other marks of punctuation go inside the quotation marks only when such items (question mark, dash, exclamation) are actually part of the quoted materials. Semicolons and colons generally fall outside the quotation marks.

Roman Numerals   Use capital or small Roman numerals as shown below:

```
Act II          Bk. x
Vol. III        Chap. xi
Part IV         scene xii
Div. V          canto xiii
Plate VI        pp. xiv-xvii
Table VII
```

A list of Roman numerals:

	UNITS	TENS	HUNDREDS
1	i	x	c
2	ii	xx	cc
3	iii	xxx	ccc
4	iv	xl	cd
5	v	l	d
6	vi	lx	dc
7	vii	lxx	dcc
8	viii	lxxx	dccc
9	ix	xc	cm

Shakespearean Plays For use in parenthetical documentation, the editorial board of the *Shakespeare Quarterly* has approved the following abbreviations of titles of Shakespearean works: *Ado; Ant.; AWW; AYL; Cor.; Cym.; Err.; Ham.; 1H4; 2H4; H5; 1H6; 2H6; 3H6; H8; JC; Jn; LLL; Lr.; Mac.; MM; MND; MV; Oth.; Per.; R2; R3; Rom.; Shr.; TGV; Tim.; Tit.; Tmp.; TN; TNK; Tro.; Wiv.; WT; LC; Luc.; PhT; PP; Son.; Ven.*

Slang Enclose in double quotation marks any words to which you direct attention.

Underlining Underline the following: books, bulletins, pamphlets, periodicals, plays, motion pictures, newspapers, operas, ships, symphonies, and yearbooks. If separately published, underline the following: essays, lectures, poems, proceedings, reports, sermons, and stories.

Word Division When necessary, divide a word with a hyphen so that the break comes between two syllables, but avoid one-letter and two-letter division (for example, "o-ver" or "separate-ly"). When in doubt about the proper division of a word, always consult a dictionary.

APPENDIX II
List of General Reference
Books and Journals

Applied and Physical Sciences

GENERAL

Books

American Library Association. *Guide to the Selection of Computer-Based Science and Technology Reference Services in the U.S.A.* Chicago: American Library Association, 1969.

Applied Science and Technology Index. New York: H. W. Wilson, 1958–date. Before 1958, see *Industrial Arts Index.*

Besterman, Theodore. *Technology.* 2 vols. Totowa, N.J.: Rowman, 1971.

Bibliographic Guide to Technology. Boston: G. K. Hall, 1977.

Bolton, Henry C. *Catalogue of Scientific and Technical Periodicals, 1665–1895.* 2nd ed. 1897; rpt. New York: Johnson Reprint, 1974.

Ching-Chih, Chen. *Scientific and Technical Information Sources.* Cambridge, Mass.: The MIT Press, 1977.

Darrow, Ken, and Rick Pam. *Appropriate Technology Sourcebook.* Rev. ed. 2 vols. Stanford, Calif.: Volunteers in Asia, 1978.

Dorian, Angelo F. *Dorian's Dictionary of Science and Technology.* 2nd rev. ed. New York: Elsevier-North Holland, 1978.

Ferguson, Eugene S., comp. *Bibliography of the History of Technology.* Cambridge, Mass.: The MIT Press, 1968.

Gerrish, Howard H. *Technical Dictionary.* Text ed. South Holland, Ill.: Goodheart-Willcox, 1976.

Grogan, Denis. *Science and Technology: An Introduction to the Literature.* 3rd ed. Hamden, Conn.: Shoe String, 1976.

Hawkins, R. R., ed. *Scientific, Medical, and Technical Books Published in the United States of America.* 2nd ed. Washington, D.C.: National Academy of Sciences, 1958.

Industrial Arts Index. New York: H. W. Wilson, 1913–57. Superseded by *Applied Science and Technology Index.*

Lasworth, Earl J. *Reference Sources in Science and Technology.* Metuchen, N.J.: Scarecrow, 1972.

McGraw-Hill Encyclopedia of Science and Technology. Rev. ed. 15 vols. New York: McGraw-Hill, 1966.

McGraw-Hill Yearbook of Science and Technology. New York: McGraw-Hill, annually.

Mitcham, Carl, and Robert McKay. *Bibliography of the Philosophy of Technology.* Chicago: Univ. of Chicago Press, 1973.

Owen, Dolores, and Marguerite Hanchey. *Abstracts and Indexes in Science and Technology: A Descriptive Guide.* Metuchen, N.J.: Scarecrow, 1974.

Powell, Russell H., ed. *Handbooks and Tables in Science and Technology: A Bibliography and Index with Selected Annotations.* Phoenix, Ariz.: Oryx, 1978.

Rider, Kenneth J. *History of Science and Technology: A Select Bibliography for Students.* 2nd ed. New York: International Publications Service, 1970.

Scientific & Technical Books & Serial in Print 1979. Ann Arbor: Bowker, 1978.

Statistical Techniques in Technological Research: An Aid to Research Productivity. New York: Halsted, 1968.

Susskind, Charles. *Understanding Technology.* Baltimore: Johns Hopkins, 1973.

Swanson, Gerald, ed. *Technology Book Guide: 1974.* Boston: G. K. Hall, 1974.

Technical Book Review Index. New York: Special Libraries Association, 1935–date.

CHEMICAL ENGINEERING

Books

Bourton, K. *Chemical and Process Engineering: Unit Operations, a Bibliographical Guide.* New York: Plenum, 1968.

Brown, R., and G. A. Campbell. *How to Find Out About the Chemical Industry.* Elmsford, N.Y.: Pergamon, 1969.

Clason, W. E. *Elsevier's Dictionary of Chemical Engineering.* 2 vols. New York: Elsevier-North Holland, 1969.

Considine, Douglas M. *Chemical and Process Encyclopedia.* New York: McGraw-Hill, 1974.

Davalloo, P. S., ed. *Chemical Engineering.* 2 vols. New York: Elsevier-North Holland, 1974.

Ernst, Richard. *Dictionary of Chemistry, Including Chemical Engineering and Fundamentals of Allied Sciences.* 2 vols. New York: International Publications Service, 1969.

Kent, James A. *Riegel's Handbook of Industrial Chemistry.* 7th ed. New York: Reinhold, 1973.

Peck, Theodore P., ed. *Chemical Industries Information Sources.* Detroit: Gale, 1978.

Perry, John H., and C. H. Chilton. *Chemical Engineers Handbook.* 5th ed. New York: McGraw-Hill, 1973.

Weekman, Vern W., Jr., ed. *Annual Reviews of Industrial and Engineering Chemistry.* Washington, D.C.: American Chemical Society, 1972–date.

Journals

Chemical and Engineering News (Chem. & Eng. N.)
Chemical and Process Engineering (Chem. & Process Eng.)
Chemical Engineering (Chem. Eng.)
Chemical Engineering Progress (Chem. Eng. Prog.)
Chemical Technology (Chem. Tech.)
Chemistry and Industry (Chem. & Ind.)
Industrial and Engineering Chemistry Fundamentals (Ind. and Eng. Chem. Fundamentals)
Industrial and Engineering Chemistry Process Design and Development (Ind. and Eng. Chem. Process Design)
Industrial and Engineering Chemistry Product Research and Development (Ind. and Eng. Chem. Product Res. and Develop.)
Petro/Chem Engineer (Petro/Chem Eng.)

CHEMISTRY

Books

Abd-El-Wahed, Anwar, comp. *Technical Dictionary: Chemical Technology.* New York: Adler's, 1976.

American Chemical Society. *Searching the Chemical Literature.* Washington, D.C.: American Chemical Society, 1961.

Bennett, Harry, ed. *Concise Chemical and Technical Dictionary.* 2nd ed. New York: Chemical Publications, 1973.

Bottle, R. T., ed. *Use of Chemical Literature.* 2nd ed. Hamden, Conn.: Shoe String, 1969.

Burman, C. R. *How to Find Out in Chemistry.* 2nd ed. Elmsford, N.Y.: Pergamon, 1966.

Clark, George L., et al. *The Encyclopedia of Chemistry.* 2nd ed. New York: Reinhold, 1966.

Cooke, Edward I. *Chemical Synonyms and Trade Names.* 7th ed. Cleveland: CRC Press, 1971.

Crane, Evan Jay, et al. *A Guide to the Literature of Chemistry.* 2nd ed. New York: Wiley, 1957.

Dean, John A. *Lange's Handbook of Chemistry.* Rev. 11th ed. New York: McGraw-Hill, 1973.

Grant, Julius. *Hackh's Chemical Dictionary.* 4th ed. New York: McGraw-Hill, 1973.

Hampel, Clifford A., and Gessner G. Hawley, eds. *The Encyclopedia of Chemistry.* 3rd ed. New York: Reinhold, 1973.

Handbook for Authors of Papers in the Journals of the American Chemical Society. Washington, D.C.: American Chemical Society, 1967.

Hodgman, Charles D., ed. *Handbook of Chemistry and Physics.* Cleveland: CRC Press, 1913–date.

Literature Resources for Chemical Process Industries. Washington, D.C.: American Chemical Society, 1954.

Mellon, M. G. *Chemical Publications.* 4th ed. New York: McGraw-Hill, 1965.

Merck Index. Ed. Martha Windholz. 9th ed. Rahway, N.J.: Merck, 1976.

Selected Titles in Chemistry. 4th ed. Washington, D.C.: American Chemical Society, 1977.

Singer, T. E., and Julian F. Smith. *Literature of Chemical Technology.* Washington, D.C.: American Chemical Society, 1968.

Weast, Robert C., and S. M. Selby, eds. *CRC Handbook of Chemistry and Physics.* 53rd ed. Cleveland: CRC Press, 1972.

Journals

Accounts of Chemical Research (Acc. of Chem. Res.)
Analytical Chemistry (Analyt. Chem.)
Biochemistry (Biochem.)
Chemical Abstracts (Chem. Abstracts)
Chemical News (Chem. N.)
Chemical Reviews (Chem. Rev.)
Chemical Society, Proceedings (Chem. Soc. Proc.)
Chemical Titles (Chem. Titles)
Chemistry (Chem.)
Current Contents
Inorganic Chemistry (Inorg. Chem.)
Journal of the American Chemical Society (J. Am. Chem. Soc.)
Journal of Chemical and Engineering Data (J. Chem. Eng. Data)
Journal of Chemical Documentation (J. Chem. Document.)
Journal of Chemical Education (J. Chem. Educ.)
Journal of the Chemical Society, London (J. Chem. Soc., London)
Journal of Organic Chemistry (J. Org. Chem.)
Journal of Physical Chemistry (J. Phys. Chem.)

ELECTRONICS

Books

Annotated Bibliography of Electronic Data Processing. Gainesville: Univ. of Florida Press, 1968.

Buchsbaum, Walter H. *Buchsbaum's Complete Handbook of Practical Electronics Reference Data.* 2nd ed. Englewood Cliffs, N.J.: Prentice-Hall, 1978.

Carter, Harley. *Dictionary of Electronics.* Blue Ridge Summit, Pa.: TAB Books, 1972.

Electronic Properties of Materials: A Guide to the Literature. 3 vols. New York: Plenum, 1967–71.

Goedecke, W. *Dictionary of Electrical Engineering, Telecommunications, and Electronics.* 3 vols. New York: Ungar, 1974.

Gotterer, Malcolm H. *KWIC Index: A Bibliography of Computer Management.* Philadelphia: Auerbach, 1970.

Graf, Rudolf F. *Modern Dictionary of Electronics.* 5th ed. Indianapolis: Howard Sams, 1977.

Harper, Charles A. *Handbook of Materials and Processes for Electronics.* New York: McGraw-Hill, 1969.

Mandl, Matthew. *Handbook of Modern Electronic Data.* Englewood Cliffs, N.J.: Reston, 1973.

Markus, John. *Electronics and Nucleonics Dictionary.* 3rd ed. New York: McGraw-Hill, 1967.

Meacham, Stanley, and Donald Herrington. *Handbook of Electronic Tables and Formulas.* 4th ed. Indianapolis: Howard Sams, 1973.

Moore, C. K., and K. J. Spencer. *Electronics: A Bibliographical Guide.* New York: Plenum, 1965.

Morrill, Chester, Jr. *Computers and Data Processing Information Sources.* Detroit: Gale, 1969.

National Computing Centre Ltd. *International Computer Bibliography.* 2 vols. New York: International Publications Service, 1968–72.

Prudhomme, Bill. *Electronics Sourcebook.* Metairie, La.: Technical Publications, 1977.

Randle, Gretchen R., ed. *Electronic Industries Information Sources.* Detroit: Gale, 1968.

Shiers, George. *Bibliography of the History of Electronics.* Metuchen, N.J.: Scarecrow, 1972.

Journals

Electrical Engineer
Electrical News and Engineering
Electrical Review
Electrical World
Electronic Engineer
Electronic Engineering
Electronic News
Electronics
Electronics Abstracts Journal
Electronics World

ENGINEERING

Books

Anderson, J. C., et al. *Data and Formulae for Engineering Students.* 2nd ed. Elmsford, N.Y.: Pergamon, 1969.

Classed Subject Catalog of the Engineering Societies Library. 10th Supplement. Boston: G. K. Hall, 1974.

Engineering Index Annual. New York: Engineering Index, annually.

Guest, G. Martin. *Brief History of Engineering.* Philadelphia: International Ideas, 1974.

Jones, Franklin D., and Paul B. Schubert. *Engineering Encyclopedia.* 3rd ed. New York: Industrial Press, 1963.

Malinowsky, H. R., et al. *Science and Engineering Literature: A Guide to Reference Sources.* 2nd ed. Littleton, Colo.: Libraries Unlimited, 1976.

Matarazzo, James M., and James M. Kyed, eds. *Scientific, Engineering and Medical Societies Publications in Print 1976–1977.* 2nd ed. Ann Arbor: Bowker, 1976.

Mount, Ellis, ed. *Guide to Basic Information Sources in Engineering.* New York: Halsted, 1976.

Oppermann, Alfred. *Dictionary of Modern Engineering.* 3rd ed. 2 vols. New York: International Publications Service, 1972–73.

Parke, Nathan G. *Guide to the Literature of Mathematics and Physics.* Rev. ed. New York: Dover, 1958.

Parsons, S. A. *How to Find Out About Engineering.* Elmsford, N.Y.: Pergamon, 1972.

Schenck, Hilbert. *Introduction to the Engineering Research Project.* New York: McGraw-Hill, 1969.

----------. *Theories of Engineering Experimentation.* 2nd ed. New York: McGraw-Hill, 1968.

Souders, Mott. *Engineer's Companion.* New York: Wiley, 1966.

Yakovlev, K. P., et al. *Handbook for Engineers.* 2 vols. Elmsford, N.Y.: Pergamon, 1965.

Journals

Engineer
Engineering
Engineering and Science
Engineering and Science Review
Engineering Designer
Engineering Digest
Engineering Forum
Engineering Index
Engineering Journal
Engineering Materials and Design
Engineering News
Engineering Review
International Journal of Engineering Science
Journal of Engineering Education
Professional Engineer (U.S.)

GEOLOGY

Books

American Geological Institute. *Dictionary of Geological Terms.* Rev. ed. Garden City, N.Y.: Doubleday, 1976.

Challinor, John. *A Dictionary of Geology.* New York: Oxford Univ. Press, 1974.

Corbin, John B. *Index of State Geological Survey Publications Issued in Series.* Metuchen, N.J.: Scarecrow, 1965.

Gary, Margaret, et al. *Glossary of Geology.* Falls Church, Va.: American Geological Institute, 1972.

Hall, Vivian S. *Environmental Geology: A Selected Bibliography.* Boulder, Colo.: Geological Society of America, 1975.

Kieffer, F. V. *An Annotated Bibliography of Geology and Land Use Planning, No. 1230.* Monticello, Ill.: Council of Planning Librarians, 1977.

Mason, Shirley L. *Source Book in Geology, Fourteen Hundred to Nineteen Hundred.* Ed. Kirtley F. Mather. Cambridge, Mass.: Harvard Univ. Press, 1970.

Siegrist, Marie, et al. *Bibliography and Index of Geology Exclusive of North America.* 30 vols. Boulder, Colo.: Geological Society of America, 1933–65.

U.S. Geological Survey Library. *Catalog of the U.S. Geological Survey Library.* Boston: G. K. Hall, 1964. Supplement.

Ward, Dederick, and Marjorie Wheeler. *Geologic Reference Sources: A Subject and Regional Bibliography to Publications and Maps in the Geological Sciences.* Metuchen, N.J.: Scarecrow, 1972.

Whitten and Brooks Dictionary of Geology. New York: Penguin, 1972.

Journals

American Journal of Science
Economic Geology
Geology Society Bulletin
Journal of Geology
Journal of Petroleum Technology
Mining Congress Journal
Mining Engineering
Petrol/Chem Engineer
Petroleum Engineer International
Society of Petroleum Engineers Journal

MATHEMATICS

Books

Aaboe, Asger. *Episodes from the Early History of Mathematics.* Washington, D.C.: Mathematical Association, 1975.

American Mathematical Society. *Index to Translations Selected by the AMS.* Providence, R.I.: American Mathematical Society, 1966.

----------. *Mathematical Reviews Cumulative Indices.* Providence, R.I.: American Mathematical Society, 1966–date.

Baker, Cyril C. *Dictionary of Mathematics.* New York: Hart, 1970.

Bell, J. L., and A. B. Slomson. *Models and Ultraproducts: An Introduction.* New York: Elsevier-North Holland, 1972.

Carr, George S. *Formulas and Theorems in Pure Mathematics.* New York: Chelsea, 1970.

Dick, Elie M. *Current Information Sources in Mathematics: An Annotated Guide to Books and Periodicals, 1960–71.* Littleton, Colo.: Libraries Unlimited, 1973.

Eves, Howard. *Introduction to the History of Mathematics.* 3rd ed. New York: Holt, Rinehart, & Winston, 1969.

Fang, Joong. *Guide to the Literature of Mathematics Today.* Memphis: Paideia Press, 1972.

Fletcher, Alan, et al. *An Index of Mathematical Tables.* 2nd ed. 2 vols. Reading, Mass.: Addison-Wesley, 1962.

Gellert, W., et al., eds. *The VNR Concise Encyclopedia of Mathematics.* Florence, Ky.: Reinhold, 1977.

Herland, Leo. *Dictionary of Mathematical Sciences.* 2 vols. New York: Ungar, 1974.

International Catalogue of Scientific Literature 1901–1914. Section A: Mathematics. Metuchen, N.J.: Scarecrow, 1974.

International Dictionary of Applied Mathematics. New York: Reinhold, 1960.

James, Robert C., and Edwin F. Beckenbach, eds. *Mathematics Dictionary,* 4th ed. Florence, Ky.: Reinhold, 1976.

Korn, G. A., and T. M. Korn. *Mathematical Handbook for Scientists and Engineers: Definitions, Theorems, and Formulas.* New York: McGraw-Hill, 1967.

Merritt, Fredrick S. *Mathematics Manual.* New York: McGraw-Hill, 1962.

Millington, William, and T. Alaric Millington. *Dictionary of Mathematics.* New York: Barnes & Noble, 1971.

National Council of Teachers of Mathematics. *Cumulative Index: The Mathematics Teachers, 1908–1965.* Reston, Va.: NCTM, 1967.

National Council of Teachers of Mathematics Yearbook. New York: City College, Columbia Univ., 1926–date.

Parke, Nathan G. *Guide to the Literature of Mathematics and Physics.* Rev. ed. New York: Dover, 1958.

Pemberton, J. E. *How to Find Out in Mathematics.* 2nd ed. Elmsford, N.Y.: Pergamon, 1970.

Schaaf, William L. *The High School Mathematics Library.* Rev. ed. Reston, Va.: NCTM, 1970.

Shapiro, Max S. *Mathematics Encyclopedia: A Made Simple Book.* Garden City, N.Y.: Doubleday, 1977.

Sneddon, I. N., ed. *Encyclopedic Dictionary of Mathematics for Engineers.* Elmsford, N.Y.: Pergamon, 1976.

The Universal Encyclopedia of Mathematics. New York: Simon & Schuster, 1964.

Journals

ACTA Mathematica (ACTA Math.)
American Journal of Mathematics (Am. J. Math.)
American Mathematical Monthly (Am. Math. Monthly)
American Mathematical Society, Bulletin (Bull. Am. Math. Soc.)
American Mathematical Society, Proceedings (Proc. Am. Math. Soc.)
American Mathematical Society, Transactions (Trans. Am. Math. Soc.)
Annals of Mathematics (Ann. of Math.)
Arithmetic Teacher
Canadian Journal of Mathematics (Canad. J. Math.)
Canadian Mathematical Bulletin (Canad. Math. Bull.)
Duke Mathematics Journal (Duke Math. J.)
Duodecimal Bulletin (Duodecimal Bul.)
The Fibonacci Quarterly (Fibonacci Q.)
Journal of Algebra (J. Algebra)
Journal of Computer and Systems Sciences (J. Computer & Systems Sci.)
Journal of Mathematics and Physics (J. Math. & Phys.)
Journal of Research of the National Bureau of Standards (J. Res. Nat. Bur. Stand.)
Mathematical Reviews (Math. Reviews)
Mathematics Magazine (Math. Mag.)
Mathematics of Computation
Mathematics Teacher (Math. Teacher)
Pacific Journal of Mathematics (Pacific J. Math.)
Philosophia Mathematica (Philos. Math.)
Proceedings of the Royal Society, Series A (Proc. Roy. Soc. Ser. A)
Quarterly Journal of Mathematics (Q. J. Math.)
Recreational Mathematics (Recreational Math.)
Scripta Mathematica
SIAM Review
SRA New Mathematics Extension Services
SRA New Mathematics for Today's Teachers (K-6)
Two-Year College Mathematics Journal
Updating Mathematics Services

PHOTOGRAPHY

Books

Abstracts of Photographic Science and Engineering Literature. New York: Columbia Univ. Department of Graphics in cooperation with the Society of Photographic Scientists and Engineers, 1962–date.

Backhouse, D., et al. *Illustrated Dictionary of Photography*. New York: International Publications Service, 1974.

Boni, Albert. *Photographic Literature*. 2 vols. New York: Morgan & Morgan, 1962–72.

Edkins, Diana. *Photography: An Information Guide*. Detroit: Gale, 1974.

Focal Press Ltd. *Focal Encyclopedia of Photography*. Rev. ed. New York: McGraw-Hill, 1969.

Grau, Wolfgang. *Dictionary of Photography and Motion Picture Engineering and Related Topics*. New York: International Publications Service, 1968.

International Glossary of Photographic Terms. Garden City, N.Y.: American Photographic Book Pub., 1968.

Jones, Bernard E., ed. *Cassell's Cyclopaedia of Photography*. The Literature of Photography Series. 1911; rpt. New York: Arno, 1973.

Kirillou, N. I. *Problems in Photographic Research and Technology*. New York: Pitman, 1967.

Photographic Abstracts. London: Scientific and Technical Group of the Royal Photographic Society of Great Britain, 1921–61.

Stubbs, S. G. Glaxland, ed. *Modern Encyclopedia of Photography*. 2 vols. Boston: American Photographic Pub., 1938.

Glazebrook, Richard T. *A Dictionary of Applied Physics*. 5 vols. New York: Macmillan, 1922–23.
Largely replaced by Thewlis (see below).

Isaacs, A., and H. J. Gray, eds. *A New Dictionary of Physics*. 2nd ed. New York: Longman, 1975.

Mayer, Herbert. *Physik Duenner Schichten— Physics of Thin Films: Complete Bibliography*. 2 vols. New York: International Publications Service, 1972.

Michels, Walter C., et al. *International Dictionary of Physics and Electronics*. New York: Reinhold, 1956.

Parke, Nathan G. *Guide to the Literature of Mathematics and Physics*. Rev. ed. New York: Dover, 1958.

Solid State Physics Literature Guides. New York: Plenum, 1972–date.

Thewlis, J., ed. *Concise Dictionary of Physics*. Elmsford, N.Y.: Pergamon, 1973.

United Nations Atomic Energy Commission Group. *An International Bibliography on Atomic Energy*. 2 vols. Lake Success, N.Y.: United Nations, 1949–51.

Whitford, Robert H. *Physics Literature*. 2nd ed. Metuchen, N.J.: Scarecrow, 1958.

Yates, B. *How to Find Out About Physics*. Elmsford, N.Y.: Pergamon, 1965.

Journals

American Surveyor and Photogrammetrist
Aperture
British Journal of Photography
Image Technology
Industrial Photography
Infinity
Journal of Photographic Science
Leica Photography
Modern Photography
Photographic Journal
Photographic Science and Engineering
Photographic Society of America Journal
Popular Photography
Professional Photographer
Technical Photography
Visual

Journals

Advances in Physics (Advances in Phys.)
American Institute of Physics Newsletter (AIP Newsletter)
American Journal of Physics (Am. J. Phys.)
Annals of Physics (Ann. of Phys.)
JETP Letters
Journal of Applied Physics (J. Appl. Phys.)
Journal of Chemical Physics (J. Chem. Phys.)
Journal of Physics (J. of Phys.)
Journal of Physics and Chemistry of Solids (J. of Phys. & Chem. Solids)
Nuclear Physics (Nuclear Phys.)
Physical Review Letters (Phys. Rev. Letters)
Proceedings of the Royal Society, London (Proc. Royal Soc., London)
Review of Modern Physics (Rev. Mod. Phys.)
Science Abstracts (Section A—Physics)

PHYSICS

Books

Annual Review of Nuclear Science. Palo Alto, Calif.: 1952–date.

Besancon, Robert M., ed. *Encyclopedia of Physics*. 2nd ed. New York: Reinhold, 1974.

Fluegge, E., ed. *Encyclopedia of Physics*. 54 vols. New York: Springer-Verlag, 1956–date.

Art

Books

Adeline, Jules. *Adeline Art Dictionary*. New York: Ungar, 1966. Supplement.

American Federation of Arts. *American Art Directory, 1978*. Ed. Jaques Cattell Press. 47th ed. New York: Bowker, 1978.

----------. *Who's Who in American Art.* Washington D.C.: Bowker, 1935–date.

The Art Index. New York: H. W. Wilson, 1929–date.

Art-Kunst: International Bibliography of Art Books. New York: International Publications Service, 1972.

Besterman, Theodore. *Art and Architecture: Including Archaeology.* Besterman World Bibliographies Series. Totowa, N.J.: Rowman, 1971.

Britannica Encyclopaedia of American Art. Ed. Milton Rugoff. Chicago: Encyclopaedia Britannica, 1973.

Chamberlin, Mary W. *Guide to Art Reference Books.* Chicago: American Library Association, 1959.

Columbia University. *Catalog of the Avery Memorial Architectural Library.* 19 vols. Boston: G. K. Hall, 1968.

Curry, Larry. *American West: From Catlin to Russell.* Los Angeles: Los Angeles County Museum of Art Bookshop, 1972.

De La Croix, Horst. *Addendum to Listing for Gardner's Art Through the Ages.* New York: Harcourt Brace, 1977.

Encyclopedia of World Art. 15 vols. New York: McGraw-Hill, 1959–68.

Gardner, Helen. *Art Through the Ages.* New York: Harcourt Brace, 1977.

Goldman, Bernard. *Reading and Writing in the Arts: A Handbook.* Rev. ed. Detroit: Wayne State Univ. Press, 1978.

Hall, R. J. *Dictionary of Subjects and Symbols in Art.* New York: Harper & Row, 1974.

Hammond, William A. *A Bibliography of Aesthetics and of the Philosophy of the Fine Arts from 1900 to 1932.* Rev. ed. New York: Longmans, Green, 1934.

Havlice, Patricia P. *Art in Time.* Metuchen, N.J.: Scarecrow, 1970.

Huddleston, Eugene L., and Douglas A. Noverr, eds. *The Relationship of Literature and Painting: A Guide to Information Sources.* Detroit: Gale, 1978.

The Index of Twentieth Century Artists. 4 vols. New York: College Art Association, 1933–37.

Jacobs, Jay. *Color Encyclopedia of World Art.* New York: Crown, 1975.

Lemke, Antje, and Ruth Fleiss. *Museum Companion: A Dictionary of Art Terms and Subjects.* New York: Hippocrene, 1974.

Lucas, E. Louise. *Art Books: A Basic Bibliography on the Fine Arts.* Greenwich, Conn.: New York Graphic Society, 1968.

Monro, Isabel S., and Kate M. Monro. *Index to Reproductions of American Paintings.* New York: H. W. Wilson, 1948. Supplement, 1964.

----------. *Index to Reproductions of European Paintings.* 3 vols. New York: H. W. Wilson, 1956.

Munro, Eleanor C. *Encyclopedia of Art.* New York: Western, 1964.

Murray, Peter, and Linda Murray, *Dictionary of Art and Artists.* Santa Fe: Gannon, n.d.

Myers, Bernard S., and Shirley D. Myers, eds. *Dictionary of Art.* 5 vols. New York: McGraw-Hill, 1969.

Osborne, Harold, ed. *Oxford Companion to Art.* New York: Oxford Univ. Press, 1970.

Praeger Encyclopedia of Art. 5 vols. Chicago: Encyclopaedia Britannica, 1971.

Ryerson Library—Art Institute of Chicago. *Index to Art Periodicals.* 11 vols. Boston: G. K. Hall, 1962.

Smith, Ralph C. *A Biographical Index of American Artists.* 1930; rpt. Detroit: Gale, 1976.

Sokol, David M. *American Architecture and Art: A Guide to Information Sources.* Detroit: Gale, 1976.

Sturgis, Russell, and Henry E. Krehbiel. *Annotated Bibliography of Fine Art.* 1897; rpt. Boston: Longwood, 1976.

Sur, Julian. *Reflections and Impressions on Art and the Artist.* New York: Vantage, 1978.

Journals

American Artist
Apollo
Art Bibliographies/Modern
Art Bulletin
Art Education
Art Forum
Art in America
Art International
Art Journal
Art News
Art Quarterly
Artist's Proof
Arts and Activities
Arts Magazine
Arts of Asia
Burlington Magazine
CA Magazine
Connoisseur
Craft Horizons
Design Quarterly
Eastern
Eighteenth-Century Studies
Horizon
Italix
Journal of Aesthetics and Art Criticism
Magazine of Art
Metropolitan Museum of Art

Print
School Arts Magazine
Studies in Art Education
Studio

Biological Sciences

Books

Altman, Philip L., and Dorothy S. Dittmer, eds. *Biology Data Book.* 2nd ed. 3 vols. Madison, Wis.: FASEB, 1972–74.

Besterman, Theodore. *Biological Sciences.* Besterman World Bibliographies Series. Totowa, N.J.: Rowman, 1971.

Biological Abstracts. Philadelphia: Biological Abstracts, 1926–date.

Biological Abstracts: BIOSIS—The First Fifty Years. New York: Plenum, 1976.

Biological and Agricultural Index. New York: H. W. Wilson, 1947–date.

Blackwelder, Richard E. *Guide to the Taxonomic Literature of Vertebrates.* Ames: Iowa State Univ. Press, 1972.

Blake, Sidney F., and A. C. Atwood. *Geographical Guide to Floras of the World: Pt. 1; Africa, Australia, North America, South America and Islands.* 1942; rpt. New York: Hafner, 1967.

Bottle, R. T. *Use of Biological Literature.* 2nd ed. Woburn, Mass.: Butterworths, 1972.

Brooks, Stewart M. *Basic Science and the Human Body.* 4th ed. St. Louis: Mosby, 1970.

Carter, John L., and Ruth C. Carter. *Bibliography and Index of North American Carboniferous Brachiopods 1898–1968.* Boulder, Colo.: Geological Society of America, 1970.

Cowgill, R. W. *Experiments in Biochemical Research Technique.* Huntington, N.Y.: Krieger, 1957.

Frye, Royal M. *Significant Advances in Science for the Layman.* New York: Carlton, n.d.

Gray, Peter, ed. *Encyclopedia of the Biological Sciences.* 2nd ed. New York: Reinhold, 1970.

----------. *Student Dictionary of Biology.* New York: Reinhold, 1973.

Henderson, Isabella F., and W. D. Henderson. *A Dictionary of Biological Terms.* 8th ed. New York: Reinhold, 1963.

International Catalogue of Scientific Literature 1901–1914. Metuchen, N.J.: Scarecrow, n.d.

Jenkins, Frances B. *Science Reference Sources.* 4th ed. Champaign, Ill.: Illini Union Bookstore, 1965.

Orr, J. B., et al. *What Science Stands For.* New York: Arno, 1937.

Smith, R. C. *Guide to the Literature of the Zoological Sciences.* 6th ed. Minneapolis: Burgess, 1962.

Swift, Lloyd, H. *Botanical Bibliographies: A Guide to Bibliographical Materials Applicable to Botany.* Minneapolis: Burgess, 1970.

----------. *Botanical Classifications: A Comparison Angiosperm Classification.* Hamden, Conn.: Shoe String, 1974.

Van Nostrand's Scientific Encyclopedia. 5th ed. New York: Reinhold, 1976.

Willis, J. C. *A Dictionary of the Flowering Plants and Ferns.* 8th ed. New York: Cambridge Univ. Press, 1973.

Journals

Advancement of Science
Advances in Botanical Research (Advances Botan. Res.)
Advancing Frontiers of Plant Sciences
American Journal of Anatomy (Am. J. Anat.)
American Journal of Botany (Am. J. Botany)
American Journal of Physiology (Am. J. Physiol.)
American Scientist (Am. Scientist)
Animal Behavior
Annales de l'Institut Pasteur
Annals and Magazine of Natural History (Ann. & Mag. Nat. Hist.)
Annals of Botany (Ann. Botany)
Annals of the Missouri Botanical Garden (Ann. Mo. Botan. Garden)
Applied Microbiology (Appl. Microbiol.)
Archiv für Hydrobiologie
Archives of Biochemistry and Biophysics (Arch. Biochem. & Biophys.)
Audubon Field Notes
Audubon Magazine
Bacteriological Reviews (Bacteriol. Rev.)
Biochemical and Biophysical Research Commission (Biochem. & Biophys. Research Comm.)
Biochemistry (Biochem.)
Biochemistry Journal (Biochem. J.)
Biochimica et Biophysica Acta
Bioscience
Botanical Review (Botan. Rev.)
Bulletin of Aquatic Biology (Bull. Aquatic Biol.)
Bulletin of Experimental Biology and Medicine (Bull. Exptl. Biol. & Med.)
Bulletin of the Atomic Scientists (Bull. Atomic Scientists)
Canadian Journal of Botany (Canadian J. Botany)
Canadian Journal of Microbiology (Canadian J. Microbiol.)

Current Contents
DOKLADY—Biochemistry section
DOKLADY—Biological Sciences section
DOKLADY—Botanical Sciences section
Ecology
Evolution
Experimental Cell Research (Exptl. Cell Research)
Federation Proceedings (Federation Proc.)
General Science Quarterly (Gen. Sci. Quart.)
Genetics
Geological Society of America—Bulletin (Geol. Soc. Am. Bull.)
Geophysical Abstracts (Geophys. Abstr.)
Heredity
Herpetologica
Human Genetics
Hydrobiologica
International Abstracts of Biological Sciences (Intern. Abstr. Biol. Sci.)
International Bureau for Plant Taxonomy (Intern. Bur. Plant Taxonomy)
Journal of Animal Behavior (J. Animal Behavior)
Journal of Animal Ecology (J. Animal Ecology)
Journal of Bacteriology (J. Bacteriol.)
Journal of Biological Chemistry (J. Biol. Chem.)
Journal of Cellular and Comparative Physiology (J. Cellular & Comp. Physiol.)
Journal of Clinical Investigation (J. Clin. Invest.)
Journal of Ecology (J. Ecol.)
Journal of Experimental Biology (J. Exptl. Biol.)
Journal of Experimental Medicine (J. Exptl. Med.)
Journal of Experimental Zoology (J. Exptl. Zool.)
Journal of General Microbiology (J. Gen. Microbiol.)
Journal of Geology (J. Geol.)
Journal of Immunology (J. Immunol.)
Journal of Lipid Research (J. Lipid Research)
Journal of Mammology (J. Mammol.)
Journal of Molecular Biology (J. Molecular Biol.)
Journal of Paleontology (J. Paleontol.)
Journal of Physiology (J. Physiol.)
Journal of Protozoology (J. Protozool.)
Journal of Wildlife Management (J. Wildl. Mgmt.)
Linnean Society of London Journal (Linnean Soc. London J.)
Mutation Research
National Academy of Sciences—Proceedings (Proc. Nat. Acad. Sci.)
National Wildlife (Nat. Wildl.)

Naturalist
Nature
New York Academy of Sciences, Annals of (Ann. NY Acad. Sci.)
Palaeobotanist
Philosophy of Science
Physiological Reviews (Physiol. Rev.)
Physiological Zoology (Physiol. Zool.)
Plant Physiology (Plant Physiol.)
Plant World
Proceedings of the National Academy of Science (Proc. Nat. Acad. Sci.)
Radiation Research (Radiation Res.)
Review of Applied Mycology (Rev. Appl. Mycology)
Science
Science Education (Sci. Ed.)
Scientific American (Sci. Am.)
Scientific American Monthly (Sci. Am. Monthly)
Scientific Monthly (Sci. Monthly)
Soil Conservation (Soil Conserv.)
Stain Technology
Zeitschrift für Zellforschung und mickroskopische Anatomie

Business

Books

Accountants' Index. New York: American Institute of Certified Public Accountants, 1921–date.

Business Books and Serials in Print, 1977. New York: Bowker, 1977.

Business Periodical Index. New York: H. W. Wilson, 1958–date.

Clark, Donald T., and Bert A. Gottfried. *University Dictionary of Business and Finance.* New York: Apollo, 1974.

Lovett, Robert W., ed. *American Economics and Business History: Information Sources.* Detroit: Gale, 1971.

Munn, Glenn G. *Encyclopedia of Banking and Finance.* Ed. Ferdinand L. Garcia. 7th ed. Boston: Bankers, 1973.

Nemmers, Erwin E., ed. *Dictionary of Economics and Business.* 3rd ed. Totowa, N.J.: Littlefield, 1976.

Wanerman, Paul, ed. *Encyclopedia of Business Information Sources.* 3rd ed. Detroit: Gale, 1976.

Williams, Robert I., and Lillian Doris, eds. *Encyclopedia of Accounting Systems.* 5 vols. Englewood Cliffs, N.J.: Prentice-Hall, 1956–57.

Wixon, Rufus, et al., eds. *Accountants' Handbook.* 5th ed. New York: Ronald Press, 1970.

Journals

Accountants' Digest
Accounting Research
Accounting Review
Advertising Age
American Economic Review
Appraisal Journal
Barron's National Business and Financial
  Weekly
Best's Review (Life/Health Insurance Edition)
Best's Review (Property/Liability Insurance Edition)
Better Living
Business Horizons
Business Week
Changing Times
Consumers' Research Bulletin
CPA Journal
Dun's Review and Modern Industry
Economic Indicators
Employment Security Review
Factory Management and Maintenance
Federal Reserve Bulletin
Federal Tax Articles
Federal Tax Guide
Financial Executive
Forbes
Fortune
Harvard Business Review
Human Engineering
Journal of Accountancy
Journal of Accounting Research
Journal of Finance
Journal of Insurance Information
Journal of Marketing
Journal of Retailing
Kiplinger Washington Letter
Labor Market and Employment Security
Lloyd's Bank Review
Magazine of Wall Street and Business Analyst
Management Accounting
Management News
Management Review
Monthly Review
Moody's Banks and Finance
Moody's Handbook of Widely Held Common
  Stocks
Moody's Industrials
Moody's Magazine
National Tax Journal
Nation's Business
Office Executive
Operations Research
Over-the-Counter Securities Review
Personnel Administration
Personnel and Guidance Journal
Personnel Psychology
Sales Management
Social Security Bulletin

Standard and Poor's Corporation Records
Supervisory Management
Survey of Current Business
Systems
Tax Executive
Value Line
Wall Street Journal

Education

Books

Camp, William L., and Bryan L. Schwark. *Guide to Periodicals in Education and Its Academic Disciplines.* 2nd ed. Metuchen, N.J.: Scarecrow, 1975.

Current Index to Journals in Education. New York: Macmillan, 1969–date.

Dewey, John. *Dictionary of Education.* Ed. Ralph B. Winn. 1959; rpt. Westport, Conn.: Greenwood, 1972.

Ebel, R. L. *Encyclopedia of Educational Research.* 4th ed. New York: Macmillan, 1969.

Education Index. New York: H. W. Wilson, 1929–date.

Educational Resources Information Center. *Current Index to Journals in Education.* New York: Macmillan, 1969–date.

----------. *Early Childhood Education: An ERIC Bibliography.* New York: Macmillan, 1973.

----------. *Educational Documents Abstracts.* New York: Macmillan, 1968–date.

----------. *Educational Documents Index.* New York: Macmillan, 1966–date.

----------. *Educational Finance: An ERIC Bibliography.* New York: Macmillan, 1972.

Educational Technology Reviews. 12 vols. Englewood Cliffs, N.J.: Educational Technology Pub., 1973.

Encyclopedia of Education. New York: Macmillan, 1971.

Good, Carter V., ed. *Dictionary of Education.* 3rd ed. New York: McGraw-Hill, 1973.

Monroe, Paul, ed. *Cyclopedia of Education.* 5 vols. 1911; rpt. Detroit: Gale, 1968.

Powell, John P. *Philosophy of Education: A Select Bibliography.* 2nd ed. New York: Humanities, 1971.

UNESCO. *World Survey of Education.* 4 vols. Paris: UNESCO, 1955–66.

Journals

American Educational Research Journal
American School Board Journal
Bulletin of the National Association of Secondary
  School Principals
California Journal of Educational Research

Childhood Education
Educational Leadership
Elementary School Journal
Elementary School Teacher
Harvard Educational Review
Journal of Education
Journal of Educational Research
Journal of Experimental Education
Journal of Higher Education
Journal of Negro Education
Journal of Secondary Education
Journal of Teacher Education
Junior College Journal
National Elementary Principal
NEA Research Division Reports
Phi Delta Kappan
Review of Educational Research
School Executive
School Life
School Management
Teachers College Record
Theory into Practice
Today's Education

English Language and Literature

GENERAL

Books

Altick, Richard D., and Andrew Wright. *Selective Bibliography for the Study of English and American Literature.* 5th ed. New York: Macmillan, 1974.

Baldensperger, Fernand, and Werner P. Friederich. *Bibliography of Comparative Literature.* 3rd ed. 1950; rpt. New York: Russell & Russell, 1960.

Bond, Donald F. *A Reference Guide to English Studies.* 2nd ed. Chicago: Univ. of Chicago Press, 1971.

Holman, C. Hugh. *Handbook to Literature.* 3rd ed. Indianapolis: Odyssey Press, 1972.

Kennedy, Arthur G., and Donald B. Sands. *A Concise Bibliography for Students of English.* Rev. William E. Colburn. Stanford: Stanford Univ. Press, 1972.

Magill, Frank N., ed. *Masterplots.* 12 vols. New York: Salem Press, 1976. Annual Review.

Moulton, Charles Wells. *Library of Literary Criticism of English and American Authors.* 8 vols. 1901–05; rpt. Magnolia, Mass.: Peter Smith, 1935–40.

AMERICAN LITERATURE

Books

Blanck, Jacob, comp. *Bibliography of American Literature.* 6 vols. New Haven: Yale Univ. Press, 1955–73.

Clark, Harry Hayden, comp. *American Literature: Poe Through Garland.* New York: AHM, 1971.

Davis, Richard Beale, comp. *American Literature Through Bryant.* New York: AHM, 1969.

Evans, Charles. *American Bibliography.* 14 vols. Magnolia, Mass.: Peter Smith, 1967.

Gohdes, Clarence. *Bibliographical Guide to the Study of Literature of the U.S.A.* 4th ed. Durham, N.C.: Duke Univ. Press, 1976.

Hart, James D., ed. *The Oxford Companion to American Literature.* 4th ed. New York: Oxford Univ. Press, 1965.

Havlice, Patricia Pate. *Index to American Author Bibliographies.* Metuchen, N.J.: Scarecrow, 1971.

Jones, Howard Mumford, and Richard M. Ludwig. *Guide to American Literature and Its Backgrounds Since 1890.* 4th ed. Cambridge, Mass.: Harvard Univ. Press, 1972.

Kunitz, Stanley J., and Howard Haycraft, eds. *American Authors, 1600–1900.* New York: H. W. Wilson, 1938.

Leary, Lewis. *Articles on American Literature, 1900–1950.* Durham, N.C.: Duke Univ. Press, 1954.

----------. *Articles on American Literature, 1950–1967.* Durham, N.C.: Duke Univ. Press, 1970.

Nilon, Charles H. *Bibliography of Bibliographies in American Literature.* New York: Bowker, 1970.

Nyren, Dorothy, ed. *Modern American Literature.* 3rd ed. New York: Ungar, 1964.

Richard, Robert F., ed. *Concise Dictionary of American Literature.* 1955; rpt. Westport, Conn.: Greenwood, 1977.

Spiller, Robert E., et al., eds. *Literary History of the United States.* 4th ed. 3 vols. New York: Macmillan, 1974.

Tate, Allen. *Sixty American Poets.* Folcroft, Pa.: Folcroft, 1945.

Trent, W. P., et al. *Cambridge History of American Literature.* 3 vols. New York: Macmillan, 1943.

BLACK LITERATURE

Books

Black African Literature in English Since 1952: Works and Criticism. New York: Johnson Reprint, 1971.

Black List: The Concise Reference Guide to Publications, Films, and Broadcasting Media of Black America, Africa, and the Caribbean. Rev. ed. New York: Panther House, 1974.

Davis, Arthur. From the Dark Tower: Afro-American Writers from 1900 to 1960. Washington, D.C.: Howard Univ. Press, 1974.

Deodene, Frank, and William P. French. Black American Fiction Since 1952: A Preliminary Checklist. Chatham, N.Y.: Chatham Bookseller, 1970.

Hallie Q. Brown Memorial Library. Index to Periodical Articles by and About Negroes. Boston: G. K. Hall, 1971.

Hughes, Langston, and Arna Bontemps, eds. Poetry of the Negro, 1746–1970. New York: Doubleday, 1970.

Irwin, Leonard B. Black Studies. Brooklawn, N.J.: McKinley, 1973.

Mitchell, Loften. Voices of the Black Theatre. New York: T. J. White, 1975.

Office of Adult Services. No Crystal Stair: A Bibliography of Black Literature. New York: New York Public Library, 1971.

Spalding, Henry D. Encyclopedia of Black Folklore and Humor. Middle Village, N.Y.: Jonathan David, 1978.

Turner, Darwin T., comp. Afro-American Writers. Northbrook, Ill.: AHM, 1970.

Welsch, Erwin K. Negro in the United States: A Research Guide. Bloomington: Indiana Univ. Press, 1965.

Whitlow, Roger. Black American Literature: A Critical History. Chicago: Nelson-Hall, 1973.

Work, Monroe Nathan. A Bibliography of the Negro in Africa and America. New York: Octagon, 1966.

Journals

Bibliographic Survey: The Negro in Print
Black Scholar
Black World
Crisis
Ebony
Journal of African Studies
Journal of Black Studies
Journal of Negro History
Negro Heritage
Negro History Bulletin

BRITISH LITERATURE

Books

Arnold, James F., and J. W. Robinson. English Theatrical Literature 1559–1900: A Bibliography Incorporating Lowe's Bibliographical Account. Elmsford, N.Y.: British Book Center, 1971.

Baker, Ernest A. History of the English Novel. 11 vols. New York: Barnes & Noble, 1924–67.

Cambridge Bibliography of English Literature. 5 vols. New York: Cambridge Univ. Press, 1940.

Cambridge History of English Literature. 15 vols. New York: Cambridge Univ. Press, 1961.

Courthope, William J. A History of English Poetry. 6 vols. 1895–1910; rpt. New York: Russell & Russell, 1962.

Dick, Aliki. A Student's Guide to British Literature. Littleton, Colo.: Libraries Unlimited, 1972.

Harvey, Paul, and Dorothy Eagle, eds. The Oxford Companion to English Literature. 4th ed. New York: Oxford Univ. Press, 1967.

Kunitz, Stanley J., and Howard Haycraft. British Authors Before 1800: A Biographical Dictionary. New York: H. W. Wilson, 1952.

----------. British Authors of the Nineteenth Century. New York: H. W. Wilson, 1936.

Mellown, Elgin W. A Descriptive Catalogue of the Bibliographies of Twentieth Century British Poets, Novelists and Dramatists. 2nd, rev. & enl.ed. Troy, N.Y.: Whitston, 1978.

Ray, Gordon N. Bibliographical Resources for the Study of Nineteenth Century English Fiction. Folcroft, Pa.: Folcroft, 1964.

Temple, Ruth, and Martin Tucker, eds. Twentieth Century British Literature. New York: Ungar, 1966.

Watson, George. Cambridge Bibliography of English Literature. 5 vols. New York: Cambridge Univ. Press, 1965.

Year's Work in English Studies. New York: Humanities, annually.

DRAMA

Books

Anderson, Michael, et al. Crowell's Handbook of Comtemporary Drama. New York: Crowell, 1971.

Baker, Blanch M. Dramatic Bibliography. 1933; rpt. New York: Arno, 1968.

----------. *Theatre and Allied Arts: A Guide to Books Dealing with the History, Criticism, and Technic of the Drama and Theatre, and Related Arts and Crafts.* 1953; rpt. New York: Arno, n.d.

Breed, Paul F., and Florence M. Sniderman. *Dramatic Criticism Index.* Detroit: Gale, 1972.

Chicorel, Marietta, ed. *Chicorel Theater Index to Drama Books and Periodicals, Vol. 21.* New York: Chicorel Library, 1975.

Coleman, Arthur, and Gary R. Tyler. *Drama Criticism.* 2 vols. Denver: Swallow, 1966–71.

Cumulated Dramatic Index, 1909–1949. 2 vols. Westwood, Mass.: Faxon, 1965.

Matlaw, Myron. *Modern World Drama: An Encyclopedia.* New York: Dutton, 1972.

Palmer, Helen H. *European Drama Criticism, 1900–1975.* 2nd ed. Hamden, Conn.: Shoe String, 1977.

----------., and Anne Jane Dyson. *American Drama Criticism.* Hamden, Conn.: Shoe String, 1970. Supplement, 1976.

Play Index. 4 vols. New York: H. W. Wilson, 1953, 1963, 1968, 1973.

LANGUAGE

Books

Bailey, Richard W., and Dolores M. Burton. *English Stylistics: A Bibliography.* Cambridge, Mass.: The M.I.T. Press, 1968.

Bond, Donald F. *Reference Guide to English Studies.* 2nd ed. Chicago: Univ. of Chicago Press, 1971.

A Dictionary of American English on Historical Principles. Ed. Sir William Craigie and J. R. Hulbert. 4 vols. Chicago: Univ. of Chicago Press, 1938–44.

Kennedy, Arthur G., and Donald B. Sands. *A Concise Bibliography for Students of English.* 5th ed. Stanford: Stanford Univ. Press, 1972.

Oxford English Dictionary. Ed. James A. H. Murray et al. 13 vols. New York: Oxford University Press, 1933.

MYTH AND FOLKLORE

Books

Eastman, Mary Huse. *Index to Fairy Tales, Myths, and Legends.* 2nd ed. Westwood, Mass.: Faxon, 1926. Supplements 1937, 1952.

Haywood, Charles. *A Bibliography of North American Folklore and Folksong.* 2nd ed. 2 vols. New York: Dover, 1961.

Ireland, Norma O. *Index to Fairy Tales, 1949–1972; Including Folklore, Legends, and Myths in Collections.* Westwood, Mass.: Faxon, 1973.

MacCulloch, John A., et al., eds. *Mythology of All Races.* 13 vols. 1932; rpt. New York: Cooper Square, n.d.

Thompson, Stith. *Motif Index of Folk Literature.* Rev. and enl. ed. 6 vols. Bloomington: Indiana Univ. Press, 1955–58.

NOVEL

Books

Adelman, Irving, and Rita Dworkin. *The Contemporary Novel: A Checklist of Critical Literature on the British and American Novel Since 1945.* Metuchen, N.J.: Scarecrow, 1972.

Bell, Inglis F., and Donald Baird. *The English Novel, 1578–1956: A Checklist of Twentieth-Century Criticisms.* 1959; rpt. Hamden, Conn.: Shoe String, 1974.

Bufkin, Ernest C. *Twentieth-Century Novel in English: A Checklist.* Athens: Univ. of Georgia Press, 1967.

Drescher, Horst W., and Bernd Kahrmann. *The Contemporary English Novel: An Annotated Bibliography of Secondary Sources.* New York: International Publications Service, 1973.

Gerstenberger, Donna, and George Hendrick. *The American Novel.* Denver: Swallow, 1961.

Holman, C. Hugh, and Richard Janis. *American Novel Through Henry James.* 2nd ed. Northbrook, Ill.: AHM, 1978.

Kearney, E. I., and L. S. Fitzgerald. *The Continental Novel: A Checklist of Criticism in English, 1900–1966.* Metuchen, N.J.: Scarecrow, 1968.

Kuntz, Joseph M. *Poetry Explication: A Checklist of Interpretations Since 1925 of British and American Poems Past and Present.* Rev. ed. Denver: Swallow, n.d.

Nevius, Blake. *American Novel: Sinclair Lewis to the Present.* Northbrook, Ill.: AHM, 1970.

Palmer, Helen, and Jane Dyson. *English Novel Explication: Criticisms to 1972.* Hamden, Conn.: Shoe String, 1973.

Watt, Ian. *British Novel: Scott Through Hardy.* Northbrook, Ill.: AHM, 1973.

Wiley, Paul L. *British Novel: Conrad to the Present.* Northbrook, Ill.: AHM, 1973.

Woodress, James. *American Fiction 1900–50: A Guide to Information Sources*. Detroit: Gale, 1974.

Wright, Lyle H. *American Fiction: A Contribution Towards a Bibliography*. 3 vols. San Marino, Calif.: Huntington Library, 1957–69.

POETRY

Books

English Poetry: Select Bibliographical Guides. Ed. A. E. Dyson. New York: Oxford Univ. Press, 1971.

Frizzell-Smith, Dorothy B., and Eva L. Andrews. *Subject Index to Poetry for Children and Young People, 1957–1975*. Chicago: American Lbrary Association, 1977.

Smith, William J., ed. *Granger's Index to Poetry*. 6th ed. New York: Columbia Univ. Press, 1973.

SHORT STORY

Books

Cook, Dorothy E., and Isabel S. Monro. *Short Story Index*. New York: H. W. Wilson, 1953. Supplements.

Walker, Warren S., ed. *Twentieth-Century Short Story Explication*. 3rd ed. Hamden, Conn.: Shoe String, 1977.

WORLD LITERATURE

Books

Adelman, Irving, and Rita Dworkin. *The Contemporary Novel: A Checklist of Critical Literature on the British and American Novel Since 1945*. Metuchen, N.J.: Scarecrow, 1972.

Buchanan-Brown, John, ed. *Cassell's Encyclopedia of World Literature*. New rev. ed. New York: Morrow, 1973.

Harvey, Paul, ed. *The Oxford Companion to Classical Literature*. 2nd ed. New York: Oxford Univ. Press, 1937.

----------, and J. E. Heseltine, eds. *The Oxford Companion to French Literature*. Oxford: Clarendon Press, 1959.

Hornstein, Lillian H., ed. *Reader's Companion to World Literature*. Rev. ed. New York: New American Library, 1973.

Morgan, Bayard Q. *A Critical Bibliography of German Literature in English Translation, 1481–1927*. 2nd ed. Metuchen, N.J.: Scarecrow, 1965.

Shipley, Joseph T., ed. *Dictionary of World Literature*. Rev. ed. Totowa, N.J.: Littlefield, 1972.

Smith, Horatio, ed. *Columbia Dictionary of Modern European Literature*. New York: Columbia Univ. Press, 1947.

Journals

Abstracts of English Studies
American Journal of Philology
American Literature
American Notes & Queries
American Quarterly
American Scholar
American Speech
College Composition and Communication
College English
Comparative Literature
ELH (ELH is the title)
English Language Notes
English Studies
Explicator
Journal of English and Germanic Philology
Modern Drama
Modern Fiction Studies
Modern Language Abstracts
Modern Language Forum
Modern Language Journal
Modern Language Notes
Modern Language Quarterly
Modern Language Review
Modern Philology
New England Quarterly
Nineteenth Century Fiction
Philological Quarterly
PMLA (PMLA is the title)
Renaissance News
Review of English Studies
Romance Philology
Shakespeare Quarterly
Studies in Philology
Victorian Studies

Foreign Languages

GENERAL

Books

MLA International Bibliography. New York: Modern Language Assn., 1921–date.

Nostrand, Howard L., et al. *Research on Language Teaching: An Annotated International Bibliography, 1945–64*. Rev. ed. Seattle: Univ. of Washington Press, 1965.

Year's Work in Modern Language Studies. New York: International Publications Service, annually.

Journals

Books Abroad
Modern Language Quarterly
Modern Philology
Philological Quarterly
PMLA
Romance Notes
Romance Philology
Studies in Philology
Symposium
Modern Language Review

FRENCH

Books

Barre, André. *Le Symbolisme: Bibliographie de la poésie symboliste.* 1911; rpt. New York: Burt Franklin, 1968.

Birkmaier, Emma M., and Dale L. Lange. *Selective Bibliography on the Teaching of Foreign Languages, 1920–1966.* New York: Modern Language Assn., 1968.

Bloch, Oscar, and W. Wartburg. *Dictionnaire étymologique de la langue française.* New York: French & European Publ., 1968.

Cabeen, David Clark. *A Critical Bibliography of French Literature.* 4 vols. Syracuse: Syracuse Univ. Press, 1948–61.

Cassell's French Dictionary. Ed. Denis Girard et al. New York: Macmillan, 1977.

Cioranescu, Alexandre. *Bibliographie de la littérature française du dix-huitième siècle.* 3 vols. New York: Adler's, n.d.

Dauzat, A., et al. *Nouveau dictionnaire étymologique.* Paris: Larousse, 1971.

Dubois, Marguerite, and Marie Dubois. *Dictionnaire de locutions français-anglais: Dictionary of Idioms French-English.* New ed. Paris: Larousse, 1973.

Dulong, Gaston. *Bibliographie linguistique du Canada français.* Portland, Oreg.: International Scholarly Book Service, 1966.

Golden, H. H., and S. O. Simches. *Modern French Literature and Language.* Millwood, N.Y.: Kraus Reprint, 1953.

Grand Larousse encyclopédique. 22 vols. Elmsford, N.Y.: Maxwell Science Intl., 1973. Supplements.

Harvey, Paul, and Janet E. Heseltine, eds. *Oxford Companion to French Literature.* Oxford: Clarendon Press, 1959.

Johnson, H. H. *A Short Introduction to the Study of French Literature.* Folcroft, Pa.: Folcroft, 1973.

Johnson, Nancy A. *Current Topics in Language: Introductory Readings.* Englewood Cliffs, N.J.: Winthrop, 1976.

Kettridge, Julius O. *Dictionary of Technical Terms* (Fr.-Eng., Eng.-Fr.). 2 vols. New York: French & European Publ., n.d.

La Grande Encyclopédie. Paris: Larousse, n.d.

Lanson & Tuffrau. *Manuel illustre d'histoire de la littérature française.* New York: French & European Publ., n.d.

Larousse classique. Paris: Larousse, 1967.

Littré, Emile. *Dictionnaire de la langue française.* New York: French & European Publ., n.d.

Malcles, M. *Les sources de travail bibliographique.* 3 vols. New York: French & European Publ., n.d.

Mankin, Paul, and Alex Szogyi. *Anthologie d'humour français.* Glenview, Ill.: Scott, Foresman, 1971.

Mansion, J. E., ed. *Harrap's Standard French and English Dictionary.* New York: Scribner's, 1972.

Marks, Joseph, et al., eds. *New French-English Dictionary of Slang and Colloquialisms.* New York: Dutton, 1971.

Thième, Hugo R. *Bibliographie de la littérature française de 1800 à 1930.* 3 vols. 1933; rpt. New York: International Publications Service, 1971.

Journals

L'Express
French News
French Notes and Queries
French Review
French Studies
Hommes et Mondes
Information Littéraire
Mercure de France
Le Monde (newspaper)
Le Moyen Age
Neophilologus
Nouvelle Revue Française
Les Nouvelles Littéraires (newspaper)
Réalités
Revue des Deux Mondes
Revue d'Esthétique
Revue d'Histoire Littéraire
Revue de Littérature Comparée
Revue de Paris
Revue des Sciences Humaines
Romania
Studi Francesi
Les Temps Modernes
Yale French Studies

GERMAN

Books

Albrecht, Gunter, and Gunther Dahlke, eds. *International Bibliography of the History of German Literature: Index.* New York: International Publications Service, n.d.

Betteridge, Harold T., ed. *Cassell's German Dictionary: German-English, English-German.* Rev. ed. New York: Macmillan, 1978.

Binger, Norman. *Bibliography of German Plays on Microcards.* Hamden, Conn.: Shoe String, 1970.

Bruns, Friedrich, ed. *Lese der Deutschen Lyrik: Von Klopstock bis Rilke.* New York: Irvington, 1961.

Dornseiff, Franz. *Deutsche Wortschatz nach Sachgruppen.* 7th ed. New York: DeGruyter, 1970.

Duden, R., ed. *Der Grosse Duden.* 10 vols. New York: Adler's, 1971.

Erdelyi, Gabor, and Agnes F. Peterson. *German Periodical Publications.* Stanford, Calif.: Hoover Institution Press, 1967.

Fleissner, Otto S., and E. M. Fleissner. *Deutsches Literaturlesebuch.* 4th ed. New York: Appleton, 1968.

Grimm, Jacob, and Wilhelm Grimm. *Deutsches Woerterbuch.* 32 vols. New York: Adler's, 1973.

Groeg, Otto J., ed. *Who's Who in Germany: A Biographical Dictionary.* 7th ed. New York: International Publications Service, 1978.

Hankamer, Paul. *Deutsche Literaturgeschichte.* 1930; rpt. New York: AMS, 1970.

Jones, Trevor, ed. *The Oxford Harrap Standard German-English Dictionary.* 3 vols. Oxford: Oxford University Press, 1978.

Keller, Howard H. *A German Word Family Dictionary: Together with English Equivalents.* Berkeley: University of California Press, 1978.

Kohlschmidt, Werner, and Werner Mohr, eds. *Reallexikon der deutschen Literaturgeschichte.* 2nd ed. 3 vols. New York: DeGruyter, 1958–77.

Kopp, W. LaMarr. *German Literature in the United States, 1945–60.* Chapel Hill: Univ. of North Carolina Press, 1968.

Lockwood, W. B. *An Informal History of the German Language.* Boulder, Colo.: Westview, 1977.

Magill, C. P. *German Literature.* New York: Oxford Univ. Press, 1974.

Morgan, Bayard Q. *Critical Bibliography of German Literature in English Translation, 1481–1927.* 1938; rpt. Metuchen, N.J.:

Scarecrow, 1965. (Supplement for years 1928–55. See below, Smith, Murray F., for a second supplement for years 1956–60.)

Muret, E., and D. Sanders, eds. *German and English Encyclopedic Dictionary, Vol. 1.* New York: Ungar, n.d.

Rose, Ernst. *A History of German Literature.* New York: New York Univ. Press, 1960.

Smith, Murray F. *Selected Bibliography of German Literature in English Translation, 1956–60.* Metuchen, N.J.: Scarecrow, 1972.

Springer, Otto, ed. *Langenscheidt's New Muret-Sanders German-English Encyclopedic Dictionary.* 2 vols. New York: Hippocrene, 1963–1974.

Vexler, Robert I. *Germany: A Chronology and Fact Book.* Dobbs Ferry, N.Y.: Oceana, 1973.

Wahrig, Gerhard. *Grosse Deutsche Woerterbuch.* New York: Adler's, 1977.

Wer Ist Wer? 17th ed. 2 vols. New York: International Publications Service, 1973.

Journals

German Documentation Literature
German International
German Life and Letters
German News
German Quarterly
German Tribune
Germanic Review
Germanistik
Germany
Kulturbrief
Kunst und Literatur
Kürbiskern
Literat
Ran
Scala International
Spiegel
Stein
Welt und Wort
Wiesbadener Leben

LATIN

Books

Cole, A. T., and D. O. Ross, eds. *Studies in Latin Language and Literature.* New York: Cambridge Univ. Press, 1972.

Faider, Paul. *Repertoire des index et lexiques d'auteurs latins.* 1926; rpt. New York: Burt Franklin, 1971.

Glare, P. G., ed. *Oxford Latin Dictionary*. New York: Oxford Univ. Press, 1968–1975.

Graesse, Johann G. *Orbis Latinus: Lexikon lateinischer geographischer Namen des Mittelalters und der Neuzeit*. 3 vols. New York: International Publications Service, 1970.

Hammond, Mason. *A Historical and Linguistic Handbook*. Cambridge, Mass.: Harvard Univ. Press, 1976.

Lewis, Charlton T., and Charles Short. *Latin Dictionary: Founded on Andrews' Edition of Freund's Latin Dictionary*. 1879; rpt. New York: Oxford Univ. Press, 1974.

MacDonald, Gerald, ed. *Antonio de Nebrija: Vocabulario de romance en latin*. Philadelphia: Temple Univ. Press, 1973.

Mackail, John W. *Latin Literature*. Folcroft, Pa.: Folcroft, 1973.

Mantinband, James H. *Dictionary of Latin Literature*. Totawa, N.J.: Littlefield, 1964.

Norton, Mary E., comp. *Selective Bibliography on the Teaching of Latin and Greek, 1920–69*. New York: Modern Language Assn., n.d.

Journals
American Classical Review
American Journal of Philology
AREPO
Arethusa
Arion
Athenaeum
Classical Bulletin
Classical Journal
Classical Outlook
Classical Philology
Classical Quarterly
Classical Review
Classical World
Greek, Roman and Byzantine Studies
Hellenism
Modern Greek Studies Association Bulletin
Nestor
Philological Quarterly
Phoenix
Quarterly Check-List of Classical Studies
Ramus

RUSSIAN

Books
Alford, M. H., and V. L. Alford. *Russian-English Scientific and Technical Dictionary*. 2 vols. Elmsford, N.Y.: Pergamon, 1970.

Blum, Alexander. *Concise Russian-English Scientific Dictionary for Students and Research Workers*. Elmsford, N.Y.: Pergamon, 1965.

Gilbert, Martin. *Russian History Atlas*. New York: Macmillan, 1972.

Harkins, William E. *Dictionary of Russian Literature*. 1956; rpt. Westport, Conn.: Greenwood, 1971.

Horecky, Paul L. *Basic Russian Publications: A Selected and Annotated Bibliography on Russian and the Soviet Union*. Chicago: Univ. of Chicago Press, 1962.

Institute for the Study of the U.S.S.R., et al. *Who Was Who in the U.S.S.R.* Metuchen, N.J.: Scarecrow, 1972.

Line, Maurice B., et al. *Bibliography of Russian Literature in English Translation to 1945*. 1963; rpt. Totowa, N.J.: Rowman, 1972.

Maichel, Karol. *Guide to Russian Reference Books*. 5 vols. Stanford, Calif.: Hoover Institution Press, 1962–67.

Muller, V. K., ed. *English-Russian Dictionary*. Rev. ed. New York: Dutton, 1973.

Parker, W. H. *Historical Geography of Russia*. Chicago: Aldine, 1969.

Smirnitsky, A. I., ed. *Russian-English Dictionary*. 3rd ed. New York: Saphrograph, n.d.

Worth, Dean S. *A Bibliography of Russian Word-Formation*. Columbus: Slavica, 1977.

Zenkovsky, Serge A., and David L. Armbruster, eds. *Guide to the Bibliographies of Russian Literature*. Nashville: Vanderbilt Univ. Press, 1970.

SPANISH

Books
Aquino-Bermudez, et al. *Mi diccionario ilustrado: edicion bilingue*. New York: Lothrop, 1972.

Bryant, Shasta M. *The Spanish Ballad in English*. Lexington: Univ. Press of Kentucky, 1973.

Celorio, Marta, and Annette C. Barlow. *Handbook of Spanish Idioms*. New ed. New York: Regents, 1974.

Chatham, James R., and Enrique Ruiz-Fornells. *Dissertations in Hispanic Languages and Literatures: 1876–1966*. Lexington: Univ. Press of Kentucky, 1970.

DeLeon, Fidel. *Español: material para el hispano*. Manchaca, Tex.: Sterling Swift, 1978.

Fitzmaurice-Kelly, J. *Chapters on Spanish Literature*. Folcroft, Pa.: Folcroft, 1973.

Flores, A. *Spanish Literature in English Translation: A Bibliographical Syllabus*. Staten Island: Gordon, n.d.

MacCurdy, Raymond. *The Tragic Fall: Don Alvaro DeLuna & Other Favorites in Spanish Golden-Age Drama*. Chapel Hill: Univ. of North Carolina Press, 1978.

McCready, Warren T. *Bibliografía temática de estudios sobre el teatro español antiguo*. Toronto: Univ. of Toronto Press, 1966.

Medina, Jeremy T. *Introduction to Spanish Literature: An Analytical Approach*. New York: Harper & Row, 1974.

Newmark, Maxim. *Dictionary of Spanish Literature*. Totowa, N.J.: Littlefield, 1970.

Peers, Edgar A., ed. *Cassell's Spanish Dictionary: Spanish-English, English-Spanish*. New York: Macmillan, 1977.

Wilson, M. *Spanish Drama of the Golden Age*. Elmsford, N.Y.: Pergamon, 1969.

Zimmerman, Irene. *Guide to Current Latin American Periodicals: Humanities and Social Sciences*. Gainesville, Fla.: Kallman, 1961.

Journals

Actualidad Española
Bulletin of Hispanic Studies
Cosmopolis
Cuaderno Cultural
Cultura Hispánica
Eco
Ediciones el Caracol Marino
Época
Exilio
Gaceta Ilustrada
Hispania
Hispanic Review
Hispanofila
Journal of Spanish Studies
Latin American Literary Review
Latin American Theatre Review
Lecturas
Lookout
Mexico Quarterly Review
Pan American Review
Revista Chicano-Requeña
Revista De Estudios Hispánicos
Semana
Spain Today
Spanish Today

Health and Physical Education

Books

American Alliance for Health, Physical Education and Recreation. *Abstracts of Research Papers*. Washington, D.C.: AAHPER, 1971–1975.

----------. *Annotated Bibliography on Perceptual-Motor Development*. Washington, D.C.: AAHPER, 1972.

----------. *Completed Research in Health, Physical Education and Recreation*. Vol. 16. Washington, D.C.: AAHPER, 1974.

----------. *Dance Facilities*. Washington, D.C.: AAHPER, 1972.

----------. *Kinesiology*. Washington, D.C.: AAHPER, 1974.

----------. *Research in Dance*. Washington, D.C.: AAHPER, 1973.

Barrow, Harold M., and Rosemary McGee. *A Practical Approach to Measurement in Physical Education*. 2nd ed. Philadelphia: Lea & Febiger, 1971.

Belknap, Sara. *Guide to Dance Periodicals*. 7 vols. Univ. Presses of Fla., 1950–date.

Besford, Pat. *Encyclopedia of Swimming*. 2nd ed. New York: St. Martin's, 1977.

Brander, Michael. *Dictionary of Sporting Terms*. New York: Humanities, 1968.

Bucher, Charles A. *Foundations of Physical Education*. 8th ed. St. Louis: Mosby, 1979.

Chujoy, Anatole, and P. W. Manchester, comps. and eds. *The Dance Encyclopedia*. Rev. and enl. ed. New York: Simon & Schuster, 1978.

Lovell, Eleanor C., and Ruth M. Hall. *Index to Handicrafts, Modelmaking, and Workshop Projects*. Westwood, Mass.: Faxon, 1936. Supplements, 1943, 1950, 1965, 1969, 1975.

Magriel, Paul David. *A Bibliography of Dancing*. New York: Arno, 1936.

Menke, Frank G. *The Encyclopedia of Sports*. 6th ed. New York: Barnes & Noble, 1978.

Rosenthal, Gary. *Spalding Guide to Fitness for the Weekend Athlete*. Cambridge, Mass.: Dorison House, 1976.

Sportsman's Encyclopedia. New York: Grosset & Dunlap, 1971.

Van Dalen, Deobold B., et al. *World History of Physical Education: Cultural, Philosophical, and Comparative*. 2nd ed. Englewood Cliffs, N.J.: Prentice-Hall, 1971.

Weber, Jerome C., and David R. Lamb. *Statistics and Research in Physical Education*. St. Louis: Mosby, 1970.

Williams, Kathleen N., comp. *Health and Development: An Annotated Indexed Bibliography*. N.p.: Department of International Health, 1972.

Journals

American Journal of Public Health and the Nation's Health
American Recreation Journal

American Recreation Society Newsletter
Aquatic Artist
Athletic Journal
Ballroom Dance Magazine
Collegiate Baseball
Dance Magazine
Dance Observer
Dance Perspectives
Dance Scope
Field and Stream
Health Bulletin
Health, Education, and Welfare Indicators
Health, Education, and Welfare Trends
Hygeia
Hygiene and Physical Education
International Journal of Physical Education
Journal of Health and Physical Education
Journal of Health, Physical Education and
Recreation
Journal of Hygiene
Journal of School Health
Modern Gymnast
Physical Education Newsletter
Physical Educator
Playground
Public Health Reports
Outdoor Life
Outing
Recreation
Research Quarterly of AAHPER
Scholastic Coach
School Health Review
Sports Illustrated
Today's Health
Track and Field News
Update
World Health
World Tennis

Home Economics

Books

Axford, Lavonne, ed. *English Language Cookbooks*. Detroit: Gale, 1976.

Bitting, Katherine Golden. *Gastronomic Bibliography*. San Francisco: priv. pr. 1939; rpt. Detroit: Gale, 1971.

Burns, Scott. *The Household Economy: Its Shape, Origins, and Future*. Boston, Mass.: Beacon Press, 1977.

Catalogs of the Home Economics Library. Boston: G. K. Hall, 1977.

Compton, Norma, and Olive Hall. *Foundations of Home Economic Research: A Human Ecology Approach*. Minneapolis: Burgess, 1972.

Dodd, Marguerite. *America's Homemaking Book*. Rev. ed. New York: Scribner's, 1974.

Forsman, John, ed. *Recipe Index, 1971: The Eater's Guide to Periodical Literature*. Detroit: Gale, 1972.

Gourley, James E. *Regional American Cookery, 1884–1934: A List of Works on the Subject*. New York: New York Public Library, 1936.

Hauser, Gaylord, and Ragnar Berg. *Dictionary of Foods*. Simi Valley, Calif.: Lust, 1971.

Heggestad, Arnold A., ed. *Public Regulation of Financial Services: Costs and Benefits to Consumers—a Bibliography*. Boulder, Colo.: Westview, 1978.

Iowa State College of Agriculture and Mechanic Arts. *Basic Books and Periodicals in Home Economics*. Ames: Iowa State College Library, 1942. Supplement, 1949.

Johnson, Arnold, and Martin Peterson. *Encyclopedia of Food Technology*. Milwaukee: Aviation, 1974.

Lincoln, Waldo. *American Cookery Books, 1742–1866*. Rev. and enl. by Eleanor Lowenstein. Worcester, Mass.: American Antiquarian Society, 1954.

Lowenstein, Eleanor. *Bibliography of American Cookery Books, 1742–1860*. New York: Corner, 1972.

Montagné, Prosper. *The New Larousse Gastronomique Encyclopedia of Food, Wine, and Cooking*. Ed. Charlotte Turgeon. New York: Crown, 1977.

Robertson, Annie I. *Guide to the Literature of Home and Family Life*. 1924; rpt. Detroit: Gale, 1971.

Simon, André. *Bibliotheca Bacchica Wine and Cooking Bibliography*. 2 vols. West Orange, N.J.: Saifer, 1974.

----------. *Bibliotheca Gastronomica: A Catalogue of Books and Documents on Gastronomy*. London: Wine and Food Society, 1953.

----------, and Robin Howe. *Dictionary of Gastronomy*. New York: McGraw-Hill, 1970.

Stevenson, Bob, and Vera Stevenson. *Illustrated Almanac for Homemakers*. New York: Grossett & Dunlap, 1974.

Treves, Ralph. *The Homeowner's Complete Guide*. New York: Dutton, 1974.

U.S. Dept. of Agriculture. *Home Economics Research Report*. Washington, D.C.: GPO, 1957–date.

Vicaire, Georges. *Bibliographie Gastronomique*. New York: Burt Franklin, 1890.

Ward, Artemus. *Encyclopedia of Food*. 1923; rpt. Ann Arbor: Finch Press, 1974.

Journals

AHEA Newsletter
Better Homes and Gardens
Canadian Home Economics Journal
Changing Times

Consumer Reports
Cookbook Digest
Cuisine et vins de France
Domestic Science
Family Economics Review
Food and Cookery Review
Good Housekeeping
Home Economics Research Abstracts
Home Economics Research Journal
Homemaker
Journal of Food Science
Journal of Home Economics
Journal of Marriage and the Family
Journal of Nutrition
McCall's
Mademoiselle
Vogue
What's New in Home Economics
Woman's Day

Music

Books

Apel, Willi. *Harvard Dictionary of Music*. 2nd rev. ed. Cambridge, Mass.: Harvard Univ. Press, 1969.

Bahle, Bruce, ed. *The International Cyclopedia of Music and Musicians*. 10th ed. New York: Dodd, Mead, 1975.

Baker, Theodore. *Baker's Biographical Dictionary of Musicians*. 5th ed. New York: Schirmer, 1958. Supplement, 1971.

----------. *Dictionary of Musical Terms*. New York: Schirmer, 1923.

Besterman, Theodore. *Music and Drama*. Totowa, N.J.: Rowman, 1971.

Bingley, William. *Musical Bibliography*. 2 vols. 1934; rpt. New York: DaCapo, 1971.

Blom, Eric. *General Index to Modern Musical Literature in the English Language Including Periodicals for the Years 1915–1926*. 1927; rpt. New York: Da Capo, 1970.

Champlin, John. *Cyclopedia of Music and Musicians*. 3 vols. New York: Gordon, 1974.

Charles, Sydney R. *Handbook of Music and Music Literature*. New York: Free Press, 1972.

Clough, Francis F., and G. J. Cuming. *The World's Encyclopaedia of Recorded Music*. 3 vols. Westport, Conn.: Greenwood, 1952. Supplements, 1953, 1957.

Curcio, Louise. *Musician's Handbook*. New York: J. Patelson Music, 1968.

Davies, J. H. *Musicalia: Sources of Information in Music*. 2nd ed. Elmsford, N.Y.: Pergamon, 1969.

Duckles, Vincent. *Music Reference and Research Materials*. 2nd ed. New York: Free Press, 1974.

Duncan, Edmond S. *Dictionary of Musicians*. Saint Clair Shores, Mich.: Scholarly, 1976.

Feather, Leonard. *Encyclopedia of Jazz in the Sixties*. New York: Horizon, 1967.

Fuller-Maitland, John A. *A Consort of Music*. New York: Arno, 1973.

Grant, W. Parks. *Handbook of Music Terms*. Metuchen, N.J.: Scarecrow, 1967.

Loewenberg, Alfred. *Annals of Opera, 1597–1940*. 2 vols. Saint Clair Shores, Mich.: Scholarly, 1972.

Mixter, K. E. *General Bibliography for Music Research*. 2nd ed. Detroit: Information Coordinators, 1975.

Oxford History of Music. Ed. William H. Hodow. 8 vols. 1929–38; rpt. London: Oxford Univ. Press, 1973.

Pratt, Waldo Selden. *The New Encyclopedia of Music and Musicians*. Rev. ed. Saint Clair Shores, Mich.: Scholarly, 1929.

Roxon, Lillian. *Rock Encyclopedia*. New York: Grosset & Dunlap, 1971

Sainsbury, John S. *Dictionary of Musicians from the Earliest Time*. 1825; rpt. Saint Clair Shores, Mich.: Scholarly, 1976.

Scholes, Percy A. *Concise Oxford Dictionary of Music*. 2nd ed. New York: Oxford Univ. Press, 1964.

Shapiro, Nat. *Popular Music: An Annotated Index of American Popular Songs*. 6 vols. New York: Adrian, 1973.

Stambler, Irwin. *Encyclopedia of Pop, Rock, and Soul*. New York: St. Martin's, 1977.

Strunk, Oliver, ed. *Source Readings in Music History*. 5 vols. New York: Norton, 1950.

Thompson, Kenneth. *St. Martin's Dictionary of Twentieth-Century Composers 1910–1971*. New York: St. Martin's, 1973.

Thompson, Oscar, ed. *International Cyclopedia of Music and Musicians*. 10th rev. ed. New York: Dodd, Mead, 1975.

Vinton, John, ed. *The Dictionary of Contemporary Music*. New York: Dutton, 1974.

Weichlein, William J. *A Checklist of American Music Periodicals, 1850–1900*. Detroit: Information Coordinators, 1970.

Westrup, J. A., and F. L. Harrison, eds. *New College Encyclopedia of Music*. New York: Norton, 1976.

Who's Who in Music and Musicians' International Directory. Saint Clair Shores, Mich.: Scholarly, 1935.

Journals

ACTA Musicologia
American Music Teacher
Brass and Percussion
British Catalogue of Music
Choral Journal
Clavier
Current Musicology
Educational Music Magazine
Journal of the American Musicological Society
Journal of Band Research
Journal of Music Theory
Journal of Music Therapy
Journal of Renaissance and Baroque Music
Journal of Research in Music Education
Modern Music
Music and Letters
Music Index
Music Journal
Music Journal Biographical Cards
Music Review
Musica Disciplina
Musical America
Musical Quarterly
Musical Record
Musical Times
Musician
Notes
Opera Journal
Piano Quarterly
Sonorum Speculum

Philosophy

Books

Baldwin, James M., et al. *Dictionary of Philosophy and Psychology.* New York: Gordon, 1977.
Bibliography of Philosophical Bibliographies. Ed. Herbert Guerry. Westport, Conn.: Greenwood, 1977.
Borchardt, D. H. *How to Find Out in Philosophy and Psychology.* Elmsford, N.Y.: Pergamon, 1968.
Copleston, Frederick. *A History of Philosophy.* 9 vols. Garden City, N.Y.: Doubleday, 1977.
Davidson, R. F. *Philosophies Men Live By.* 2nd ed. New York: Holt, Rinehart, & Winston, 1974.
Edwards, Paul, ed. *The Encyclopedia of Philosophy.* 4 vols. New York: Free Press, 1973.
Higgins, Charles L. *Bibliography of Philosophy.* Ann Arbor: Campus, 1965.
Lucey, A. R. *A Dictionary of Philosophy.* Boston: Routledge & Kegan, 1976.
Nauman, St. Elmo, Jr. *Dictionary of American Philosophy.* Totowa, N.J.: Littlefield, 1974.

Passmore, John. *A Hundred Years of Philosophy.* Baltimore: Penguin, 1978.
Philosophy Documentation Center. *The Philosopher's Index: A Retrospective Index to U.S. Publications from 1940.* 2 vols. Bowling Green, Ohio: Philosophy Documentation Center, 1978.
Rand, Benjamin, comp. *Bibliography of Philosophy, Psychology and Cognate Subjects.* 2 vols. New York: Macmillan, 1905.
Runes, Dagobert D., ed. *The Dictionary of Philosophy.* Totowa, N.J.: Littlefield, 1965.
Steenbergen, G. J., and Johan Groofen. *New Encyclopedia of Philosophy.* Ed. and trans. Edmond Van Den Bossche. New York: Philosophical Library, 1972.

Journals

American Philosophical Society, Proceedings
Bibliography of Philosophy
Diogenes
Ethics
Humanist
International Journal of Ethics
Journal of Existentialism
Journal of the History of Ideas
Journal of Philosophy
Journal of Philosophy, Psychology, and Scientific Method
Journal of Symbolic Logic
Journal of Thought
Mind
Pacific Philosophy Forum
Personalist
Philosopher's Index
Philosophia Mathematica
Philosophical Quarterly
Philosophical Review
Philosophical Studies
Philosophy and Phenomenological Research
Philosophy of Science
Review of Metaphysics
Self-Realization Magazine
Southwestern Journal of Philosophy
Soviet Studies in Philosophy
Studies in Soviet Thought

Psychology

Books

Annual Review of Psychology. Palo Alto, Calif.: Annual Reviews, 1950–date.
Bachrach, Arthur J. *Psychological Research: An Introduction.* 3rd ed. New York: Random House, 1972.
Beigel, Hugo G. *Dictionary of Psychology and Related Fields.* New York: Ungar, 1974.

Bell, James E. *A Guide to Library Research in Psychology.* Dubuque: William C. Brown, 1971.

Columbia University. *Cumulated Subject Index to Psychological Abstracts, 1927–1960.* 2 vols. Boston: G. K. Hall, 1966. Supplements.

English, Horace B., and Ava C. English. *A Comprehensive Dictionary of Psychological and Psychoanalytical Terms.* New York: McKay, 1958.

Eysenck, H. J., et al. *Encyclopedia of Psychology.* 3 vols. New York: Seabury, 1972.

Goldenson, Robert M. *Encyclopedia of Human Behavior.* 2 vols. Garden City, N.Y.: Doubleday, 1974.

Grinstein, Alexander. *The Index of Psychoanalytic Writings.* 5 vols. New York: International Universities, 1956–60. Supplements, 1964–. (In progress through vol. 14)

Harvard University Psychologists. *Harvard List of Books in Psychology.* 4th ed. Cambridge, Mass.: Harvard Univ. Press, 1971.

Kiell, Norman, ed. *Psychiatry and Psychology in the Visual Arts and Aesthetics: A Bibliography.* Madison: Univ. of Wisconsin Press, 1965.

Louttit, Chauncey M. *Bibliography of Bibliographies on Psychology, 1900–1927.* 1928; rpt. New York: Burt Franklin, 1970.

----------. *Handbook of Psychological Literature.* New York: Gordon, 1974.

Murchison, C. A., ed. *Handbook of Social Psychology.* 1935; rpt. New York: Russell & Russell, 1967.

Narramore, Clyde M. *Encyclopedia of Psychological Problems.* Grand Rapids: Zondervan, 1966.

Psychological Abstracts. Lancaster, Pa.: American Psychological Assn., 1927–date.

Psychological Index, 1894–1935. 42 vols. Princeton, N.J.: Psychological Review Co., 1895–1936. (superseded by *Psychological Abstracts)*

Scott, William A., and Michael Wertheimer. *Introduction to Psychological Research.* New York: Wiley, 1962.

Wilkening, Howard E. *The Psychology Almanac: A Handbook for Students.* Monterey, Calif.: Brooks-Cole, 1973.

Journals

American Journal of Psychology
American Journal of Psychotherapy
American Psychologist
Annual Review of Psychology
Behavioral Science
Child Development Abstracts and Bibliography
Contemporary Psychology
Journal of Abnormal & Social Psychology
Journal of Applied Behavioral Science
Journal of Applied Psychology
Journal of Clinical Psychology
Journal of Educational Psychology
Journal of Experimental Psychology
Journal of General Psychology
Journal of Individual Psychology
Journal of Psychology
Journal of Social Psychology
Menninger Quarterly
Psychological Bulletin
Psychological Monographs
Psychological Record
Psychological Review

Religion

Books

Adams, Charles J., ed. *A Reader's Guide to the Great Religions.* 2nd ed. Riverside, N.J.: Free Press, 1977.

Attwater, Donald, ed. *A Catholic Dictionary.* 3rd ed. New York: Macmillan, 1961.

Bach, Marcus. *Major Religions of the World: Their Origins, Basic Beliefs, and Development.* New York: Abingdon, 1977.

Beckh, Hermann. *From Buddha to Christ.* Spring Valley, N.Y.: St. George Book Service, 1978.

Broderick, Robert. *Catholic Encyclopedia.* Appleton, Wis.: Nelson, 1976.

Buttrick, George A., et al. *The Interpreter's Bible,* 12 vols. New York: Abingdon, 1951–57.

----------, and Keith R. Crim. *The Interpreter's Dictionary of the Bible.* 5 vols. New York: Abingdon, 1976.

The Catholic Periodical and Literature Index. Ed. Catherine M. Pilley. 18 vols. New York: Catholic Library Association, 1934–date.

Cross, F. L., and Elizabeth A. Livingstone. *The Oxford Dictionary of the Christian Church.* New York: Oxford Univ. Press, 1974.

Ellison, John W., ed. *Nelson's Complete Concordance to the Revised Standard Version of the Bible.* New York: Nelson, 1978.

Ferm, Vergilius. *An Encyclopedia of Religion.* 1945; rpt. Westport, Conn.: Greenwood, 1976.

Frazer, James George. *The New Golden Bough.* Ed. Theodore H. Gastner. Abridged ed. New York: S. G. Phillips, 1959.

Gibb, H. A., and J. H. Kramers, eds. *Shorter Encyclopedia of Islam.* Ithaca, N.Y.: Cornell Univ. Press, 1953.

Hawes, G., and S. Knight. *Atlas of Man and Religion*. Elmsford, N.Y.: British Book Center, 1976.

Hick, John, ed. *Philosophy of Religion*. 2nd ed. Englewood Cliffs, N.J.: Prentice-Hall, 1973.

Hutchinson, John A. *Paths of Faith*. New York: McGraw-Hill, 1969.

Jacquet, Constant H., Jr., ed. *Yearbook of American and Canadian Churches*. New York: Abingdon, 1978.

Joy, Charles R., ed. *Harper's Topical Concordance*. Rev. ed. New York: Harper & Row, 1976.

Kaster, Joseph. *Putnam's Concise Mythological Dictionary: A Dictionary of the Deities of All Lands*. New York: Putnam, 1964.

Kuenen, Abraham. *National Religions and Universal Religions*. New York: AMS, 1978.

Landman, Isaac. *Universal Jewish Encyclopedia and Reader's Guide*. 11 vols. New York: Ktav, 1944.

Lives of the Saints. Ed. Thurston Attwater. 4 vols. Westminister, Md.: Christian Classics, 1976.

Marx, Herbert L., ed. *Religions in America*. New York: Wilson, 1977.

May, Herbert G., and G. H. S. Hunt, eds. *Oxford Bible Atlas*. New York: Oxford Univ. Press, 1974.

Mazar, Benjamin, and Michael Avi-Yonah, eds. *Illustrated World of the Bible Library*. 5 vols. Hartford: Davey, Daniel, & Co., 1961.

McKenzie, John L. *Dictionary of the Bible*. New York: MacMillan, 1965.

Mead, Frank Spencer. *Handbook of Denominations in the United States*. 6th ed. New York: Abingdon, 1975.

Melton, J. Gordon. *Encyclopedia of American Religions*. 2 vols. Wilmington, N.C.: McGrath, 1978.

Mensching, Gustav. *Structure and Pattern of Religion*. Mystic, Conn.: Verry, 1976.

Miller, Madeleine S., and J. Lane Miller. *Harper Bible Dictionary*. New York: Harper & Row, 1973.

Morris, Raymond P. *A Theological Book List*. Cambridge, Mass.: Greeno, Hadden, 1971.

Novak, Michael. *Ascent of the Mountain Flight of the Dove: An Invitation to Religious Studies*. New York: Harper & Row, 1978.

Parrinder, Geoffrey. *A Dictionary of Non-Christian Religions*. Philadelphia: Westminster, 1973.

----------. *Faiths of Mankind: A Guide to the World's Living Religions*. New York: Crowell, 1965.

----------. *Introduction to Asian Religions*. New York: Oxford University Press, 1976.

Reese, William. *Dictionary of Philosophy and Religion, Eastern and Western*. Atlanta, Ga.: Humanics, 1978.

Religious Reading. Wilmington, N.C.: McGrath, 1977.

Rice, Edward. *Ten Religions of the East*. New York: Scholastic Book Service, 1978.

Smith, Huston, et al. *Great Religions of the World*. Story of Man Library. Washington, D.C.: National Geographic, 1978.

Strong, James, ed. *Strong's Exhaustive Concordance of the Bible*. Nashville: Abingdon, 1977.

Tylor, Edward. *Religion in Primitive Culture*. Gloucester, Mass.: Peter Smith, 1972.

Wach, Joachim. *Types of Religious Experience*. Chicago: Univ. of Chicago Press, 1972.

Wigoder, Geoffrey, and Itzhak Karpman. *The New Standard Jewish Encyclopedia*. New York: Doubleday, 1977.

Wright, George E., and Floyd V. Filson. *The Westminster Historical Atlas to the Bible*. Rev. ed. Philadelphia: Westminster, 1956.

Zaehner, Robert C., ed. *The Concise Encyclopedia of Living Faiths*. Boston: Beacon, 1959.

Journals

America
American Judaism
The Biblical Archaeologist
Catholic Digest
Christian Century
Christian Herald
Christian Scholar
Christianity and Crisis
Church History
Commentary
Commonweal
Cross Currents
Dialog
Ecumenical Review
Ecumenist
Encounter
The Expository Times
Hibbert Journal
History of Religions
International Journal of Religious Education
International Review of Missions
Interpretation: A Journal of Bible and Theology
Journal for the Scientific Study of Religion
Journal of Religion
Motive
Religion in Life
Religious and Theological Abstracts
Religious Education
Risk

Social Sciences

GENERAL

Books

Belson, W. A., and B. A. Thompson. *Bibliography on Methods of Social and Business Research*. New York: Halsted, 1973.

Clarke, Jack A., ed. *Research Materials in the Social Sciences*. 2nd ed. Madison: Univ. of Wisconsin Press, 1967.

Ducharme, Raymond A., et al. *Bibliography for Teachers of Social Studies*. New York: Teachers College Press of Columbia Univ., 1968.

Ferman, Gerald S., and Jack Levin. *Social Science Research: A Handbook*. Cambridge, Mass.: Schenkman, 1977.

Gopal, M.H. *Introduction to Research Procedure in Social Sciences*. 2nd ed. New York: Asia, 1970.

Gould, Julius, and W. J. Kolb. *UNESCO Dictionary of the Social Sciences*. 2nd ed. New York: Free Press, 1970.

Hoselitz, Bert F., ed. *A Reader's Guide to the Social Sciences*. Rev. ed. New York: Free Press, 1972.

International Index. New York: H. W. Wilson, 1907–65.

London Bibliography of the Social Sciences. London: London School of Economics, 1931–date.

Rothschild, Max, ed. *Jewish Social Studies Cumulative Index*. New York: Ktav, 1968.

Rzepecki, Arnold. *Book Review Index to Social Science Periodicals*. Ann Arbor: Pierian, 1978–date.

Seligman, Edwin R., ed. *Encyclopedia of the Social Sciences*. 8 vols. New York: Macmillan, 1937.

Sills, D. E., ed. *International Encyclopedia of the Social Sciences*. 17 vols. New York: Macmillan, 1968.

Simon, Julian. *Basic Research Methods in Social Science*. 2nd ed. New York: Random House, 1978.

Social Sciences and Humanities Index. 27 vols. New York: H. W. Wilson, 1965–74.

Social Sciences Index. New York: H. W. Wilson, 1974–date.

U.S. Library of Congress. *Monthly Checklist of State Publications*. Washington, D.C.: GPO, 1912–date.

U.S. Superintendent of Documents. *Monthly Catalog of United States Government Publications*. Washington, D.C.: GPO, 1895–date.

White, Carl M., et al. *Sources of Information in the Social Sciences*. 2nd ed. Chicago: American Library Association, 1973.

ECONOMICS

Books

Batson, Harold E. *Select Bibliography of Modern Economic Theory 1870–1929*. Clifton, N.J.: Kelley, 1930.

Belson, W. A., and B. A. Thompson. *Bibliography on Methods of Social and Business Research*. New York: Halsted, 1973.

Berenson, Conrad, and Raymond Colton. *Research and Report Writing for Business and Economics*. New York: Random House, 1970.

Cohen, J. *Special Bibliography in Monetary Economics and Finance*. New York: Gordon, 1976.

Cumulative Bibliography of Economic Books: 1954–1962. New York: Gordon, 1965.

Dasgupta, A. K., ed. *Methodology in Economic Research*. New York: Asia, 1974.

Dorfman, Robert, and Nancy S. Dorfman. *Economics of the Environment: Selected Readings*. 2nd ed. New York: Norton, 1977.

Geiger, H. Kent. *National Development 1776–1966: A Selective and Annotated Guide to the Most Important Articles in English*. Metuchen, N.J.: Scarecrow, 1969.

Greenwood, Douglas. *The McGraw-Hill Dictionary of Modern Economics: A Handbook of Terms and Organizations*. 2nd ed. New York: McGraw-Hill, 1973.

Houston, Samuel R., et al., eds. *Methods and Techniques in Business Research*. New York: MSS Information, 1973.

Hughes, Catherine, ed. *Economic Education: A Guide to Information Sources*. Detroit: Gale, 1977.

Kooy, Marcelle, ed. *Studies in Economics and Economic History*. Durham, N.C.: Duke Univ. Press, 1972.

Murdick, Robert G. *Business Research: Concept and Practice*. New York: Harper & Row, 1969.

Sloan, Harold S., and Arnold J. Zurcher, eds. *Dictionary of Economics*. 5th ed. New York: Barnes & Noble, 1970.

United Nations Bureau of General Economic Research and Policies. *World Economic Survey*. New York: United Nations Dept. of Economic and Social Affairs, 1945–47–date.

Journals

ACES Bulletin
American Economic Review
American Economist
Barron's
Business Economics
Economic and Business Digest
Economic and Business Review

Economic Bulletin
Economic Indicators
Economic Journal
Economic News
Economic Notes
Economic Studies
Federal Reserve Bulletin
Journal of Economic Abstracts
Journal of Economic Education
Journal of Economic Literature
Journal of Political Economy
Quarterly Check-List of Economics and Political
    Science
Quarterly Journal of Economics
Review of Economics and Statistics
Southern Economic Journal
Wall Street Journal
Western Economic Journal

GEOGRAPHY

Books

American Geographical Society Library. *Research Catalogue of the American Geographical Society.* 15 vols. Boston: G. K. Hall, 1962.

Brewer, J. Gordon. *The Literature of Geography: A Guide to Its Organization and Use.* Hamden, Conn.: Shoe String, 1973.

Goode's World Atlas. Ed. Edward B. Espenshade. 15th ed. Chicago: Rand McNally, 1977.

Harris, Chauncy D., and Jerome D. Fellmann. *International List of Geographical Serials.* 2nd ed. Chicago: Univ. of Chicago, Dept. of Geography, 1971.

Lock, Muriel. *Geography and Cartography: A Reference Handbook.* 3rd ed. Hamden, Conn.: Shoe String, 1976.

Monkhouse, F. J. *A Dictionary of the Natural Environment.* Ed. John Small. Rev. ed. New York: Halsted, 1977.

The Statesman's Yearbook. New York: St. Martin's, 1961–date.

The Times Atlas of the World. Comprehensive ed., produced by *The Times of London.* New York: Times Books, 1975.

United Nations. *Statistical Yearbook.* New York: United Nations, 1961–date.

United Nations Statistical Office. *Demographic Yearbook.* New York: International Publications Service, 1962–date.

U.S. Bureau of the Census. *Current Population Reports.* Washington, D.C.: GPO, 1970–date.

----------. *Statistical Abstract of the United States.* Washington, D.C.: GPO, 1878–date.

U.S. Department of Commerce. *Census of Agriculture.* Washington, D.C.: GPO, 1972.

Journals

Annales de geographie
Annals of the Association of American Geographers
Die Erde
Economic Geography
Geographical Review
Journal of Geography
Journal of Regional Science
Landscape
The Professional Geographer

HISTORY

Books

Beers, Henry Putney. *Bibliographies in American History.* New York: H. W. Wilson, 1942; rpt. New York: Octagon, 1973.

Bengtson, Hermann. *Introduction to Ancient History.* Trans. R. I. Frank and Frank D. Gilliard. Berkeley: Univ. of California Press, 1976.

Besterman, Theodore. *History and Geography.* Besterman World Bibliographies Series. 4 vols. Totowa, N.J.: Rowman, 1972.

Bradford, T. C. *Bibliographers Manual of American History.* 5 vols. New York: Gordon, n.d.

Britannica Book of the Year. Ed. James Ertel. Chicago: Encyclopaedia Britannica. 1938–date.

Brooks, Philip C. *Research in Archives: The Use of Unpublished Primary Sources.* Chicago: Univ. of Chicago Press, 1969.

Cooper, William R. *Archaic Dictionary.* 1876; rpt. Detroit: Gale, 1969.

Facts on File Master Indexes. New York: Facts on File, 1946–date.

Facts on File Yearbook. New York: Facts on File, 1941–date.

Howe, George F., et al. *Guide to Historical Literature.* New York: Macmillan, 1961.

International Bibliography of Historical Sciences. New York: H. W. Wilson, 1930–date.

Langer, William Leonard, comp. and ed. *An Encyclopedia of World History: Ancient, Medieval, and Modern.* 5th ed. Boston: Houghton Mifflin, 1972.

Laqueur, W., and G. L. Mosse. *The New History: Trends in Historical Research and Writing Since World War Two.* Santa Fe: Gannon, 1970.

Martin, Michael, and Leonard Gelber. *Dictionary of American History*. Rev. ed. Totowa, N.J.: Littlefield, 1978.

McDermott, John F., ed. *Research Opportunities in American Cultural History*. 1961; rpt. Westport, Conn.: Greenwood, 1977.

Morris, Richard B., and Graham W. Irwin, eds. *Harper Encyclopedia of the Modern World: A Concise Reference History from 1760 to the Present*. New York: Harper & Row, 1970.

New York Public Library. *Dictionary Catalog of the History of the Americas Collection*. 28 vols. Boston: G. K. Hall, 1961.

Poulton, Helen J., and Marguerite S. Howland. *The Historian's Handbook*. Norman: Univ. of Oklahoma Press, 1977.

Radice, Betty. *Who's Who in the Ancient World*. Baltimore: Penguin, 1973.

Schlesinger, Arthur M., and Dixon R. Fox, eds. *A History of American Life*. 12 vols. New York: Macmillan, 1927–55.

Williamson, Derek. *Historical Bibliography*. Hamden, Conn.: Shoe String, 1967.

Winso, Justin, ed. *Narrative and Critical History of America*. 8 vols. 1889; rpt. New York: AMS, 1978.

Journals
American Historical Review
Economic History Review
English Historical Review
Hispanic American Historical Review
History
History Today
Journal of American History
Journal of Economic History
Journal of the History of Ideas
Journal of Modern History
Journal of Southern History
New Statesman
North American Review
Pacific Historical Review
Past and Present
Renaissance News
Social Studies
Speculum

POLITICAL SCIENCE

Books
Baier, C. W., et al., eds. *Documents on American Foreign Relations*. Mystic, Conn.: Verry, 1966.

Bergholt, Joan, and Alfred De Grazia, eds. *The Universal Reference System*. New York: Plenum, 1967. Annual Supplements.

Brock, Clifton. *The Literature of Political Science: A Guide for Students, Librarians, and Teachers*. New York: Bowker, 1969.

Garceau, Oliver, ed. *Political Research and Political Theory*. Cambridge, Mass.: Harvard Univ. Press, 1968.

Garson, G. David. *Handbook of Political Science Methods*. 2nd ed. Boston: Holbrook, 1976.

Griffith, Ernest S., ed. *Research in Political Science*. Port Washington, N.Y.: Kennikat, 1969.

Harmon, Robert B. *Methodology and Research in Political Science: An Annotated Bibliography*. N.p.: Bibliographical Information, 1972.

----------. *Political Science: A Bibliographical Guide to the Literature*. Metuchen, N.J.: Scarecrow, 1965. Supplements, 1968, 1972, 1974.

----------. *Political Science Bibliographies*. 2 vols. Metuchen, N.J.: Scarecrow, 1973–1976.

Holler, Frederick L. *The Information Sources of Political Science*. 2nd rev. ed. 5 vols. Santa Barbara: ABC-Clio, 1975.

Holt, Robert T., and John E. Turner, eds. *The Methodology of Comparative Political Research*. New York: Free Press, 1970.

International Bibliography of Political Science, 1976. Vol. 25. New York: International Publications Service, 1978.

McLaughlin, Andrew C., and Albert B. Hart, eds. *Cyclopedia of American Government*. 3 vols. 1914; rpt. Gloucester, Mass.: Peter Smith, 1949.

Roberts, G. K. *Dictionary of Political Analysis*. New York: St. Martin's, 1971.

Sperber, Hans, and Travis Trittschuh. *American Political Terms: An Historical Dictionary*. Detroit: Wayne State Univ. Press, 1962.

The Statesman's Yearbook. New York: St. Martin's Press, 1961–date.

Schwarzenberger, Georg, and George W. Keeton, eds. *Yearbook of World Affairs*. 32 vols. Boulder, Colo.: Westview, 1947–date.

Stebbins, Richard P. *Political Handbook and Atlas of the World*. New York: Simon & Schuster, 1970.

Yearbook of the United Nations. Lake Success, N.Y.: United Nations, 1947–date.

Journals
Administrative Science Quarterly
American Bar Association Journal
American Political Science Review
Annals of the American Academy of Political and Social Science

Atlantic Community Quarterly
Canadian Journal of Political Science
Center Magazine
China Quarterly
Columbia Law Review
Commentary
Comparative Political Studies
Comparative Politics
Comparative Studies in Society and History
Congressional Digest
Congressional Quarterly Almanac
Congressional Quarterly Weekly Report
Congressional Record
Cornell Law Review
Current History
Daedalus
Dissent
Foreign Affairs
Government and Opposition
International Affairs (Great Britain)
International Review of Administrative Sciences
International Social Science Journal
International Studies Quarterly
Journal of Applied Behavioral Science
Journal of Inter-American Studies
Journal of Inter-American Studies and World Affairs
Journal of Law and Economics
Journal of Political Economy
Journal of Politics
Journal of Public Law
Journal of Social Issues
Midwest Journal of Political Science
Orbis
Parliamentary Affairs
Political Science Quarterly
Political Science Review
Political Studies
Politics
Politics and Society
Polity
Public Administration Review
Public Interest
Public Opinion Quarterly
Review of Politics
Science & Society
State Government
State Government Administration
Studies in Soviet Thought
Urban Affairs Quarterly
Washington Monthly
Western Political Quarterly
World Affairs
World Politics
Yale Review

SOCIOLOGY

Books

Fairchild, Henry Pratt, ed. *Dictionary of Sociology and Related Sciences*. Totowa, N.J.: Littlefield, 1977.

Goslin, David A., ed. *Handbook of Socialization Theory and Research*. Chicago: Rand McNally, 1969.

March, James G., ed. *Handbook of Organizations*. Chicago: Rand McNally, 1965.

Social Sciences and Humanities Index. New York: H. W. Wilson, 1965–74.

Social Sciences Index. New York: H. W. Wilson, 1974–date.

Sociological Abstracts. New York: Sociological Abstracts, 1952–date.

Statistical Abstract of the United States. Washington, D.C.: GPO, annually.

Theodorson, George, and Achilles G. Theodorson. *A Modern Dictionary of Sociology*. Scranton, Pa.: Apollo, 1969.

Turner, John, ed. *Encyclopedia of Social Work*. New York: National Association of Social Workers, 1965–date.

Journals

American Journal of Sociology
American Sociological Review
British Journal of Sociology
Contemporary Sociology
Human Organization
International Social Science Journal
Journal of Educational Sociology
Journal of Health and Social Behavior
Journal of Marriage and the Family
Social Education
Social Science
Social Science Abstracts
Social Science Review
Sociological Quarterly
Sociology and Social Research
Sociometry

WOMEN'S STUDIES

Books

Davis, Audrey B. *Bibliography on Women: With Special Emphasis on Their Roles in Science and Society*. New York: Science History, 1974.

Ireland, Norma. *Index to Women of the World from Ancient to Modern Times. Biographies and Portraits*. Westwood, Mass.: Faxon, 1970.

Krichmar, Albert, et al., *The Women's Rights Movement in the Seventies: An International English-Language Bibliography*. Metuchen, N.J.: Scarecrow, 1977.

----------. *Women's Rights Movement in the U.S., 1948–1970: A Bibliography and Sourcebook*. Metuchen, N.J.: Scarecrow, 1972.

Lerner, Gerda. *Black Women in White America*. New York: Pantheon, 1972.

Wheeler, Helen Rippier. *Womanhood Media: Current Resources About Women*. Metuchen, N.J.: Scarecrow, 1972.

Who's Who of American Women. Chicago: A. N. Marquis, 1958–date.

Journals

Collegiate Woman's Career Magazine
Ms.
Womanpower
Woman Activist
Woman's Journal
Women Studies Abstracts
Women's Studies
Women's World

Speech and Drama

Books

Auer, John J. *Introduction to Research in Speech*. 1959; rpt. Westport, Conn.: Greenwood, 1977.

Berlo, David K. *The Process of Communication*. New York: Holt, Rinehart, & Winston, 1960.

Besterman, Theodore. *Music and Drama*. Besterman World Bibliographies Series. Totowa, N.J.: Rowman, 1971.

Chicorel, Marietta. *Chicorel Theater Index to Plays in Anthologies, Periodicals, Discs, and Tapes*. 8 vols. New York: Chicorel Library, 1970–1973.

Connor, John M., and Billie M. Connor. *Ottemiller's Index to Plays in Collections*. 6th ed. Metuchen, N.J.: Scarecrow, 1976.

Cooper, Lane, trans. *The Rhetoric of Aristotle*. Englewood Cliffs, N.J.: Prentice-Hall, 1960.

Cumulated Dramatic Index, 1909–1949. 2 vols. Boston: G. K. Hall, 1965.

Duker, Sam. *Time-Compressed Speech*. 3 vols. Metuchen, N.J.: Scarecrow, 1974.

Firkins, Ina T. E., comp. *Index of Plays, 1800–1926*. 2 vols. 1927; rpt. New York: AMS, 1972.

Gassner, John, and Edward Quinn, eds. *Reader's Encyclopedia of World Drama*. New York: Crowell, 1969.

Granville, Wilfred. *Theater Dictionary: British and American Terms in the Drama, Opera, and Ballet*. Westport, Conn.: Greenwood, 1974.

Greg, W.W. *A Bibliography of the English Printed Drama to the Restoration*. London: Oxford Univ. Press, n.d.

Haberman, Frederick W., and James W. Cleary, comps. *Rhetoric and Public Address: A Bibliography: 1947–1961*. Madison: Univ. of Wisconsin Press, 1964. (Continued annually in *Speech Monographs*.)

Harbage, Alfred. *Annals of English Drama, 1575–1700*. Rev. S. Schoenbaum. Univ. of Penn. Press, 1964.

Hiler, Hilaire, and Meyer Hiler, comps. *Bibliography of Costume*. 1939; rpt. New York: Arno, 1967.

Index to Full-Length Plays. 3 vols. Westwood, Mass.: Faxon. 1956–65.

Keller, Dean H. *Index to Plays in Periodicals*. Metuchen, N.J.: Scarecrow, 1971. Supplement, 1973.

Logasa, Hannah, and Winifred Ver Nooy, comps. *An Index to One-Act Plays, 1900–1924*. Westwood, Mass.: Faxon, 1924. Supplements, 1932–date.

McCavitt, William E. *Radio and Television: A Selected, Annotated Bibliography*. Metuchen, N.J.: Scarecrow, 1978.

Mulgrave, Dorothy, et al. *Bibliography of Speech and Allied Areas, 1950–1960*. Westport, Conn.: Greenwood, 1972.

New York Public Library. *Catalog of the Theatre and Drama Collections*. Boston: G. K. Hall, 1967. Supplement, 1973.

The New York Times Theatre Reviews 1920–1974. 10 vols. New York: Arno, 1974.

Smith, Bruce L., and Chitra M. Smith. *International Communication and Political Opinion*. Westport, Conn.: Greenwood, 1972.

Stratman, Carl J. *Britian's Theatrical Periodicals, 1720–1967: A Bibliography*. 2nd ed. New York: New York Public Library, 1972.

----------. *Bibliography of English Printed Tragedy*. Carbondale: Southern Illinois Univ. Press, 1966.

----------. *Bibliography of Medieval Drama*. New York: Ungar, 1972.

Summers, Montague. *A Bibliography of the Restoration Drama*. 1934; rpt. New York: Russell & Russell, 1970.

Journals

Audio-Visual Communication Review
Business Screen
Education Theatre Journal
Film News
Film Quarterly
Modern Drama
New York Guide and Theatre Magazine
New York Theatre Critic's Reviews
Quarterly Journal of Speech
Radio and Television News
Speech Monographs
The Speech Teacher
Studies in Public Communication
Television Magazine
Television Quarterly
Theatre
Theatre Arts
Theatre Arts Monthly
Tulane Drama Review

Index